Tsunami Recovery in Sri Lanka

The Indian Ocean Tsunami, which devastated 70 percent of Sri Lanka's coastline and killed an estimated 35,000 people, was remarkable both for the magnitude of the disaster and for the unprecedented scale of the relief and recovery operations mounted by national and international agencies. The reconstruction process was soon hampered by political patronage, by the competing efforts of hundreds of foreign humanitarian organizations, and by the ongoing civil war.

This book is framed within this larger political and social context, offering descriptions and comparisons between two regions (southwest vs. eastern coast) and four ethnic communities (Sinhalese, Tamils, Muslims, and Burghers) to illustrate how disaster relief unfolded in a culturally pluralistic political landscape. Approaching the issue from four disciplinary perspectives – anthropology, demography, political science, and disaster studies – chapters by experts in the field analyse regional and ethnic patterns of post-tsunami reconstruction according to different sectors of Sri Lankan society. Demonstrating the key importance of comprehending the local cultural contexts of disaster recovery processes, the book is a timely and useful contribution to the existing literature.

Dennis B. McGilvray is Professor and Chair of the Department of Anthropology, University of Colorado at Boulder. His research focuses on Tamil-speaking Hindus and Muslims of eastern Sri Lanka, including caste identities, matrilineal family patterns, popular religious traditions, and ethnic conflict. He is the author of *Crucible of Conflict: Tamil and Muslim Society on the East Coast of Sri Lanka* (2008).

Michele R. Gamburd is Professor of Anthropology at Portland State University. She has performed ethnographic research in Sri Lanka since 1992 and her theoretical interests focus on globalization, gender relations, violence, and social change. Her most recent book is *Breaking the Ashes: The Culture of Illicit Liquor in Sri Lanka* (2008).

Routledge Contemporary South Asia Series

Tsunami Recovery in Sri Lanka

Ethnic and regional dimensions

Edited by Dennis B. McGilvray and Michele R. Gamburd

Routledge
Taylor & Francis Group

LONDON AND NEW YORK

First published 2010 by Routledge
2 Park Square, Milton Park, Abingdon, Oxfordshire OX14 4RN

Simultaneously published in the USA and Canada
by Routledge
711 Third Avenue, New York, NY 10017

Routledge is an imprint of the Taylor & Francis Group, an Informa business

First issued in paperback 2011

Typeset in Times New Roman by
Pindar NZ, Auckland, New Zealand

British Library Cataloguing in Publication Data
A catalogue record for this book is available from the British Library

Library of Congress Cataloging in Publication Data
Tsunami recovery in Sri Lanka : ethnic and regional dimensions / edited by Dennis B. McGilvray and Michele R. Gamburd.
    p.cm — (Routledge contemporary south Asia series ; 27)
    Includes bibliographical references and index.
    1. Disaster relief—Asia, Southeast. 2. Tsunamis—Asia, Southeast. 3. Indian Ocean Tsunami, 2004. I. McGilvray, Dennis B. II. Gamburd, Michele Ruth, 1965-
    HV603 2004. S644 T78 2010
    363.34'948095493—dc22   2009035634

ISBN13: 978-0-415-77877-8 (hbk)
ISBN13: 978-0-415-50001-2 (pbk)
ISBN13: 978-0-203-85651-2 (ebk)

In memory of those who perished in the Indian Ocean Tsunami

Contents

x *Contents*

Illustrations

Figures

Tables

Contributors

Georg Frerks, Professor of Disaster Studies at Wageningen University, The Netherlands and Professor in Conflict Prevention and Conflict Management at Utrecht University.

As a sociologist and policy analyst, Frerks focuses on disaster and conflict-induced vulnerabilities and local responses as well as on policies and interventions implemented at international and national levels. He did his PhD research on popular participation in local level development in the Matara District, Sri Lanka in the early 1980s, and has been working on the Sri Lankan conflict for the past ten years. Frerks acts as an advisor to several governmental and non-governmental organisations. Recent books include *Mapping Vulnerability: Disasters, Development & People* (London: Earthscan 2004; co-editors Greg Bankoff and Dorothea Hilhorst); *Refugees and the Transformation of Societies. Agency, Policies, Ethics and Politics. Studies in Forced Migration – Volume 13.* (Oxford: Berghahn Books 2004, Co-editors: P. Essed and J. Schrijvers), *Dealing with Diversity, Sri Lankan Discourses on Peace and Conflict* (The Hague: Netherlands Institute of International Relations 'Clingendael' 2005; co-editor Bart Klem); *Gender, Conflict and Development* (Washington, D.C.: World Bank 2005; co-authors Tsjeard Bouta and Ian Bannon); and *Human Security and International Insecurity* (Wageningen: Wageningen Academic Publishers 2007; co-editor: Berma Klein Goldewijk). Frerks has also published articles on the Sri Lankan conflict and the 2004 tsunami, including "Tsunami Response in Sri Lanka: Civil-Military Cooperation in a Conflictuous Context" in *Managing Civil-Military Cooperation, A 24/7 Joint Effort for Stability* (S.J.H. Rietjens and M.T.I.B. Bollen (eds.), pp. 67–79, Aldershot: Ashgate.

Timmo Gaasbeek, PhD candidate in Disaster Studies and Irrigation Engineering, Wageningen University, the Netherlands; Policy Development Officer with a Dutch humanitarian agency.

Gaasbeek has extensive background in development program evaluation and management, and has served as a consultant in South Asia, Southeast Asia, and Africa. He has worked in the humanitarian sector in Sri Lanka since September 2000, mostly in the North and East of the country. His PhD research, started in 2003, focuses on positive inter-ethnic interaction in Kottiyar Pattu, an area in the conflict zone in eastern Sri Lanka. Gaasbeek was in the coastal town of Batticaloa when the tsunami hit, and was involved in the humanitarian response from half an hour after the waves struck. Following his hands-on immediate relief work, he worked actively in the national-level co-ordination of the shelter sector. Gaasbeek also has an M.Sc. in Tropical Land Use, with specialization in Irrigation and Water Management and Political Science.

Michele R. Gamburd, Professor of Anthropology at Portland State University.
    Gamburd, a cultural anthropologist, earned her PhD in Anthropology from the University of Michigan in 1995. She has performed ethnographic research in Sri Lanka since 1992. She has received fellowships from the Mellon Foundation, the National Science Foundation, the Oregon Council for the Humanities, and the American Institute for Sri Lankan Studies. Her theoretical interests focus on globalization, gender relations, violence, and social change. Topics of study include the migration of labor from Sri Lanka to West Asia (the Middle East), the use and abuse of alcohol, and the aftermath of the 2004 Indian Ocean Tsunami. She is the author of *The Kitchen Spoon's Handle: Transnationalism and Sri Lanka's Migrant Housemaids* (Cornell University Press, 2000) and *Breaking the Ashes: The Culture of Illicit Liquor in Sri Lanka* (Cornell University Press, 2008).

Alan Keenan, Senior Analyst for the International Crisis Group.
    As Senior Analyst for the International Crisis Group, Keenan is based in Colombo, Sri Lanka. He has been working in and on Sri Lanka since 2000. Prior to joining the Crisis Group, he was a Visiting Scholar at the University of Pennsylvania's Solomon Asch Center for the Study of Ethnopolitical Conflict and was from 2003–5 a Mellon Postdoctoral Fellow in Peace and Conflict Studies at Bryn Mawr College, where he taught courses on human rights, conflict, democratization, and transitional justice. Before coming to Bryn Mawr, Alan spent much of the previous four years in Sri Lanka as a Visiting Fellow at the International Centre for Ethnic Studies, Colombo. In addition to his academic research, Alan has also worked as a consultant for the Programme on Human Rights and Conflict at the Law and Society Trust in Colombo and with the International Centre for Transitional Justice in New York. Alan received his PhD in political theory from Johns Hopkins University, and has taught political, legal, and social theory at the Universities of California at Berkeley and at Santa Cruz, and in the Committee on Degrees in Social Studies at Harvard University. He is the author of *Democracy in Question: Democratic Openness in a Time of Political Closure* (Stanford University Press, 2003), as well as articles on both political theory and on Sri Lankan politics in various academic journals and edited volumes. His research on the politics of tsunami relief and reconstruction follows directly from his work on the activities of local and international NGOs in the context of Sri Lanka's ongoing civil war. He is currently finishing a manuscript entitled "Between the Devil and the Deep Blue Sea: The Politics of Human Rights and Peacebuilding in Sri Lanka."

Randall Kuhn, Assistant Professor and Director of the Global Health Affairs Program at the Josef Korbel School of International Studies, University of Denver.

With a joint PhD in Demography and Sociology from the University of Pennsylvania (1999), Kuhn has directed his work at understanding family and community responses to the challenges and opportunities posed by migration and fertility decline, political and economic crisis, ecological crisis, social and health interventions, and disease epidemics. Combining two years of qualitative fieldwork and extensive quantitative analysis of survey and demographic registration data, Kuhn has chronicled how the opportunities and risks posed by rural-urban and international migration intersect with land resources, social networks, family norms, and natural disaster risks to create often unexpected opportunities and risks for migrant and non-migrant households in the rural Matlab region of Bangladesh. This work increasingly led him to address the social, economic, and health consequences of unanticipated "shocks" such as flood control embankments in Matlab, currency crisis in Russia, and the HIV/AIDS epidemic in South Africa. His work on the Sri Lanka tsunami leverages these interests in community responses to disaster, political crisis, and his extensive field data collection experience, as well as an emerging interest in aid effectiveness and the political determinants of resource allocation. A new project entitled "The Misery Dividend" looks to identify the conditions under which national crises such as conflict and disaster can lead to rejuvenated or successful drives to human and political development.

Patricia Lawrence, Consultant for the UNOPS Applied Social Research Unit in Sri Lanka.

Prior to consulting for the United Nations, Lawrence taught in the Department of Anthropology and the Program in Peace and Conflict Studies at the University of Colorado in Boulder for more than a decade. She has conducted field research, and worked for international and local humanitarian organizations, in eastern Sri Lanka since the early 1990s in coastal areas that were devastated by both the civil war and the Indian Ocean Tsunami. She received a PhD in cultural anthropology at the University of Colorado at Boulder in 1997. She has received fellowships from the MacArthur Foundation, Fulbright-Hayes, and Rockefeller Foundation. Her published writings about Sri Lanka's eastern region concentrate on the healing rituals of Hindu oracles in eastern Sri Lanka, conflict transformation, recovery in contexts of complex emergency, women and agency, and children's recovery from war trauma. Her essay entitled "Violence, Suffering, Amman: The Work of Oracles in Sri Lanka's Eastern War Zone" appeared in Veena Das, Arthur Kleinman, *et al.* eds.*Violence and Subjectivity* (University of California Press, 2000). She is the author of *The Ocean of Stories* and is a co-editor with Monique Skidmore of *Women and the Contested State: Religion, Violence and Agency in South and Southeast Asia* (University of Notre Dame Press, 2007).

Dennis B. McGilvray, Professor and Chair of Anthropology, University of Colorado at Boulder.

After receiving his PhD in anthropology from the University of Chicago in 1974, McGilvray taught at Cambridge University and was a Mellon Postdoctoral Fellow at Cornell University before joining the University of Colorado faculty in 1980. His ethnographic fieldwork in the Tamil-speaking Hindu and Muslim communities of eastern Sri Lanka began in 1969 and has continued to the present, focusing on regional Hindu caste hierarchies, matrilineal kinship and matrilocal household patterns, ethnomedical knowledge and gender ideologies, popular traditions of Hinduism and Islam, cultural identities and ethnic conflict. From 2005–2008 he served as Principal Investigator on the team-based NSF-funded project which is the foundation for this edited volume. His books include *Caste Ideology and Interaction* (edited, Cambridge University Press, 1982), *Symbolic Heat: Gender, Health, and Worship among the Tamils of South India and Sri Lanka* (Ahmedabad: Mapin Publishing, 1998), *Muslim Perspectives on the Sri Lankan Conflict* (with Mirak Raheem, Washington DC: East-West Center, 2007), and *Crucible of Conflict: Tamil and Muslim Society on the East Coast of Sri Lanka* (Duke University Press, 2008).

Acknowledgments

For their help with gathering demographic data and assisting in ethnographic research, the editors would like to thank Nilam Hamead, R.B.H. "Siri" de Zoysa and Peter Franklin. We thank Jennifer Haynes-Clark for her assistance in researching background literature for the introduction and for her work compiling the bibliography and formatting the manuscript. We also thank Kerry Robarge for producing the maps and Jason Newcomer and Genevieve Meyer for data preparation assistance.

Many contributing authors were part of an interdisciplinary research project entitled "The Sri Lankan Tsunami: Societal Resilience in Two Coastal Regions," funded by the Human and Social Dynamics Program of the National Science Foundation (grant number SES-0525260). Dennis McGilvray was the principal investigator on the grant, Michele Gamburd and Randall Kuhn served as Co-PIs, and Patricia Lawrence and Alan Keenan served as Co-Investigators. We gratefully acknowledge the support provided for this research.

Abbreviations

CFA	Cease Fire Agreement
CHF	Cooperative Housing Foundation International
DPMP	Disaster Prevention, Mitigation, and Preparedness
DS	District Secretariat
GN	Grama Niladhari (formerly Grama Sevaka, or precinct headman)
GoSL	Government of Sri Lanka
IDNDR	International Decade for Natural Disaster Reduction
IDP	Internally displaced persons
IFRC	International Federation of Red Cross and Red Crescent Societies
INGO	International non-governmental organization
IPKF	Indian Peace-Keeping Force
ISDR	International Strategy for Disaster Reduction
ISGA	Interim Self-Governing Authority
JHU	Jatika Hela Urumaya (National Sinhala Heritage Party)
JVP	Janata Vimukti Peramuna (People's Liberation Front)
LTTE	Liberation Tigers of Tamil Eelam ("Tamil Tigers")
MP	Member of Parliament
MSF	Medicins Sans Frontières (Doctors Without Borders)
NERF	North East Reconstruction Fund
NGO	Non-governmental organization
P-TOMS	Post-Tsunami Operational Management Structure
RADA	Reconstruction and Development Agency
SIHRN	Subcommittee on Immediate Humanitarian Rehabilitation Needs
SLFP	Sri Lanka Freedom Party
SLMC	Sri Lanka Muslim Congress
SLMM	Sri Lanka Monitoring Mission
SN	Samurdhi Niyamaka (poverty-alleviation program worker)
TAFREN	Task Force for the Reconstruction of the Nation
TEC	Tsunami Evaluation Coalition
TO	Technical Officer
TRO	Tamils Rehabilitation Organization

UNHCR	United Nations High Commission for Refugees
UNICEF	United Nations Children's Fund
UNOCHA	United Nations Office for the Coordination of Humanitarian Affairs
UNP	United National Party
UPFA	United People's Freedom Alliance
UTHR	University Teachers for Human Rights
WHO	World Health Organization

Introduction

Michele R. Gamburd and
Dennis B. McGilvray

The Indian Ocean Tsunami, which devastated 70 percent of Sri Lanka's coastline and killed an estimated 35,000 people on 26 December 2004, was remarkable both in the magnitude of the disaster and in the scale of the relief and recovery operations mounted by national and international agencies.[1] This edited volume explores the aftermath of the tsunami in two culturally distinct coastal regions of Sri Lanka, the east and the southwest.

The disastrous ocean waves caused by an undersea subduction earthquake off the western coast of Sumatra fatally struck the coast lines of most nations bordering the Indian Ocean. However, the greatest catastrophic damage and death toll occurred in the Indonesian province of Aceh, the islands of southern Thailand, the Indian territory of the Andaman Islands, the south Indian state of Tamil Nadu, and the island nation of Sri Lanka. Coastal settlements and villages within 1 to 3 kilometers of the sea were reduced to rubble within a period of 20 minutes, and tens of thousands of victims died. All told, over 220,000 people died and over 2.4 million people were affected (Telford, Cosgrave and Houghton 2006: 33; Renner and Chafe 2007: 11; Le Billon and Waizenegger 2007: 411). An estimated 436,000 houses were damaged or destroyed and 1,850,000 people displaced (Sarvananthan and Sanjeewanie 2008: 340). It was an experience for which no one was remotely prepared.[2]

Disasters unfold within pre-existing economic, social, and political contexts. In this volume, the authors examine the social and political aftermath of the tsunami. Drawing from interdisciplinary research performed in 2005–8 in Sri Lanka, the contributors present analysis from diverse scholarly perspectives. Oliver-Smith suggests that "The multiple forms, enactments, and constructions that a disaster may take also elicit multiple interpretations from many disciplinary approaches, each with widely varying methodological tools and theoretical and practical goals" (1999: 21). This volume brings together experts from anthropology, political science, demography, and disaster studies to explore the multifaceted nature of tsunami relief and recovery in Sri Lanka.

What's been written about the tsunami

The scale of the Indian Ocean Tsunami is rivaled by the diverse and varied wave of publications that it has triggered. Stories of the disaster abound, including moving

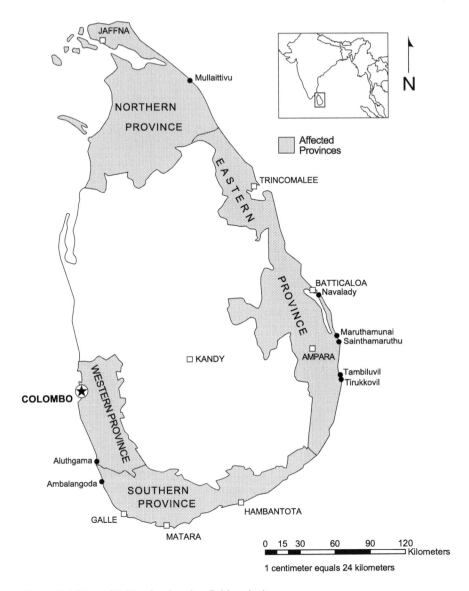

Figure 0.1 Map of Sri Lanka showing fieldwork sites.

tales of harrowing experiences and heart-shattering losses. For example, Erich Krauss (2006), a specialist in natural disasters, provides a first-hand account of the tsunami in Thailand for a popular audience; and Joe Funk's edited volume (2005) provides photographs of the event, accompanied by hair-raising tales of survival. Reporters quickly wrote up human interest stories, and relief workers captured the humanitarian efforts in the aftermath of the tsunami. In this vein, Ann Morris (2005) and a UNICEF photographer document the story of a Thai family before and after the tsunami disaster, and Carrie Lock (2006) writes a thoughtful, respectful narrative about her experience as a relief worker in southern Sri Lanka. People have also written fictional accounts of the event, including a moving volume of Sri Lankan short stories (Rajapakse 2007).

Experts and practicing professionals have also evaluated events in the aftermath of the tsunami. Disaster specialists have studied the response, the relief efforts, and the recovery process in a variety of nations (Athukorala, *et al.* 2005; Cashman 2006; Cheng 2007; Frerks and Klem 2005c; Hassmiller 2007; Manning 2006; Phillips 2008; Telford, Cosgrave and Houghton 2006; Zhang 2006). Documenting institutional responses to the disaster, non-governmental organizations (NGOs), inter-governmental institutions, and government bodies have written reports about their activities (Anderson 2008; Couldrey and Morris 2005; Crespin 2006; Walton 2008). Publications include Congressional hearing transcripts on the costs of relief aid, NGO and INGO reports, and governmental agency analyses (Center for Disease Control and Prevention (US) 2005; Horobin 2005; Mamadough 2008; Preston 2008; Telford 2007; United States 2005a, 2005b). The Human Rights Center (2005) reviews human rights situations in five hard-hit countries, including Sri Lanka; and in India, the People's Tribunal also discussed the human-rights implications of the tsunami (Muricken and Kumar 2005).

Academics have chimed in from a variety of perspectives. For example, natural scientists have written about the geological factors involved in the tsunami, and the event's effects on natural systems (such as coral reefs, mangrove swamps, and sea creatures) (Barbier 2008; Brodie 2008; Danielsen 2005; Shaw 2008). Scholars have published geophysical materials on plate tectonics (McCaffrey 2009; Okal 2008; Wijetunge 2008), discussed ecological effects on coastal zones in the aftermath of the tsunami (Kerr 2007; Phongsuwan 2007), and reviewed proposals about coastal zone protections (Olwig 2007). Engineering and technical reports cover the effect of tidal waves on buildings, wells, and other infrastructure, and some include hazard maps, survival guides, descriptions of warning systems, and documents on preparedness (Geist 2006; Goff 2005; Green 2006; Hodgson 2006; International Water Management Institute 2005; Samarajiva 2005; Srinivas 2008; Tomita 2006).

In addition to addressing damage to the natural and built environment, scholars have documented the social consequences of the disaster. Mental health specialists have addressed issues of post-traumatic stress disorder and grieving (Domroes 2006; Hawkins and Rao 2008). Health professionals and social workers discuss human health issues, including mental health studies concerning post-traumatic stress disorder and other psychological effects (Galappatti 2005). One report suggests the importance of understanding non-Western cultures and the value of community-based services in dealing with social trauma (Hawkins and Rao 2008: 33). Another report (Rajkumar, Premkumar and Tharyan 2008) notes that adverse long-term mental health consequences of the tsunami in coastal India were observed nine months after the disaster at much lower rates than had originally been predicted. Individuals relied on culturally specific coping mechanisms and meaning-making strategies rather than formal, Western professional interventions (2008: 844, 852).

Providing information specific to Sri Lanka, scholars have contributed insightful analysis of the local situation. Swarna Jayaweera (2005) provides a short statistical study of the tsunami's impact at the household level in two Sri Lankan districts on the south and west coast, and Sarvananthan and Sanjeewanie (2008) and Moonesinghe (2007) present results of surveys done in tsunami-affected areas. De Mel and Ruwanpura (2006) focus specifically on Sri Lankan women's experiences in the tsunami. Rajan Philips (2005) considers the power struggles between the tourism industry and local fishing communities regarding access to beachside property, and Nandini Gunawardena discusses allegations that "tsunami rehabilitation is being used to promote big business and tourism at the expense of local communities" (2008: 77).[3] Muttukrishna Sarvananthan (2005) passionately discusses his views of corruption in the distribution of tsunami aid in the north and east. Jayadeva Uyangoda offers trenchant political analysis (2005a, 2005b), and K. Tudor Silva (2009) examines the long-term effects of disaster management. In sum, the international community of academics and humanitarian workers has amply documented the Indian Ocean Tsunami and its aftermath.

Sri Lanka, South Asia, and the Indian Ocean

To understand the tsunami and its aftermath, it is useful to situate Sri Lanka within the wider frameworks of Asia and the Indian Ocean. South Asia has been the center of old-world trade for millennia, and merchants used routes on both land and sea. As traders made their way around the Indian Ocean, they transported not only goods but also people and philosophies. For example, first Hinduism and then Buddhism spread from India to Sri Lanka and Southeast Asia by maritime routes; later Islam arrived in South India and Sri Lanka by means of Persian and Arab trade across the Indian Ocean (Schmidt 1995: 122; McGilvray 1998a). Located at the tip of the Indian subcontinent, Sri Lanka has been central to this trans-Asiatic cultural exchange for centuries.

When Vasco da Gama rounded the tip of Africa in 1498 and landed on the southwest coast of India, he initiated the extension of the ocean trade and heralded the colonial incursions of European powers into the Indian Ocean. Sri Lanka was colonized successively for about 150 years apiece by the Portuguese (1505–1658), the Dutch (1658–1796), and the British (1796–1948), achieving independence in 1948 (Peebles 2006). Since that time, the island nation's international connections have continued, and Sri Lanka is now closely integrated into the global economy through the export of tea and garments (Hewamanne 2007; Institute of Policy Studies 2005; Lynch 2007), the flow of transnational laborers to the Gulf (Gamburd 2000), and the influx of foreign tourists to its tropical beaches.

Global economic dynamics affect Sri Lanka as they affect many developing countries; Sri Lanka has borrowed heavily from foreign donors. To help the country pay back its debt, the International Monetary Fund has periodically imposed

Structural Adjustment Programs, and a number of nations in the Global North provide funding and advice for development (Gunawardena 2008: 72; Ruwanpura 2000: 10). Alongside this economic development (and some say caused thereby), Sri Lanka fell into ethnic conflict and civil war (Richardson 2005; Winslow and Woost 2004). Regional and global powers have sought to bring an end to the conflict, with minimal success.

The Indian Ocean Tsunami brought home in vivid detail the shared interests of those who dwell on this ocean's shores, uniting the region in tragedy. In the aftermath of the tsunami, transnational connections again came into play, as the international community offered unprecedented amounts of financial help for reconstruction (Renner and Chafe 2007: 11). The disaster and its aftermath both reveal and challenge many of the social, economic, and political relations that predate the tsunami. As we discuss the theoretical perspectives that shape the analysis in this volume, we examine these relations in turn.

Theoretical perspectives

The ample materials published about the tsunami document what happened in the natural and social worlds. This level of detailed information is both valuable and overwhelming. Several theoretical perspectives provide key insights for spotting patterns and identifying larger dynamics in the data on human relations. The following three theoretical frameworks have been useful for our study.

Disaster construction: the social basis of community vulnerability

Rigg, Grundy-Warr, Law, and Tan-Mullins suggest that "Natural hazards only become disasters when humans are involved" (2008: 137). It comes as no surprise, then, that human social dynamics impinge on disaster relief and recovery. The field of disaster studies provides a framing context for this volume. In particular, we are interested in demonstrating what ethnographic insights can offer to the study of disasters (Frerks and Klem 2005c). Susanna M. Hoffman and Anthony Oliver-Smith have edited two excellent volumes (1999, 2002) on disasters from an anthropological perspective. Their theoretical position, political ecology, is one that we use in this volume.

Hoffman and Oliver-Smith suggest that disasters are "all-encompassing occurrences" (1999: 1) that affect multiple dimensions of life, including the environment, human technologies, and various aspects of society. Disasters highlight human relationships with the environment. Sudden catastrophic shifts in the environment (whether natural or manmade) reveal the fundamental organization of society, including inequalities and antagonisms (Hoffman and Oliver-Smith 1999: 4–6). As people deal with the social disturbance caused by a disaster, concerns about property, identity, morality, and legality arise. Allegiances and alliances shift and change in the face of social upheaval. Interventions by individuals, groups, organizations, and governments can and do shape fundamental changes in society at these crucial junctures. Although the natural sciences may provide an ample explanation of hazards, it is the social sciences that elucidate hazards' effects on individuals and their communities.

As an Oxfam International report suggests, "Disasters, however 'natural,' are profoundly discriminatory. Wherever they hit, pre-existing structures and social conditions determine that some members of the community will be less affected while others pay a higher price" (Hyndman 2008: 101–2). Marginalized groups often suffer more and get less help for recovery. For example, researchers suggest that in Somalia, the tsunami compounded an existing humanitarian crisis (UNOCHA Somalia office 2005) and that in India, members of certain castes and communities received less than others (Hawkins and Rao 2008: 41; Thangaraj 2005: 85). Similarly, some scholars found evidence of patronage, favoritism, and corrupt distribution practices in Sri Lanka (Sarvananthan 2005; Sarvananthan and Sanjeewanie 2008: 343; Moonasinghe 2007: 63). Disasters often affect the poor, the marginalized, and the disempowered more than they do the rest of a population. For this and other reasons, the humanitarian community has since 1997 set out to improve the quality and accountability of disaster assistance under the Sphere project and its Humanitarian Charter and Minimum Standards in Disaster Response (Sphere 2004; see Kuhn this volume).

Gender identity forms a common basis for differential treatment. Various scholars have explored gender issues, showing that women suffered more than men did from the tsunami (Hines 2007; Ruwanpura 2008a). Renner and Chafe report that two thirds of the Sri Lankan deaths and over seventy percent of fatalities in Indonesia were female (2007: 14). Similarly, Hawkins and Rao report that in India, "three times more women than men died" (2008: 36). The Tsunami Evaluation Coalition's authoritative Synthesis Report indicates that children and the elderly also suffered disproportionately (2006: 35). At play here are biological factors such as age and sexual dimorphism. Also of note, however, are cultural conditions that keep women and girls from learning how to swim or climb trees, put women in charge of caring for (and saving) children, and dictate that women dress in clothing that impedes running and grow long hair that catches on barbed wire (de Mel and Ruwanpura 2006: 36; Hyndman 2008: 109; Rigg, *et al.* 2008: 142; see also Lawrence this volume).

After the immediate hazard passed, gender roles continued to affect men and women differently. Gender issues affected women's lives in tsunami camps and temporary shelters. For example, Renner and Chafe suggest that some women experienced embarrassment, harassment, and abuse in temporary camps (2007: 14). Furthermore, even development programs implemented for humanitarian purposes such as disaster relief are deeply gendered (Hyndman 2008: 103). For example, de Mel and Ruwanpura suggest that post-tsunami training programs relegated women's work to the informal sector (2006: 44). In addition, state policies on property deeds disadvantaged women; preexisting gender inequalities affected the distribution of property deeds for donor-given houses, as well as disbursement of relief money to female-headed households (Renner and Chafe 2007: 14; see also McGilvray and Lawrence this volume). Outside the sphere of formal governance, Jennifer Hyndman (2008) suggests that gender roles have shaped remarriage prospects differently for widows and widowers in eastern Sri Lanka, with men remarrying at a higher percentage and more freely than women do. Gender distinctions and other forms of identity politics actively affect how individuals recover from catastrophes.

Long-term ethnographic fieldwork provides the social context against which to understand the aftermath of disasters. Furthermore, scholarly insights into the local political economy can help critique post-disaster interventions.

Disaster capitalism: economic opportunity and political influence

Economic inequalities and underdevelopment increase vulnerability to disasters and exacerbate the negative consequences of a natural event. Oliver Smith argues, "Disasters do not simply happen; they are caused. The high correlation between disaster proneness, chronic malnutrition, low income, and famine potential has led many researchers to the conclusion that the root cause of disasters can be attributed to the structural imbalances between rich and poor countries" (1999b: 74). What counts as a disaster for one group of people might be weathered without stress by another depending on preexisting vulnerabilities in the social environment.

But the causal arrow between disasters and adverse economic development can run both ways. Recently, a number of scholars have explored how capitalist elites use extreme events to further neoliberal agendas (Klein 2008). Le Billon and Waizenegger write, "Disasters reshape 'governable spaces'" (2007: 423). Kelman suggests that giving aid is a way of asserting dominance (2005). Schuller (2008) argues that disasters can and do trigger social change; often this change comes in the form of neo-liberal economic reform. He defines disaster capitalism as the "instrumental use of catastrophe ... to promote and empower a range of private, neoliberal capitalist interests" (Schuller 2008: 20). relate to Columbia

NGOs, international donors, and inter-governmental organizations have all stepped in after the tsunami to aid in Sri Lanka's relief and recovery operations. Along with material aid and technological advice, these organizations bring economic and political ideologies (e.g. democratic forms of government and neoliberal economic regulations) (Bastian 2005: 22–23; Le Billon and Waizenegger 2007: 413). Schuller notes that aid – including aid distributed after disasters – has world-ordering functions and may be used "for advancing the political, ideological, and economic interests of a transnational capitalist class" (2008: 22), particularly when urgent needs pave the way to implement policies without participation or debate. These tactics blur the boundaries between aid and politics, and they run against principles of participatory, rights-based reconstruction (Leckie 2005).

Analysis of the "disaster capitalism" of the tsunami focuses on how this natural hazard affected economic relations. Disaster specialists have long known that catastrophes are "instruments of change in the structure and organization of societies" (Hoffman and Oliver-Smith 1999: 9) because individuals, organizations, and social groups interact in new ways after a disaster. For example, in the aftermath of the tsunami Rigg, *et al.* (2008: 148) show how the government in a Thai village repossessed a stretch of valuable land "under the aegis of the 'common good.'" The article suggests, "Local people believed that this effort was designed to permit well-connected businesspeople to gain access to some of the best tourist development land on the island, evacuating the pre-tsunami operators under the cloak of hazard and disaster management and mitigation" (Rigg, *et al.* 2008: 148). Gunawardena (2008) and Silva (2009) suggest that a similar process may have taken place in Sri Lanka.

Soon after the tsunami, economists in Sri Lanka recognized the dramatic transformative effect this event could have on the nation's economy (Steele 2005). The disaster also affected political relations, particularly those related to Sri Lanka's ongoing civil war.

Disaster diplomacy: peace and conflict in the distribution of relief aid

Having recognized that scholars must focus on social structures in order to understand the effects of disasters, and having noted the interconnections between disasters and economic systems, we now turn to the topic of disaster diplomacy, or the interconnections between disasters and situations of conflict. Scholars have studied the conjunction of disaster relief and civil strife in many societies. Kelman suggests that disasters can either improve or worsen political conditions, and he hypothesizes that "disaster diplomacy inevitably provides an opportunity which is rarely grasped because non-disaster reasons dominate diplomatic interactions" (2005: 5.4).

Since disasters can prompt political change, theorists have studied the effects of the tsunami on two chronic civil conflicts: the insurgency in Aceh, Indonesia, and the long-standing war in Sri Lanka's north and east. Tsunami deaths in Aceh and Sri Lanka accounted for 90 percent of all tsunami-related fatalities (Le Billon and Waizenegger 2007: 411). In both cases, the tsunami unsettled the existing power relations and provided a "pivotal point motivating change" (Hoffman and Oliver-Smith 1999: 10), but only in Aceh did the disaster lead to successful peace-making.

In Aceh, the tsunami facilitated the settlement of a civil conflict nearly 30 years old. Within eight months of the tsunami, the Free Aceh Movement (Gerakan Aceh Merdeka, or GAM) and the government of Indonesia signed a Memorandum of Understanding (MoU). Scholars suggest that although peace talks were already underway, the tsunami and subsequent international attention to the area facilitated negotiations (Renner and Chafe 2007: 22).

The political and economic conflict in Aceh centered on dueling concepts of national identity (whether the disputed territory was Acehnese or Indonesian) and which group was entitled to benefit from extraction of oil and timber resources (McCarthy 2007: 315). Structural violence in the form of regional inequalities and unjust exploitation by the Indonesian state prompted the GAM's separatist movement in 1976. McCarthy sums up the conflict in Aceh by stating: "Wider populations can observe the prospect of high rents generated from the resource industry flowing to the state, multinational corporations and outside investors while the environmental and social costs – large-scale pollution and loss of productive customary landholdings – are borne by local agrarian populations" (2007: 316). Economic inequalities facilitated secessionist resistance, which the Indonesian state met with violent military repression.

When the tsunami struck Aceh, democratic and decentralizing reforms had been underway in Indonesia for some years (Renner and Chafe 2007: 21; Le Billon and Waizenegger 2007: 415, 420). At the same time, GAM had suffered a series of military setbacks and had little civilian support (McCarthy 2007: 326). GAM was unable to administer any tsunami aid, and the Indonesian government gained legitimacy in the eyes of the local population by controlling this humanitarian endeavor while simultaneously continuing to repress GAM's insurgency (Le Billon and Waizenegger 2007: 418). International diplomacy and pre-existing conditions created a context in which the disputing parties could reach a peace accord that promised "extensive autonomy and a package of economic concessions" for Aceh (McCarthy 2007: 326). This package addressed many Acehnese grievances yet in turn enhanced local legitimacy of the Indonesian state.

Events surrounding the tsunami succeeded in jump-starting the peace process in Aceh, but continued progress will depend on equitable control over resources and local benefits from development activities. Despite demobilization of the rebel fighters, economic inequalities and political tensions remain. For example, the 2006 law that formalized the 2005 peace agreement watered down key provisions of the MoU. Still at issue are the distribution of revenues from Aceh's resources of timber, oil, and natural gas; the degree of regional autonomy in Aceh; and impunity granted to the Indonesian government and military for past human rights violations (Renner and Chafe 2007: 25). Continued peace in the region will depend on whether the Indonesian state returns sufficient development benefits (economic justice and substantive public goods) and political autonomy (legitimate public authority) to the area in exchange for ongoing resource extraction.

In contrast to the successful peace process in Aceh, in Sri Lanka the tsunami exacerbated existing tensions in the civil war and may have accelerated the return to conflict. A separatist guerrilla movement had been fighting the central government for over two decades. The so-called Eelam Wars – fought between the Sri Lankan military and the Liberation Tigers of Tamil Eelam (LTTE) – had a major impact on society, but one that was significantly different between the north and east on the one hand and the southwest on the other. Thus Sri Lanka's tsunami relief and recovery operations took place within a polity fraught with intense internal conflicts.

When the tsunami struck in December 2004, the ceasefire that had been signed in early 2002 was already crumbling. The subsequent politicization of disaster relief further undermined peace efforts (Le Billon and Waizenegger 2007: 418). Specifically, disputes over who would control tsunami aid enhanced existing political tensions, as the Government of Sri Lanka sought to centralize the distribution of international aid throughout the island, while the LTTE argued that it should control the distribution of aid in the territories it controlled through its own organization, the Tamils Rehabilitation Organization (TRO) (Silva 2009: 67). This dispute, crystallized in litigation and political unrest surrounding the notorious Post-Tsunami Operational Management Structure (P-TOMS) agreement of July 2005, echoed ongoing disagreements about sovereignty. In particular, the P-TOMS agreement was reminiscent of a 2003 discussion of the LTTE's proposal for an "Interim Self-Governing Authority," which many in the Sinhala-Buddhist southwest saw as a prototype or a proxy for an independent state of Tamil Eelam (Centre for Policy Alternatives 2005: 29). Sri Lanka's Muslim minority was also concerned about the P-TOMS proposal, viewing it as further evidence that neither the government of Sri Lanka nor the LTTE were sincerely interested in bringing the Muslims directly into the peace process (McGilvray and Raheem 2007).

The tsunami was but the latest (and perhaps not the worst) in a series of catas- trophes to affect the inhabitants of northern and eastern Sri Lanka. The tsunami killed about 35,000 people, compared to an estimated 86,000 killed or missing in the civil war; and the tsunami displaced over 500,000 people along two-thirds of Sri Lanka's coastline, compared to 800,000 people displaced at the peak of the war (Renner and Chafe 2007: 27). This led to questions about which displaced people most required aid, and why some were seen as more deserving than others (Kuar Grewal 2006). As Le Billon and Waizenneger write, "Disasters ... are prone to causing or deepening inequalities along pre-existing fault lines in societies, increas- ing grievances and disaffection and possibly heightening the risk of (renewed) conflict" (2007: 415).

In Sri Lanka, post-tsunami wrangling over territorial authority and the distribu- tion of relief and recovery funds quickly fell into familiar and unproductive ruts – ruts that had theretofore impeded the peace process and thereafter slowed and politicized the distribution of aid, particularly to the war-weary north and east. Political influence of the majority population in the southwest, combined with logistical difficulties in reaching the north and east, created a situation where reconstruction processes moved forward more quickly in the Sinhala south (Renner and Chafe 2007: 30; Silva 2009: 70). Such conditions impeded the trust necessary for a successful post-tsunami peace effort (Stokke and Shanmugaratnam 2005). Le Billon and Waizenegger write, "It is arguably in response to the failure of ter- ritorializing an alternative 'sovereign' and truly 'humanitarian' space that the logic of war ultimately prevailed" (2007: 422). Reflecting increased political tensions, violations of the ceasefire escalated during the summer of 2006. When the ceasefire was officially abrogated in early 2008, the Sri Lankan military began an eighteen month campaign, culminating in May 2009 with the complete reacquisition of territory formerly held by the LTTE.

Although disasters can open a window for political change, "Pre-disaster political trends play a major role in the outcome of disasters" (Le Billon and Waizenegger 2007: 412). Political marginality and economic underdevelopment in Aceh and in the northern and eastern areas of Sri Lanka made them especially vulnerable in the aftermath of the tsunami disaster. But in Indonesia, the momen- tum was towards peace, while in Sri Lanka the peace process was already failing. In both Aceh and Sri Lanka, the tsunami has brought about social, economic, and political change that has strengthened the government's position. In Aceh, the tsunami led to a ceasefire; in Sri Lanka the tsunami destabilized a ceasefire and weakened the LTTE's hold over the north and east. Le Billon and Waizenegger write, "Many governments have exploited disasters to increase their strength, improve their image and maintain the status quo, notably through major foreign contributions to relief efforts and occasionally under false pretence of post-disaster 'transformation' of society rather than the 'reconstruction' of previous inequalities" (2007: 414). Scholars now debate the role of the tsunami in allowing the government of Sri Lanka to unite the island under its sole control in 2009 (See Keenan this volume).

What this book offers

Given that so much has already been written about the tsunami, the reader may wonder what new knowledge and insight can be gained from this volume. This book offers an interdisciplinary discussion of a range of issues spurred by the tsunami as it affected Sri Lanka. The tsunami was a complex disaster, a "total-izing event" (Oliver-Smith 1996: 304) that affected a nation already fractured by poverty and ethnic conflict. In this volume, we explore to what extent "culture matters" in responses to a natural disaster. We offer a well rounded, triangulated, multidisciplinary overview of the island as it was before the tsunami, during the events of the tsunami, and during the relief and reconstruction process that followed the disaster.

In a single book, we bring together wide interdisciplinary skills and detailed comparative knowledge, combining in-depth local ethnographic fieldwork with broader demographic and political analysis of the Sinhala-speaking Buddhist and Catholic south-western coast in the Galle district, and the Tamil-speaking Hindu and Muslim eastern coastal districts of Batticaloa and Ampara. Contributing authors have extensive pre-tsunami experience in Sri Lanka and South Asia and have collaborated in a long-term interdisciplinary NSF-sponsored research project begun shortly after the disaster. Through rich and detailed qualitative data, three anthropologists explore the role played by family structure, kinship loyalties, caste affiliations, religious beliefs and institutions, non-governmental organizations, political networks, and local community associations in the post-tsunami relief and recovery process. At the same time, the volume recognizes and assesses the importance of larger macro-level factors, which are explored through chapters contributed by a sociological demographer, a political scientist, and two disaster specialists.

Overview of chapters

This volume has nine chapters divided into three main sections. The first section opens with a country-wide overview of the tsunami disaster written by political scientist Alan Keenan, followed by a comparative quantitative analysis written by demographer Randall Kuhn. The middle section of the book offers three ethno-graphic case-studies of the aftermath of the tsunami drawn from the fieldwork of Michele Gamburd, who works in the Sinhala-speaking Galle District along Sri

Lanka's southwest coast; Patricia Lawrence, who works in the Tamil-speaking Batticaloa District on the east coast; and Dennis McGilvray, who works with Tamil-speaking Muslims and Hindus in the hard-hit eastern Ampara District. Together, these ethnographic portraits reveal important contrasts between different sides of the island and describe the experiences of different ethnic communities with tsunami relief and recovery. The third section of the book focuses on relief activities from an NGO and a disaster studies perspective. Timmo Gaasbeek writes about post-tsunami NGO outreach in eastern Sri Lanka and the culture of donor organizations. Georg Frerks examines the tsunami from a disaster-studies perspective, evaluating the recovery process by current global standards. The volume ends with a conclusion that summarizes the main points of the collected works and points to the benefits of interdisciplinary approaches in disaster research.

Keenan

Sri Lanka is an island united by natural disaster but divided by ongoing ethnic antagonisms. In the first chapter of the volume, political scientist Alan Keenan provides a synopsis of the political context in which post-tsunami relief and recovery operations unfolded. Keenan writes, "The Indian Ocean tsunami burst onto a fractured and deeply divided political landscape in Sri Lanka. In the immediate wake of the disaster, people came together and cooperated across ethnic and regional and political lines. Within weeks, however, old divisions reasserted themselves, fueled by new resources and a new set of grievances." Fleshing out this scenario, Keenan provides background on the various ethnic groups and political parties; on the history of the civil war, including the 2002 ceasefire and its 2008 abrogation; on the contents of the controversial Post-Tsunami Operational Management Structure (P-TOMS) agreement; and on the anti-NGO political rhetoric that has circulated in Sri Lanka over the past few years. He also shows how the difficult political situation that prevailed on the island at the time of the tsunami hampered efforts to respond to the disaster and complicated the delivery of aid. Delays and perceived inequities in turn exacerbated the complex conflict dynamics, encouraging a renewal of fierce combat between opposing parties in Sri Lanka's ongoing civil war.

Kuhn

In an interdisciplinary study, both qualitative and quantitative data are of value. Demographer Randall Kuhn sets up a quantitative framework for evaluating broad-scale regional differences in pre- and post-tsunami Sri Lanka, thus providing a population-level backdrop against which to view the qualitative, ethnographic data presented in subsequent chapters. Kuhn explores the literature on socioeconomic and ethnic variations in disaster impact and recovery. He then describes the methodologies used in Sri Lanka for collecting local-level quantitative data and discusses the problems of data reliability inherent in a project of this scale. He presents the preexisting socioeconomic differentials among affected and unaffected communities, taking account of ethnic backgrounds. His data highlight pre-tsunami patterns of advantage and vulnerability (in dwellings, occupation of marginal land, and economic wellbeing). In particular, the data reveal how a minority within a minority area, such as Tamils in Muslim-dominated coastal areas of Ampara District, faced elevated levels of vulnerability and exposure to tsunami impact – a point that is largely ignored in other post-tsunami literature. His data also capture the unprecedented magnitude of the international post-tsunami relief effort, which swamped the role of community-level factors and introduced new sources of ethnic differential. His analysis reveals patterns of ethnic and community variations in both objective and perceived indicators of long-term tsunami impact. Kuhn concludes with some comments on the relevance of these findings for Sri Lanka's recovery process and for future community-level analysis of disaster recovery programs.

In Sri Lanka, the tsunami struck coastal communities that differ significantly in terms of social structure, economy, language, religion, kinship patterns, and cultural identity. Hoffman and Oliver-Smith write, "Anthropology's long-term perspective and in-depth fieldwork have added significantly to comprehending the protracted repercussions calamities provide. The anthropological eye has further enhanced comprehension of factors that lead to people's vulnerability, bringing to light such matters as age, gender, social class, language, religion, ethnicity, and other distinctions" (1999: 3). The anthropologists contributing to this volume show how social practices led particular groups to be especially vulnerable to the tsunami, and how on-the-ground micro-politics have affected how tsunami recovery takes place. Issues of note include religious rituals of protection; domestic property rights, dowry and marriage patterns; jealousy and accusations of corruption; and interactions with institutions including the government, NGOs, religious organizations, and political parties.

Gamburd

Cultural anthropologist Michele Gamburd reports on events that took place within a year after the tsunami on Sri Lanka's predominantly Sinhala-Buddhist southwest coast. The village in the Galle District where Gamburd does fieldwork is a mile from the ocean; its dwellings were untouched by the tsunami, but its residents were on the front lines of recovery efforts. Local residents called the relief windfall "a golden wave" (*ratarang raellak*) of aid. Gamburd sets the context by discussing the support provided for tsunami-affected families. She then explores the local and national renegotiation of social hierarchies. Situating her analysis within South Asian understandings of class and caste status, she examines the fine-grained status relations at stake in narratives about entitlement, immorality, favoritism, and corruption in the distribution of aid. Specifically, she considers the moral evaluation of people who took what they did not deserve, or who did not take what they were entitled to receive. She examines how government administrators used the same systems of logic to position themselves as moral agents and to defend themselves against the accusations of corruption that circulated freely after the tsunami. She also considers how discussions of entitlement affected understandings of national sovereignty and ethnicity by examining political wrangling about the Post-Tsunami Operational Management Structure (P-TOMS). Gamburd concludes with the re-envisioning of an old historical legend about the Sinhala cultural heroine Vihara Maha Devi as relief and recovery operations unfolded against the politically charged backdrop of Sri Lanka's ongoing ethnic conflict.

Lawrence

In vivid prose, Patricia Lawrence presents a series of interweaving stories told by residents of the Tamil fishing village of Navalady in Batticaloa District to illustrate the religious responses of the community to devastating personal loss and to slow post-tsunami reconstruction. Navalady was a mixed Hindu and Catholic village to begin with, but because they were located near the beach, the temples of Hindu goddesses suffered the main brunt of the tsunami. The seeming inability of traditional Tamil *amman* ("mother") deities, especially the village sea goddess and a local cobra goddess, to protect the village from the catastrophic waves generated anger and religious doubt among many Hindus. At the same time, the nearby Catholic church for Our Lady of Good Voyages – which was spared by the tsunami – grew in popularity. However, Lawrence shows how all of the religious responses to the tsunami have shared an enduring cultural allegiance to the protective powers of the divine feminine, whether by the force of Hindu *sakti* or by the blessings of the Virgin Mary, or both. Some survivors in Navalady have also erected elaborate family tsunami shrines to commemorate their lost family members, which have helped them face the necessity of returning to sea fishing as a livelihood. Conditioning all of the post-tsunami traumas and readjustments in Navalady was the intermittent Sri Lankan civil war, which resulted in a regime of self-censorship and fear within ordinary Tamil families. Surprisingly, Lawrence suggests that the descriptions of gruesome deaths and mutilated corpses caused by the tsunami – bodies often entangled in military razor wire – were exempt from this self-censorship, giving people license to speak openly of death in a way that proved cathartic. Over a period of three years following the tsunami, Lawrence documents the gradual healing of religious faith in Navalady, and the resumption of productive fishing activities.

McGilvray and Lawrence

More information from the east coast is provided by anthropologists Dennis McGilvray and Patricia Lawrence as they examine the effects of post-tsunami housing programs on women's ownership of dwellings and domestic property among the Tamils, Muslims, and Burghers of Ampara and Batticaloa districts. After the tsunami, the national government and a competing welter of international donors began constructing new permanent dwellings for those families who had lost everything. Many families were prohibited from rebuilding on their original beachfront house sites because they fell within the fluctuating government-designated "buffer zones." As the authors describe, finding new land for resettlement projects farther away from the shore caused huge difficulties and delays. Once land and houses were procured, tsunami housing programs island-wide commonly assumed that the "head of household" and the "owner" of a damaged dwelling would be a male, not a female, person – typically a father, a husband, or a son. The fact that traditionally mothers, wives, and daughters held sole title – or joint title with their husbands – to domestic dwellings in eastern Tamil, Muslim, and Burgher communities was largely overlooked by government and foreign NGO relief agencies. This posed a potential threat to women's traditional property rights on the matrilineal-matrilocal east coast, where land and houses are considered women's dowry property to be handed down from parents to daughters at marriage. Illustrating their fieldwork findings with a series of case studies, McGilvray and Lawrence reveal that the pre-existing system of matrilocal residence and transfer of dowry-house property to daughters continues despite the emergency period when reconstruction funds and NGO house deeds were transferred to men. In the post-tsunami era, Tamil, Muslim, and Burgher families continue to plan strategically to acquire the matrilocal dowry houses needed for their daughters to get married, and this seems likely to restore women's domestic property rights in the next generation if not sooner.

Gaasbeek

Much of the tsunami literature pertains to NGO activities in the aftermath of the disaster. Examining this literature critically in context of his own relief and recovery experiences, disaster studies expert Timmo Gaasbeek provides an NGO insider's eye-witness account of what happened in the Batticaloa area from the moment the waves hit the beaches of Batticaloa until the tail-end of the reconstruction process. Gaasbeek describes the coordinated activities by locally present local and international humanitarian agencies in the immediate aftermath of the tsunami; the well meaning efforts by local citizens to help; the government initiatives to restore power and transportation services and to coordinate the administration of aid; and the activities of disaster specialists and INGO workers. While ultimately lauding these accomplishments in post-disaster relief and recovery, Gaasbeek points out cases of corruption, inefficiency, incompetence, and competition. In particular, he argues that three crucial aspects of the tsunami response have been misrepresented or ignored in the common discourses on the topic. First, the initial response (at least in eastern Sri Lanka) was effective and, though hectic, not chaotic. This was due to a pre-existing NGO co-ordination mechanism and efficient sharing of resources, and to the government's success in restoring within days the roads and the supply of fuel and electricity. Initially the response capabilities of the various actors formed an almost natural symbiosis. Over the next three years, the bulk of the post-tsunami needs were met, but with avoidable wastage. Second, Gaasbeek comments on the way in which international NGOs operated. Caught in a struggle for their institutional reputations back home, INGOs engaged in open competition and in sometimes unnecessary high-visibility projects. In the process, the international normative debate on global standards of aid-delivery became a strategic rhetorical resource for agencies that were unable to mount a quick response. Third, Gaasbeek discusses the role of expatriates on the ground. Many aid workers either had insufficient experience or were used to working in failed states. They often worked with language barriers and a poor understanding of local cultural dynamics. Together with highly visible but culturally inappropriate ways of spending leisure time, the behavior of foreign NGO personnel sometimes led to local misunderstandings and misgivings.

Frerks

Using the criteria of international disaster policy standards, Georg Frerks judges the effectiveness of Sri Lankan governmental efforts to provide relief to its citizens in the aftermath of the tsunami catastrophe. He discusses the Sri Lankan case along four general dimensions that are prominent in the disaster studies literature: 1) sensitivity to political complexity and conflict; 2) assessment of community vulnerability and resilience; 3) awareness of local perceptions and popular discourses; and 4) impacts of political culture and patronage. He finds that the complexity of the Sri Lankan tsunami relief process was overwhelmingly conditioned by the pre-existing civil-military conflict between the Government of Sri Lanka and the LTTE Tamil rebels, who were unable to agree on a joint tsunami relief modality. He observes that the north and the east, regions already suffering chronic civilian displacement and violence, were disproportionately affected by the tsunami. Local perceptions and discourses in the wake of the tsunami exhibited diverse reinterpretations of traditional religious beliefs along with widespread suspicions of insider profiteering, and the influence of patronage politics in the immediate disbursement of tsunami relief was striking. In his conclusion, Frerks is highly critical of the tsunami relief efforts of the Sri Lankan government, asserting that it amounted to "an ethnicized, politicized, and communalized distribution of aid based on politically charged patron-client relations."

Notes

1 Estimates of the Sri Lankan death toll continue to vary, even years after the disaster. The Tsunami Evaluation Coalition estimates the toll at 35,322 (Telford, Cosgrave and Houghton 2006: 33); Saravananthan and Sanjeewanie put the number at 36,858 (2008: 340); and Le Billon and Waizenegger suggest the figure 39,000 (2007: 417).
2 For a useful set of research web-links on the Indian Ocean Tsunami, go to the following University of Colorado Natural Hazards Center URL: http://www.colorado.edu/hazards/resources/web/tsunamis.html
3 Although it points out important issues, Gunawardena's discussion romanticizes fishing communities and exaggerates their poverty and vulnerability.

1 Building the conflict back better

The politics of tsunami relief and reconstruction in Sri Lanka[1]

Alan Keenan

Introduction

The Indian Ocean tsunami burst onto a fractured and deeply divided political landscape in Sri Lanka. In the immediate wake of the disaster, people came together and cooperated across ethnic, regional, and political lines. Within weeks, however, old divisions reasserted themselves, fuelled by new resources and a new set of grievances. Efforts to respond to the disaster quickly met difficult political challenges that affected the quality and speed of assistance. This chapter, based in part on interviews with aid workers and international donor officials in February 2006, explores the political factors that complicated tsunami relief efforts. It also examines how various forms of aid delivery aggravated the political conflicts that have trapped Sri Lanka in civil war for more than 25 years.

Pre-tsunami politics and the civil war

The Indian Ocean tsunami had its most devastating impact in Sri Lanka in the predominantly Tamil and Tamil-speaking Northern and Eastern Provinces. These two provinces, merged into one administrative unit at the time of the tsunami, make up the bulk of the "Tamil homeland" claimed by many Sri Lankan Tamil nationalists. As a result, the north and east were the scene of intense fighting and large-scale destruction from the 1980s onwards. Hundreds of thousands of Tamils – and also large numbers of Muslims and Sinhalese – were uprooted during the various rounds of war between Tamil militants and the Sri Lankan government, and at the time of the December 2004 tsunami many of them remained displaced throughout the north and east. Although the majority of deaths from the tsunami occurred in the north and east, there was extensive damage and many lives lost in the predominantly Sinhalese south and west as well. The complex political relationships between all three communities – Tamils, Muslims, and Sinhalese – that were central to Sri Lanka's three decades of violent ethnic conflict were also at the heart of how tsunami relief and reconstruction operations were regarded and managed politically.

Sinhala and Tamil nationalisms

The violent struggle to establish a separate state in the name of the Tamil people of Sri Lanka, ultimately led by the Tamil Tigers (officially known as the Liberation Tigers of Tamil Eelam, or LTTE) began in the mid-1970s. It originated in the failure of Sri Lanka's post-independence political leadership to agree on a political system that would grant citizens of all ethnicities equal access to the resources and protections of the state.

Within a decade of independence from the British in 1948, Sinhalese politicians had discovered the benefits of using the state to rectify what many of the predominantly Buddhist Sinhalese (74 percent of the population) saw as the humiliations and disadvantages they had suffered under British colonial rule. Their grievances centered on the loss of prestige accorded to Buddhism, the dominance of English as the language of the elite and of economic opportunity, and the disproportionate number of Tamils holding civil-service jobs and gaining entrance to universities. Exploiting popular conceptions of democracy as unrestrained majority rule and popular myths about the essentially Buddhist character of the island, Sinhalese politicians from the 1950s through the 1970s passed a series of laws that effectively defined the state as Sinhalese and Buddhist. The Sinhala Only Act passed by Parliament in 1956 made Sinhala the sole official language for government work and forced many Tamil-speaking bureaucrats from their jobs while imposing major burdens on Tamil speakers throughout the island. The 1972 constitution granted Buddhism a special, semi-official status, while affirmative action policies in the 1970s permitted Sinhalese students to gain admission to university with lower marks than many Tamils. This policy was a major blow to the career prospects of Tamil youth, especially those in the northern Jaffna peninsula, where Tamil nationalist militancy soon emerged. State-sponsored irrigation and settlement schemes from the 1940s into the 1980s, which brought many landless Sinhalese peasants into the Eastern Province and fundamentally changed the demographic balance of that Tamil-majority region, were another important cause of Tamil alienation and anger.

A series of compromises between Sinhalese and Tamil politicians – granting limited autonomy for the Tamil dominated north and east and equal status to the Tamil language – were abandoned after national protest campaigns by Sinhala opposition parties. The Bandaranaike-Chelvanayagam Pact of 1957 – signed by the Sri Lanka Freedom Party (SLFP) leader, Prime Minister S.W.R.D. Bandaranaike, and S.J.V. Chelvanayakam, the Tamil leader of the Federal Party – was abrogated after protests led by the United National Party (UNP). A similar agreement in 1965 between Chelvanayakam and the UNP Prime Minister, Dudley Senanayake, was defeated after protests by the SLFP. From 1956 onward, non-violent Tamil protests against their second-class citizenship were met with increasingly violent repression by government forces. Tamils were victims of violent mob attacks, with increasing degrees of state-support, in 1956, 1958, 1977, 1979, 1981, and worst of all in 1983.

Physical insecurity and the failure to reach lasting agreements with Sinhala political leaders radicalized many Tamils. Demands for limited forms of political autonomy for the combined Northern and Eastern Provinces, where Tamil speakers (mostly Hindu, but also Christian and Muslim) combine to form a majority, eventually became demands for a separate state. The Vaddukoddai Resolution of 1976 enshrined separatism as the official policy of the major Tamil political parties, whose senior leaders faced increasing pressure from militant youth.

Small-scale anti-state violence by various groups of Tamil youth in the north eventually exploded into full-scale war. A Tamil Tiger ambush of an army truck that killed 13 Sinhalese soldiers was the pretext for massive state-sanctioned anti-Tamil violence in July 1983, first in Colombo and then throughout the island. Over the course of nearly two weeks of violence, an estimated 500 to 2000 Tamils were killed, thousands of houses and businesses burned and looted, and tens of thousands made internal refugees (Tambiah 1986: 13–33). Tamil militant groups, including the LTTE, received a flood of new recruits. From this violence originated the global Tamil diaspora, ultimately numbering some one million people, which went on to play a crucial role in funding the separatist struggle of various militant groups, particularly the LTTE.

A series of pauses and peace talks punctuated Sri Lanka's decades of warfare. The first talks in 1985, brokered by the Indian government and held in Thimpu, Bhutan, quickly broke down, but gave birth to the "Thimpu principles," which set out the basic demands of Tamil nationalists and were endorsed by all major Tamil militant groups of the time.[2] The Indo-Lanka accord of 1987 briefly brought a halt to the fighting again. This agreement, forced upon Sri Lanka by the Indian government of Rajiv Gandhi, led to the 13th Amendment to the Sri Lankan Constitution, which established Provincial Councils throughout the island, including a merged Northeast council which eventually functioned for less than a year in 1998. The Indian Peacekeeping Force (IPKF), brought in to guarantee the agreement, soon found itself fighting the LTTE, which alone among the five major Tamil militant groups rejected the accord. The IPKF ultimately withdrew from the island after stiff military resistance from the LTTE as well as political resistance from the Sri Lankan government, pressured by a violent uprising in the south of the island by the Sinhala nationalist and Maoist People's Liberation Front (known by its Sinhala initials as the JVP). A brief period of peace in the north and east was achieved in 1990, as then-President Premadasa used the lull in fighting with the Tigers to crush the JVP uprising. By then a number of other Tamil militant groups had abandoned separatism and joined with the government to fight the LTTE.[3]

A new peace initiative began in 1994 with the election of the SLFP's candidate for President, Chandrika Bandaranaike Kumaratunga. After a few months of cease-fire, peace talks collapsed in April 1995 when the LTTE returned to war, arguing that the government had never been serious about peace. Kumaratunga responded with a "war for peace" strategy. This saw an initially successful military campaign coupled with a series of proposals for constitutional reforms that would have devolved large amounts of power to the north and east and instituted other forms of power-sharing designed to address the grievances of Tamils and other minorities. By 2000, however, many of the government's military gains of the proceeding six years had been reversed. Its constitutional reforms had also failed to gain support from the UNP, which held the balance of power in the Parliament.

Throughout this period of heightened violence, all parties to the conflict nurtured a range of fears and grievances. While Tamils complained of their denial of equal language rights, adequate share of political power, and their continued vulnerability to state-sanctioned violence, Sinhalese had their own demographic and historical concerns. Brutal LTTE suicide attacks committed in the name of a Tamil separatist political project awakened deep-seated fears among many Sinhalese of eventually losing their distinctive cultural and political autonomy to the 60 million Tamils living in South India. Histories and myths of invasions from medieval South Indian dynasties are still invoked by many Sinhala nationalists and have a particular resonance given the collective sense of humiliation that remains after 500 years of Western colonialism.

There is also the important community of Muslims (or "Moors") who make up seven to eight percent of the population and who live throughout the island, with nearly a third residing in the Eastern Province. Mostly Tamil-speaking, yet seeking to divorce themselves from the Tamil separatist cause, the Muslims have played a shrewd and equivocal role in Sri Lanka's ethnic politics. Having suffered greatly at the hands of the LTTE – most grievously in the forced expulsion of 90 thousand Muslims from the Jaffna peninsula and other areas of the north in 1990 – Muslims began over the course of the war to develop their own reactive form of nationalism. With the LTTE and Tamil nationalists claiming the northeast as their ethnic homeland (Tamil Eelam), activist Muslims from the east also began to call for an autonomous administrative unit of their own (McGilvray and Raheem 2007: 26–28).

Even as the Tigers fought the Sinhalese-dominated state, they also killed thousands of Tamils aligned with rival political and militant movements. The Tigers enforced their claim to be "the sole representative of the Tamil people" through fear and violence, including the assassinations of the most prominent Tamil politicians of the past three decades. Indeed, political violence in Sri Lanka has taken place among and between all communities, and all have suffered from it. At the time of the tsunami, the separatist war had led to the deaths of an estimated 70,000 people and displaced upwards of one million others, out of a population of less than 20 million. Violence became deeply embedded in the everyday practices of the state, with torture and brutality a basic aspect of the police and political authority (Lawrence 2008).[4]

Ceasefire and the peace process of 2002–2006

The victory of the UNP and its allies in the parliamentary elections of December 2001 paved the way for the signing of a formal ceasefire agreement (CFA) between the Sri Lankan government and the LTTE in February 2002.[5] The agreement, facilitated by the Norwegian government, brought a temporary end to hostilities between the two warring parties and established a team of Nordic ceasefire monitors, known as the Sri Lanka Monitoring Mission (SLMM). By granting the LTTE exclusive access to large areas of the north and east, the agreement formalized Sri Lanka's division into two separate jurisdictions. It also effectively recognized the LTTE's de-facto – and highly authoritarian – state of Tamil Eelam, which featured courts of law, a police force, a tax system, and other administrative departments. At the same time, the central government continued to provide large amounts of humanitarian assistance to the civilian population and to fund basic public services – schools, hospitals, state banks – managed by its own civil servants in a unique system of dual administration. Although the CFA denied government forces access to large areas under LTTE control, the agreement allowed the LTTE to send its operatives into government controlled areas to do "political work." The agreement thus allowed the Tigers to strengthen the institutions of their proto-state, consolidate their control in other areas of the north and east, and gain greater international acceptance as the legitimate representative of the Tamil people. Achieving this latter objective was one of the central goals of the peace process for the LTTE.

From September 2002 to early 2003, the LTTE and the government, led by UNP Prime Minister Ranil Wickremasinghe, held six rounds of peace talks with Norwegian facilitation. The high point of the talks came in December 2002, when the LTTE agreed to explore a political settlement along the lines of a federal political system within a united Sri Lanka. This was the closest the LTTE had come to announcing that it might accept something less than a separate state, and many observers hailed it as a potential breakthrough. Initial rounds of negotiations also focused on establishing interim administrative arrangements through which the LTTE and the government could work together to "normalize" the situation in the north and east and improve the living standards for populations in LTTE areas. The government and LTTE eventually agreed to establish the Subcommittee on Immediate Humanitarian and Rehabilitation Needs (SIHRN), made up of equal representatives from both the LTTE and the government, with the aim of administering tangible aid to the Tamil civilians caught in the midst of the civil war in the northern Vanni region (Rainford and Sathkunanathan 2009: 36–42).

Central to international engagement in support of peace in Sri Lanka was financial support for the reconstruction and economic development of the north and east. The high point of international engagement came in Tokyo in June 2003 at a meeting of donor nations co-chaired by Japan, Norway, the European Union and the United States. Following an extensive needs assessment of the north and east carried out by the United Nations, the World Bank and the Asian Development Bank, more than 40 donors pledged some US $4.5 billion in assistance to Sri Lanka.

The Tokyo Donor Conference took place despite the absence of the LTTE, which had pulled out of peace talks in April 2003, ostensibly due to anger at being excluded from a previous donor meeting held in Washington DC.[6] In its April 2003 letter withdrawing from talks, the LTTE also expressed its frustration with what it said was the government's lack of cooperation in "normalizing" conditions for the civilian population in the north and east (Tamilnet 2005). For the LTTE, this would have required the full resettlement of the hundreds of thousands of Tamils displaced from their homes and thus the removal of the numerous High Security Zones established by the Sri Lankan military and the withdrawal of troops from Tamil areas in the north and east.

Eventually, the LTTE demanded that the government come up with a new, more effective mechanism to help "rehabilitate the war affected people of the northeast," one which would give the LTTE substantial powers, including control over inter-national financial assistance (Tamilnet 2005). Bound to remain within the terms of the Sri Lankan constitution and reluctant to strengthen the LTTE's power, the government's three successive proposals all fell short of LTTE demands (Rainford and Satkunanathan 2009: 87–90). At the end of October 2003, the LTTE proposed an "Interim Self-Governing Authority" (ISGA) for a merged north and east, on the basis of which it offered to restart talks with the government. Under its plan, the LTTE would appoint a majority of ISGA members, and the LTTE-controlled ISGA in turn would administer all matters relating to police, land, natural resources, taxes, revenue, development aid and certain judicial matters. Elections to the ISGA would not be held for five years and the ISGA would remain in force until a final settlement between the LTTE and the Sri Lankan government was reached (Rainford and Satkunanathan 2009: 91–4). While some viewed the ISGA proposal as the LTTE's opening gambit in what was expected to be a longer negotiation process, many Sinhalese saw it as a blueprint for a separate state in all but name. The ISGA would merely be the first step in the LTTE's quest to gain full control of the northeast through undemocratic means.

Although the UNP expressed reservations about the ISGA proposal, it said it would be willing to discuss it. Already frustrated, however, by what she saw as Prime Minister Wickremasinghe's overindulgence of the LTTE, President Kumaratunga, leader of the rival SLFP, reacted quickly and negatively to the ISGA. Within days of its announcement, in early November 2003, Kumaratunga suspended parliament and took control of four essential ministries – including the defense ministry – arguing that the UNP's stewardship of the peace process had endangered national security. What had been a quiet struggle for power between the President and the Prime Minister was now more bitter and more public. For the next five months, the peace process was essentially suspended. Eventually the President used her broad executive powers to call for a new parliamentary election. Running in coalition with the Sinhala nationalist JVP, which actively campaigned against the ceasefire agreement, the President's SLFP won a narrow victory in April 2004, though it failed to win a majority of seats.

The peace process and the CFA on which it was built had from the beginning been a source of contestation and division among the Sinhala parties. The President and the Prime Minister had distinct visions of how to achieve peace and how to engage with the LTTE, and their relationship was further undermined by a long-standing lack of trust on both sides and by the Prime Minister's lack of consultation with the President at crucial moments. Both the JVP and the right-wing Buddhist National Sinhala Heritage party (JHU) were deeply opposed to the ceasefire agree-ment and to negotiation with the LTTE from the beginning.

Opposition to the peace process from Sinhala nationalist parties – and from many average Sinhalese – grew in reaction to the LTTE's repeated and egregious violations of the ceasefire, ranging from their continued smuggling of arms and illegal taxation of businesses in the north and east to their forced recruitment of thousands of children and their systematic assassination of members of rival Tamil political parties and of Tamil and Muslim government intelligence officers.[7] The lack of a strong and effective response from the SLMM ceasefire monitors and from the Norwegian mediators weakened their reputation as impartial and helped undermine the credibility of the peace process as a whole. (Keenan 2007). At a deeper level, many Sinhalese were angered – and humiliated – by the way in which the ceasefire agreement and the growing international engagement with the LTTE seemed to call into question Sri Lanka's sovereignty, endorsing the division of its territory and a dual system of administration.

Many Muslims, especially those in the Eastern Province, had grown increasingly restive and felt more vulnerable as the peace process went on (McGilvray and Raheem 2007). With permission under the CFA to do "political work" in government controlled territory, the LTTE had quickly asserted its control throughout the east, including in predominantly Muslim towns and villages. The LTTE stepped up its taxation of Muslim businesses, and refused to release thousands of acres of agricultural lands owned or traditionally cultivated by Muslims in LTTE areas of control. LTTE cadres clashed frequently with Muslims. At the national level, Muslim political leaders were angry at being left out of formal negotiations with the LTTE. Although some Muslim ministers attended peace talks as part of the government delegation, neither the LTTE nor the government would accept a separate Muslim delegation. Many Muslims feared that any peace deal between the LTTE and the government would come at the expense of the lands and political power of Muslims in the east and in the north. Demands for a separate administrative unit for the various Muslim majority jurisdictions in the north and east grew louder as a result.

Even as many Sinhalese and Muslims saw the LTTE as having gained power and international legitimacy through the peace process, however, the LTTE leadership was far from happy. The government's refusal even to discuss their ISGA proposal and the failure of earlier attempts at joint interim administrative arrangements for the north and east called into question the willingness of the Sri Lankan government to allow the LTTE to share any political power (Uyangoda 2005: 6). The LTTE was particularly unhappy with the new SLFP coalition government elected in April 2004, which wanted negotiations to focus on the core issues of the conflict and move towards discussion of a final peace agreement. The LTTE insisted that any new talks focus only on the ISGA, in line with their longstanding demand that "normalisation" in the north and east take precedence, to be facilitated by an interim administrative arrangement. Meanwhile, the President's coalition partners, the JVP, opposed any talks at all, unless the ceasefire agreement could be renegotiated and strengthened. The peace process remained deadlocked on this issue throughout 2004.

The LTTE was also feeling threatened by the March 2004 decision of its eastern military commander, Colonel Karuna, to leave the LTTE, along with an estimated 6,000 of the LTTE's best fighters. Karuna complained of neglect and mistreatment of eastern Tamils by the northern Tamils who dominated the Tiger leadership. The LTTE leadership responded by accusing Karuna of corruption and treason. The northern wing of the LTTE eventually attacked Karuna's troops in the east. After a few days of fighting in April 2004 Karuna sent his remaining fighters home and the LTTE appeared to have crushed the rebellion. But the LTTE never regained effective control of the east, as Karuna eventually regrouped, and with some degree of assistance from the Sri Lankan military waged a low intensity, but effective, guerrilla campaign against the LTTE in that region. Although the ceasefire and the peace process had appeared to many to strengthen the LTTE's hold over the northeast, Karuna's split and the emergence of a separate Tamil militia in the east ultimately proved a fatal blow to the Tigers. By the end of 2004, the Tiger leadership felt it was losing the peace. After an initial year of optimism and apparent progress, the CFA and the peace process built on it had eventually deepened ethnic divisions and political tensions. By the time of the tsunami in December 2004, both the ceasefire and what passed for peace in Sri Lanka were on the brink of collapse.[8]

The devastating impact of the tsunami's waves and the near universal desire to respond to the terrible suffering they left in their wake seemed initially to shift Sri Lanka's long-standing conflict dynamics. The hours and days immediately after the tsunami saw spontaneous cooperation across ethnic lines, as Tamils, Muslims and Sinhalese – including LTTE and government forces – worked together to rescue and assist those in need. This was particularly true in the north and along the multi-ethnic east coast, where more than 20,000 were killed and almost half a million were displaced (Kuhn, this volume). Soon, however, the established lines of conflict re-emerged. International aid money in particular became a source of renewed political competition, suspicion and mistrust. Ultimately, the large amounts of actual and promised international assistance for relief and reconstruction were undermined by, and went on to worsen, Sri Lanka's conflict dynamics.

P-TOMS: attempting cooperation, fueling conflict

In the same spirit of cooperation that had characterized grass roots responses across the island, representatives of the LTTE and the Government of Sri Lanka (GoSL) began discussions within days of the tsunami about a "joint mechanism" to coordinate tsunami relief operations in the north and east and to distribute the large amount of promised international financial assistance. Six rounds of direct negotiations between the GoSL and the LTTE "peace secretariats" broke down after the 7 February 2005 murder of LTTE eastern political leader E. Kaushalyan, which the LTTE blamed on the Karuna group, supported by the Sri Lankan military.[9] By the end of February, though, basic agreement on a joint mechanism to be called the Post-Tsunami Operational Management Structure (P-TOMS) had been reached with Norwegian facilitation, and by April it was ready to be signed. By then, however, strong opposition had begun to build, driven by the Sinhala nationalist JVP, who feared the agreement would further empower the LTTE and be a stepping stone to the Tigers' goal of a separate state for the northeast. Muslim political groups were also an obstacle, angry that they had not been consulted when the agreement was drafted, and that no Muslim representative was invited to sign the agreement. Many Muslims also feared the joint mechanism would allow the LTTE to expand its power in the east.

The P-TOMS would have been composed of three separate "tiers" in a complex organizational design ostensibly meant to address the needs and fears of various competing constituencies, ranging from high-level political entities to local coastal settlements in the six tsunami-affected districts of the northeast (Rainford and Satkunanathan 2009: 48–54). According to its supporters, P-TOMS would have helped to streamline the distribution of aid and ensure a more equitable distribution of assistance to the north and east, especially in LTTE-controlled areas. "A joint mechanism would have made it much easier to have the equity in distribution that Canada's constituencies demand," said one diplomat.[10] P-TOMS district committees would have taken over from the government's ad hoc district committees, whose track record was mixed. The new district committees would have "explicitly included Muslims and guaranteed representation from all groups," in the words of an international donor.[11] According to one aid agency official who was close to the negotiations, it also "would have monitored and clarified the allocation of monies. Without it, we have no central clearinghouse for monies."[12]

The JVP quit the government in protest on 16 June 2005, which severely weakened President Kumaratunga's already fragile coalition. P-TOMS was signed on 24 June 2005 by mid-level bureaucrats representing the government and the LTTE, but by then it was doomed. The JVP's lawsuit against the agreement was taken up for consideration by the Supreme Court, and on 15 July 2005, the Supreme Court issued an interim stay order blocking implementation of P-TOMS. The Supreme Court only blocked parts of the agreement, but the agreement as a whole was soon dead, especially after a further Supreme Court decision set the date for the election of a new president for November 2005, thus further weakening President Kumaratunga's political influence.[13]

P-TOMS had been presented publicly as necessary for distributing tsunami relief and reconstruction assistance, yet funds were effectively distributed without it, if less equitably and in a more complicated and opaque fashion.[14] As negotiations had dragged on without formalizing the agreement, donors were forced to find other means for distributing their huge amounts of aid. "By the time it was signed," said one aid official, "its material importance was largely over. Donors had already committed their monies through other channels. Initially, a lot of money would have been channeled through P-TOMS, but later on the money had largely been allocated via other channels."[15]

Although not always presented this way by the government, the LTTE, or international donors, the primary value of P-TOMS was in establishing cooperation in aid distribution that could have formed the foundation for a more stable peace process.[16] "The LTTE and the government publicly declared that P-TOMS wasn't about the peace process," said one influential Muslim community leader. "But everyone knew that it was. It was a way to get the LTTE engaged. You could have done tsunami reconstruction without a joint mechanism."[17] "It would have been the first occasion for various groups to sit down and work together," said one donor. "If the structure had been operationalized, it would have been a good opportunity for all the groups."[18] Another donor summed things up this way: "No one believes P-TOMS was necessary to deliver aid. It was essentially a peace-building, conflict transformation effort. This is precisely why it failed. The LTTE signed in late February or early March. Then it dragged on in the south. People recognized it for what it was – a test balloon for some kind of a future power-sharing mechanism with devolved power. There was a fear this can take on a life of its own, either leading to a separate state or simply to share power. The south didn't want P-TOMS, it's as simple as that."[19]

P-TOMS' most vocal critics were the JVP and other Sinhala nationalist parties such as the Jathika Hela Urumaya (JHU). From their perspective, the agreement would have granted significant powers and political legitimacy to a terrorist organization dedicated to establishing a separate state in the north and east. The apparently technical and administrative nature of the agreement, and the various safeguards the three-tiered structure established failed to convince them that P-TOMS did not pose a fundamental threat to the sovereignty and territorial integrity of Sri Lanka. The frequent violations of the ceasefire agreement proved, from this point of view, that the LTTE could not, in any case, be trusted to abide by its promises. The Sinhala nationalist concern with P-TOMS was shared even by those not obsessed with sovereignty issues. According to one prominent Tamil intellectual and political activist known for his criticisms of the LTTE, "P-TOMS could have been a way of moving towards establishing ISGA as *fait accompli*, with the regional fund playing the role of NERF [North East Reconstruction Fund] and the regional committee functioning much like the ISGA."[20]

These and other concerns were shared by many Muslims, whose widespread scepticism about, and in some cases opposition to, P-TOMS was a central cause of its defeat (McGilvray and Raheem 2007: 43–45). Substantively speaking, Muslim opposition was based more on past experience with the LTTE and the mistrust it had bred than on anything in the agreement itself: "LTTE attacks on Muslims and other problems with the LTTE during the CFA – killings and abductions, robberies of cars and motorcycles, land disputes … the LTTE has lost credibility among Muslims," said one prominent eastern Muslim community leader in early 2006.[21] The government argued that safeguards had been put in the P-TOMS agreement that would have protected Muslim interests. For instance, any project that representatives of one community felt threatened their vital interests would require approval by seven out of 10 votes on the regional committee. With three Muslim members of the regional committee appointed to represent Muslims and one of the government members pledged to be a Muslim, this was felt by many to be a strong protection. A number of the district committees would have had Muslim majorities.[22]

Despite these genuine concerns, Muslim opposition was primarily procedural and symbolic. The strongest complaint of Muslim political leaders was that they weren't included in the negotiations or significantly consulted as the agreement was being devised. In the words of one Muslim community leader, "It was a mistake not to include Muslims in drafting the agreement. The agreement was worked out with the LTTE. Afterwards there was tremendous consultation with various Muslim representatives, political, religious, civil society. If this amount of consultation had happened before the pact was agreed, things might have been different."[23] In the estimation of one diplomat, "Muslims might have been able to come on board if they'd been part of the process of negotiations. But they were never consulted. They were simply given the text as a *fait accompli*."[24]

Some of the force of the JVP and Muslim opposition might have been blunted if the government had chosen to argue for the P-TOMS more honestly: as a way to get the peace process back on track and draw the LTTE into a carefully managed process of very limited power-sharing. According to one prominent Tamil activist, the government would have been wiser if it had publicly stated that it "didn't really need the P-TOMS for tsunami relief. If the P-TOMS was sold as explicitly for the peace process, it would have been defensible. Without this, selling it with a spin of tsunami humanitarian relief gave ammunition to the JVP. As with selling peace at any costs without any human rights protections, this bred cynicism."[25] As Charan Rainford and Ambika Satkunanathan argue in their study of "interim arrangements" during Sri Lanka's peace process of 2002–2005, it was in part "the covert nature by which the document was shaped along ethno-political lines that made nationalist parties, like the JVP and JHU, wary of the structure" (2009: 51).

Numerous people involved in or close to the process of negotiating P-TOMS describe President Kumaratunga as conflicted and ambivalent about the deal. "Yes, the President wanted P-TOMS," said one knowledgeable diplomat, "but she wanted something else more: power."[26] As political opposition grew even among her political allies, perhaps she was happy to be rid of it. Dealing with the LTTE was, of course, a real challenge and a real gamble. According to one diplomat close to negotiations, the text of the agreement was "basically done in early February. Work still had to be done only on a few smaller points. The extra time was taken to get Muslims on board. But the longer they took, the more the opposition grew." "If Chandrika had been more decisive, she might have been able to push it through," said another diplomat, echoing the sentiments of many.[27]

In part because of her uncertainty and ambivalence, Kumaratunga pressed international donors to publicly express their support for the agreement. Bilateral donors convened at the Sri Lanka Development Forum in the central town of Kandy on 16–17 May 2005 stated their support for the joint mechanism between the government and the LTTE and pledged some US $3 billion in support (UNOCHA 2005). The donors also strongly urged the government and the LTTE to return to peace talks. Public endorsement by international donors of a joint mechanism for tsunami relief, however, was a double-edged sword at best, especially as government officials also hinted at times that the P-TOMS was forced on them by donors as a condition for financial support. The wide-spread perception that P-TOMS was being pushed by international donors seemed to many to substantiate JVP and JHU concerns that P-TOMS was part of the international conspiracy to undermine Sri Lanka's sovereignty and to assist the LTTE in establishing their Tamil Eelam in the name of "peace."

As already noted, by the time the agreement was signed it was immediately faced with the JVP's legal challenge. However, by this point, it was not clear the government really wanted P-TOMS to succeed. According to many observers, the government did not present as strong a legal defense of P-TOMS as they could have.[28] Said one aid official, "Perhaps CBK [President Kumaratunga] wanted it both ways: to present herself as pro-peace but without actually alienating the Sinhalese constituency?"[29] Similar doubts were expressed about the LTTE's position by those close to the negotiations: "One can also ask whether the Tigers wanted P-TOMS. Neither party wanted to be the one to say no first. Why not sign it first and expect the government to fail?"[30]

Although the Supreme court's 15 July 2005 interim stay order did not rule out P-TOMS entirely, political dynamics changed fundamentally after the court's announcement in August 2005 that President Kumaratunga's term in office would end in December 2005. With Kumaratunga now a lame duck and her successor as the SLFP candidate running on a platform supported by the JVP and opposed to P-TOMS, the agreement was effectively dead at that point regardless of any remaining legalities.

With P-TOMS undercut by Sinhalese, and to a lesser extent, Muslim, suspicions, the long-standing sense of discrimination and marginalization felt by many Tamils in the north and the east increased. The failure to establish P-TOMS became for many Tamils further evidence that Sinhala-dominated governments would never be willing or able to implement a deal with Tamil leaders. "The loss of P-TOMS was a huge setback and disappointment," said one representative of the Tamils Rehabilitation Organization, closely affiliated to the LTTE. "Its intended beneficiaries are especially disappointed. First with SIHRN and now with P-TOMS, their expectations have been dashed, there is lots of disillusionment ... If the government can't implement SIHRN and P-TOMS, how can they ever implement or reach a long-term settlement?"[31]

Realities of inequity, perceptions of bias

Sinhalese opposition to P-TOMS was generally born of fear that international assistance was unfairly supporting Tamils and the LTTE. At the same time, the failure of P-TOMS fed the perception by Tamils that they were not being given their fair share of aid, and Muslims had similar grievances. Beyond the P-TOMS debacle, however, there were other signs of inequity.

According to a range of sources, post-tsunami assistance was delivered in unequal ways across different regions and communities (Grewal 2006: 19–22, Silva 2009, Kuhn and Frerks this volume).[32] The number and quality of houses, boats, household goods, equipment for fishing or other livelihoods and the speed with which they were delivered to beneficiaries varied widely between regions and ethnic communities. Equally, whether or how quickly a community got a new road, school, hospital, or government building depended to some significant degree on where it was located, what language its residents spoke, and who its political leaders were.

There were two major, overlapping, axes of unequal treatment. First, among people displaced by the tsunami, those living in the north and east received relatively fewer resources than those in the south and west.[33] Second, there was even more pronounced inequity in the assistance received between those who had been previously displaced by the civil war and the more recently displaced survivors of the tsunami (Grewal 2006: 19–22).[34] People displaced by the conflict received fewer resources relative to those affected by the tsunami at least in part because most were Tamils and Muslims from the north and east, many of them living in areas under LTTE control. Other factors were also at work. The conflict-displaced received fewer resources and slower assistance because the vast majority of international assistance – especially in the initial weeks and months – was naturally dedicated to the victims of the tsunami whose plight had captured the attention of the world. Many people saw those displaced by the tsunami as more deserving: they were viewed as victims of a purely "natural" disaster, not parties to a long-standing, intractable political dispute with complicated and confusing causes. Indeed, the conflict-related displaced were already part of an existing and highly complex national and international system of aid delivery with its own rules and forms of assistance which did not initially align with systems established to assist tsunami survivors.

There were many reasons for the different treatment accorded those in the north and east, whether tsunami or war-affected, and those in the south and west. The inequities did not merely reflect ethnic or religious discrimination. Nonetheless, ethnic bias was clearly one factor at work, and many of the apparently unintentional causes of differential treatment were deeply intertwined with institutionalized aspects of Sri Lanka's violent conflicts and the unequal power of its ethnic communities.

Access and conditions for relief work in the south and west

The first and foremost cause of the regional disparities was the relative ease of working along the south and west coast for aid organizations and the Sri Lankan government. The western and southern coasts were closer to and easier to reach from Colombo, which is not only the center of political and economic activity in Sri Lanka, but also the site of the country's international airport and harbour where relief materials arrived. Popularly known as "tarmac bias" in the development and disaster literature, the better roads and airport access meant that organizations and individuals with money – whether local or international – could more easily and quickly deliver aid to the south and west. This was especially true for international organizations and ad hoc initiatives by individuals who were not familiar with Sri Lanka and not willing to deal with the more difficult work conditions in the north and east. The relative proximity of the southwest coast to Colombo also meant the situation there was more easily monitored and reported on and thus better known by potential donors. The greater knowledge about what was happening – who was available to work with, and how to transport supplies – translated directly into more assistance.

In addition, there were no language barriers for Sinhala-speaking Colombo bureaucrats or Colombo-based funders and volunteers to work in the south and west, as opposed to the Tamil-speaking east and north. In other ways, too, the Sri Lankan state was better equipped to function along the southwest coast than the north and east. Greater state resources and staff were available for work along the southern and western coasts. For instance, government staff required to approve projects, and national housing inspectors, travelled to the southwest more easily and more often (Grewal 2006: 29–30).

Obstacles in the northeast

In addition to being further away and harder to gain access to, the north and the east suffered from other disadvantages. Overall, the "transaction costs of working in parts of north and east [were] much higher than in the south and west," explained one donor.[35] Most important were political and security factors.[36] In the words of one relief worker, "The political jigsaw puzzle of the northeast allows chaos to happen and get worse. It's been virtually impossible to have a humanitarian relief effort that is coordinated and effective on top of such a complex and mistrustful political context."[37] Violence and insecurity in the north and east, but especially in Batticaloa district where forces loyal to Karuna were actively challenging the LTTE, made it harder to implement projects. Many contractors preferred to stay away, and additional checkpoints and security-based restrictions slowed down what work could be done. "The TRO is frightened to do work in the east because of Karuna," explained one Muslim activist in the east. "It's true that both the east and north have been neglected, but while the LTTE and TRO have been able to do some good work in the north, their security concerns meant they didn't make the east a priority."[38]

Relief and reconstruction efforts faced particular difficulties in LTTE-controlled areas. In addition to bad roads and particularly poor infrastructure, the LTTE's own "taxes" imposed on supplies and equipment that entered areas it controlled raised the cost and the difficulty of working in Tiger areas (Grewal 2006: 29). Government and military mistrust of the LTTE also led to the denial or restriction of any supplies or assistance that could have strengthened the Tigers. Military checkpoints and high security zones limited access to reconstruction sites in LTTE-controlled areas, and there were strict controls on the importation of cement and other crucial building materials into Tiger-held territory – and even at times into government areas in the east.[39] NGOs working in Tiger areas were generally treated with suspicion by the military and often accused of being "white tigers."[40] Obstacles were regularly placed in the way of their entering and working in LTTE areas.

"Politics is a big factor here," explained an official with UNOCHA. "There's a desire by the government to keep access difficult, for instance in Trinco north, and particularly for big infrastructure projects. People here think this is because of a desire to neglect the northeast." Although some Tamil critics took the military's restrictions as an expression of anti-Tamil bias, the government clearly had legitimate security concerns, especially as tensions with the LTTE in the north and east had been growing in the months prior to the tsunami. "The government is afraid of sending money to the east for fear of the LTTE getting a piece of it," explained one Muslim activist in Batticaloa in February 2006. "There were many instances of money coming to government administration that then got siphoned off to the LTTE."

The centralized structure of the Sri Lankan state

The centralized, Colombo-based, and predominantly Sinhala Sri Lankan state proved structurally biased not only against those within LTTE-controlled areas but also against expressions of local and regional initiative and control of any sort. This was naturally felt most acutely in the Tamil-speaking areas of the north and east farthest from Colombo. The various ad hoc administrative mechanisms established by the central government, first under President Kumaratunga and then President Rajpaksa,[41] further reduced the decision-making powers of local authorities and communities and forced costly changes in approach on the ground (Grewal 2006: 31).

The combination of ad hoc centralized control and institutionalized neglect of the north and east meant a lack of clear standards and lack of direction for those at the local level. Government offices and aid agencies in the north and east were often left unaware of the latest policies. "The north and east has trouble getting information from the central government. Government circulars and information are not sent systematically ... Many circulars haven't reached offices in the northeast, so we still don't have a clear idea about the buffer zones," explained one UN official in Trincomalee in February 2006.

In addition, the ethnicized nature of Sri Lanka's local-level administrative system –where the senior central government official is invariably of the same ethnicity as the majority of the division – contributed to the biased distribution of assistance. This was especially true for Tamils living in LTTE-controlled sections of Muslim majority divisions – as for instance in Mutur in Trincomalee district[42] – but the problem affected to some degree members of all communities.

Finally, while the centralized state structure gave great powers to Colombo and to Sinhala politicians and bureaucrats, in many ways the state was also quite weak. A general lack of staff and resources, especially for the monitoring and coordination of relief activities carried out by NGOs, was especially pronounced in the north and east (Grewal 2006: 24–6). NGOs frequently resisted even well-intentioned efforts by government officials to know the details of their relief activities. "Some NGOs have a policy *not* to share information," said the same UN official. "There's a need for strong coordination from the government," argued one local activist in Batticaloa, "but the government is too weak."[43]

Patronage politics and corruption

Sri Lanka's entrenched patronage system – by which public monies and assistance are at the disposal of politicians to distribute to their political supporters regardless of formal criteria – strengthened the effects of the centralized and Sinhala-dominated state. Given that most of Sri Lanka's most powerful politicians are Sinhalese from southern and western constituencies, the patronage system favoured aid going to the south and west.[44] "These are the constituencies of those in power in Colombo," said one donor. "It still astonishes me how much the north is not in people's consciousness." "The south has some very senior politicians. Their areas have gotten a lot of resources," explained a diplomat. "The south coast has strong politicians – Mahinda [Rajapaksa], [Mangala] Samaraweera, the JVP," seconded a Muslim activist in Batticaloa.[45] "The entire east coast was abandoned. Priority was given to other areas."[46] The almost complete lack of transparency and accountability of government institutions and political leaders made it difficult to respond to and correct the discriminatory effects of the patronage system.

In some cases patronage politics shaded into outright theft and corruption. In the most widely reported case, hundreds of thousands of dollars were said to have disappeared into the bank account of "Helping Hambantota," a charity controlled by the then Prime Minister Mahinda Rajapaksa for work in his southern hometown of Hambantota.[47] In addition to the unfair and ultimately undemocratic politics of patronage, there were more obvious forms of corruption. "You can pay to get your name on the beneficiaries list," explained one diplomat. Numerous local level government officials were accused of corruption and some were eventually prosecuted.

Too much, too fast

Even the best system of governance would have had trouble efficiently and equitably managing the huge amount of money and large number of relief organizations that poured into post-tsunami Sri Lanka. "There was so much funding that it was economically overwhelming," said one government official.[48] "The tsunami brought in billions of dollars. It was too much to deal with. Not all can be spent, and not all has been spent on valuable things."[49] Given the massive global media coverage devoted to the tsunami and its effects, there was tremendous pressure to spend quickly and to show tangible results. "Trying to spend a lot of money fast leads to corruption, centralization, raised costs and other disruptions due to the lack of local capacity to absorb the funds."[50] The pressure to deliver quick results also contributed to the unequal distribution of funds by pushing agencies to spend in the more easily accessible south and to give preference for tsunami rather than conflict-displaced IDPs (Grewal 2006: 32). "Just due to the huge number of actors, without oversight and tactical planning yet with the power to direct funds, you are bound to have pockets that are undersubscribed and others that are oversubscribed."[51]

Grievance and the political effects of inequity

Overall, there is little evidence that the unequal distribution of tsunami aid was the result of deliberate discrimination against Tamils or Muslims.[52] Mostly an effect of deep-seated structural and political dynamics, the inequity was nonetheless significant enough to feed the sense of grievance and deepen the sense of alienation experienced by many Tamils and Muslims.[53] At the same time, the massive influx of largely unregulated money and foreign organizations, coming in the midst of a slowly collapsing ceasefire characterized by widespread LTTE violations and human rights abuses, fed the suspicions and fears of loss of sovereignty among many Sinhalese. This was especially true as many of the foreign NGOs necessarily worked closely with the LTTE in the parts of the north and east it controlled.

The sense of grievance and insecurity on all sides of Sri Lanka's ethnic divides was strengthened by the more fundamental crisis of political legitimacy that affected in different ways all the major actors involved in tsunami relief: the government, the LTTE, political parties, foreign governments and multi-lateral donors, and international NGOs. None was significantly accountable to those who received aid or to the people of Sri Lanka; each was at the time plagued by fundamental questions about its legitimacy from some segment of the Sri Lankan public. To many people – and almost all Sinhalese – the LTTE was merely a ruthless terrorist group strengthening itself thanks to international assistance and support for peace negotiations. Large numbers of Sri Lankans of all ethnicities saw the government as corrupt; many Muslims and Tamils experienced it as ethnically biased. Sri Lankans from all communities increasingly viewed international and local NGOs as motivated primarily by financial gain and as carrying out the agendas of their foreign funders rather than being accountable to the people they served. Many Sinhalese in particular viewed local and international NGOs as central players in an international conspiracy to undermine Sri Lanka's sovereignty and Sinhala Buddhist heritage.

Denouement: from tsunami to military victory

Political reactions to tsunami relief played a central role in the fundamental reorientation of Sri Lanka's political and military dynamics that began in the middle of 2005 and culminated in the military defeat of the LTTE in May 2009. Support from the JVP and JHU and other Sinhala nationalist activists, strengthened by their vocal opposition to P-TOMS, the ceasefire, and the role of international organizations in supporting the peace process, was essential to the election of Mahinda Rajapaksa as president in November 2005. The victory of Rajapaksa, who ran on a platform critical of the ceasefire agreement and decrying the threats to Sri Lanka's sovereignty from the LTTE and international forces, ironically depended upon the LTTE's decision to enforce a boycott of the election within areas they controlled. The LTTE leadership, frustrated with what it had been able to gain through negotiations, apparently preferred the staunch Sinhala nationalist Rajapaksa over the more conciliatory candidate of the United National Party, Ranil Wickremasinghe, who was thought to be the overwhelming favorite of Tamils and Muslims in the north and east. That the LTTE had chosen a return to war over negotiations was made clear within weeks of Rajapaksa's election, when they launched a sustained campaign of guerrilla attacks on government security forces in the north and east. The government responded with a ruthless counterinsurgency campaign that ultimately led to the deaths and disappearance of hundreds of Tamils suspected of involvement with the LTTE (International Crisis Group 2007, 2008a).[54] Assassination attempts by the LTTE against the army commander and other military officials were followed by strategic strikes against the LTTE leadership.

Full-scale war returned to Sri Lanka in July 2006 when the military re-took by force an irrigation canal in a multi-ethnic section of Trincomalee district that had been shut down by the LTTE. The fighting that followed eventually saw the government regaining control of the entire Eastern Province a year later. By late 2007 the war had turned north. With its official abrogation of the ceasefire agreement in January 2008, the government made clear its intention to defeat the LTTE and retake the entirety of the Northern Province. In May 2009, the military recaptured the last pockets of LTTE control after killing its commander Velupillai Prabhakaran and the rest of the leadership of the LTTE near the north-eastern fishing town of Mullaittivu, site of utter tsunami devastation in 2004.

The government's military campaign in the Eastern Province saw the forced displacement of some 200,000 people and large scale destruction and looting of houses and personal property in former LTTE areas. By late 2008, all but a few thousand residents had been resettled and large-scale construction projects – roads, utilities infrastructure, housing, ports – were underway, much of it funded under plans originally launched in the wake of the tsunami. Although the east has now gotten its full share of post-tsunami aid, a deep divide persists between the wealthier coast and the inland, former LTTE areas, which remain poorer and less developed. Despite the election of the Eastern Provincial Council in May 2008 and promises of devolved power, the central government and security forces have maintained tighter control over economic and political decisions in the east than before the tsunami. (International Crisis Group 2008b, 2009).

Centralized power, and with it the sources of continued conflict along ethnic lines, is likely to be stronger in the more recently "liberated" Northern Province. The north suffered even greater destruction and even larger numbers of residents displaced by the final months of fighting than did the east. The requirements for reconstruction – including in areas to some degree rebuilt after the tsunami – are massive. The military is almost certain to play a decisive role in governing the north in the initial post-LTTE years. Security concerns and the desire to eliminate all remnants of the LTTE and any possibility of its return have been the central factor behind the prolonged internment of the nearly 300,000 civilians displaced by fighting in 2008–9. Due to well-founded fears of LTTE infiltration, the Jaffna peninsula has effectively been under martial law since early 2006 and is likely to remain tightly controlled by the military even in peacetime.

The Rajapaksa government's unexpected victory over the LTTE resulted in part from its decision to adopt a fundamentally different set of policies and style of governance from those pursued from 1994–2005 under President Kumaratunga (and during Ranil Wickremasinghe's brief period as prime minister from 2001–2004). A strident defense of the unitary state and of Sri Lanka as an essentially Sinhalese and Buddhist island has replaced public commitment to federalism and power-sharing with the regions. An already centralized government administration has become even more concentrated in the presidency and a small band of advisors and ministers, and the military has been given unprecedented power and influence over political decisions. Non-stop pro-military and pro-government propaganda generated overwhelming support for a military solution to the ethnic conflict.

With this came the government's suppression of political and civil rights and its brutal crackdown on dissent, with any who publicly challenged government policy labeled as pro-terrorist and traitors to the nation.

At the same time as the return to war fed Sinhala nationalism and restored a large degree of the government's credibility among the Sinhalese, it further undermined the legitimacy of Western-led international institutions, the UN, INGOs and foreign funded local NGOs. Attacks by the strongly Sinhala nationalist media and deliberate government and military policies effectively challenged the legitimacy of those NGOs that had worked in LTTE controlled areas. All were now labelled as pro-Tiger simply for working in areas of LTTE control and according to LTTE rules and regulations, despite having the full consent of the government then in power. The ex-post facto criminalization of those with contacts or institutional relationships with the LTTE para-state has grown even stronger in the wake of the government's military victory, with the arrests and detention of many Tamils who worked or cooperated with the LTTE, even in the absence of any evidence of involvement in military or terrorist activities. This has been combined with increasingly tight and punitive restrictions on visas for and operations of INGOs, UN agencies, journalists, and even diplomats.

The current rise in aggressive Sinhala nationalism is partly a genuine expression of ethnic identity – much of it a belated and indirect response to the humiliations of Western colonial rule – and anger at the international support the LTTE received as an integral part of the 2002 ceasefire and peace process. It is also in part an understandable reaction to the willingness of some INGOs and UN agencies working in the north to grant undue legitimacy to the LTTE's de-facto state centered in Kilinochchi and to mute their criticism of the Tamil Tigers' many abuses and undemocratic rule, including abductions of children as LTTE cadres. At the same time, it is as much or more a cynical government strategy to generate public anger at foreign enemies and to crush domestic and international opposition to their no-holds-barred counter-terrorism strategy, the centralization of power in the hands of a few, and the growing role of the military in civilian affairs.

The government's counterattacks against international critics and international NGOs occurred concurrently with a fundamental shift in its foreign policy and international relations. As a result, five years after the tsunami, the landscape of international aid to Sri Lanka has fundamentally changed. In the face of Western criticism of the human rights abuses that accompanied the war against the LTTE, the Rajapaksa government consciously cultivated support from China, Pakistan, Iran, Libya, and other non-Western economic and military partners. While Western countries withheld some of their aid in light of the government's poor respect for basic human rights,[55] China and other non-Western donors have been content to give loans and military assistance with no human rights or good governance conditions attached. Worried by China's increasing political and economic influence in Sri Lanka, even India – the country with potentially the greatest power to affect Sri Lanka's policies – and Japan – Sri Lanka's largest donor during the previous decade – did little to soften the government's brutal conduct of the war, especially in the final three months of fighting.[56] Each has pledged significant assistance to rebuild the war-torn north and east. The limited ability of donors to use international aid to affect Sri Lanka's conflict dynamics positively – seen clearly in the failure of P-TOMS and in the ineffectiveness of economic incentives for the peace process as a whole – was proven even more clearly when the war resumed in mid-2006.[57]

Nearly five years after the tsunami, the political interests and ethno-nationalist impulses that compromised the delivery of post-tsunami relief and reconstruction resources still persist. The forces set in motion during the peace process and in the immediate post-tsunami period have led to the victory of one narrow and strident majoritarian nationalism over an equally narrow and strident minority nationalism. But the government's victory has brought Sri Lanka no closer to ethnic understanding and reconciliation than before. The global outpouring of goodwill and philanthropy toward this disaster-stricken island nation ended up strengthening Sri Lanka's habits of zero-sum political calculation and ethnicized governance. In doing so, the tsunami recovery process helped "build back better" the pre-tsunami conflict.

Notes

1   "Build back better" was a phrase widely used by international agencies involved in post-tsunami relief and reconstruction. The phrase was meant to announce the commitment of international donors and contractors not simply to repair the damage done by the tsunami but to rebuild communities and infrastructure in a way that made them stronger and more resilient in the face of potential future catastrophes. For an analysis of the problems involved in understanding and effectively implementing the concept "build back better," see Kennedy, *et al.*, 2009.
2   The four Thimpu principles were: (1.) Recognition of the Tamils of Sri Lanka as a nation, (2.) Recognition of the existence of a regional homeland for the Tamils in Sri Lanka, (3.) Recognition of the right of self-determination of the Tamil nation, and (4.) Recognition of the right to citizenship and the fundamental rights of all Tamils in Sri Lanka (Wilson 2000: 144–145).
3   Chief among these were the Eelam People's Revolutionary Front (EPRLF), the Eelam People's Democratic Party (EPDP), and People's Liberation Organization of Tamil Eelam (PLOTE).
4   See also the many documents on the routine nature of police abuse and torture published by the Asian Human Rights Commission, Hong Kong, available at http://www.srilankahr.net/.
5   For a useful analysis of the limitations of the 2002 peace process see Goodhand and Klem 2005 and International Crisis Group 2006.
6   While the Sri Lankan government officials attended the meeting, the LTTE could not, thanks to their being banned in the US as a "terrorist" organization. Achieving "parity of status" with the government was one of the LTTE's fundamental demands, so their exclusion from the Washington talks was a significant blow.
7   For details on human rights violations committed during the ceasefire, see the invaluable reports of the University Teachers for Human Rights (UTHR), available at www.uthr.org. For analyses of the politics of human rights controversies during the 2002–2006 peace process, see Keenan 2006 and 2007.
8   Its collapse was probably delayed by the tsunami, but then ultimately sped up again by the weaknesses and controversies of tsunami aid delivery.
9   Interview with multilateral aid agency official, Colombo, February 2006.

10 Interview with Canadian diplomat, Colombo, February 2006.
11 Interview with British diplomat, Colombo, February 2006.
12 Interview with multilateral aid agency official, Colombo, February 2006.
13 The SLFP's candidate, Mahinda Rajapaksa, ran with JVP support on a platform opposed to P-TOMS and calling for the CFA to be renegotiated. The LTTE's August 2005 assassination of the Sri Lankan foreign minister, Lakshman Kadirgamar, further weakened the spirit of cooperation. After Rajapaksa's election in November 2005, the court case was ultimately dropped when the government formally abandoned P-TOMS.
14 "Aid [to the north and east] is still getting through," said one diplomat in February 2006, "but it takes longer, is more acrimonious, with more logistical problems." Interview with Canadian diplomat, Colombo. According to one study, some amount of aid was lost to the northeast region as some donors waited for P-TOMS before distributing money (Grewal 2006: 29).
15 Interview with multilateral aid agency official, Colombo, February 2006.
16 For a helpful discussion of the government's ambiguous public position on this point, see Rainford and Satkunanathan 2009: 50–51.
17 Interview with Javid Usuf, Peace Secretariat for Muslims, Colombo, February 2006.
18 Interview with multilateral aid agency official, Colombo, February 2006.
19 Interview with Swedish diplomat, Colombo, February 2006.
20 Interview with Kethesh Loganathan, Colombo, February 2006. Loganathan was murdered on 12 August 2006, when he was working as the Deputy Secretary General of the government's Peace Secretariat under President Rajapaksa. Most people believe his killers were sent by the LTTE.
21 Interview, Kattankudy, Batticaloa District, February 2006.
22 More generally speaking, one donor argued that "The three-tiered structure of P-TOMS would actually have offered more accountability than the single tier existing in government controlled areas." Interview with British diplomat, Colombo, February 2006.
23 Interview with Javid Usuf, Peace Secretariat for Muslims, Colombo, February 2006.
24 Interview with Canadian diplomat, Colombo, February 2006.
25 Interview with Kethesh Loganathan, Colombo, February 2006.
26 Interview with Swedish diplomat, Colombo, February 2006.
27 Interview with Canadian diplomat, Colombo, February 2006.
28 Interviews with diplomats and donor agency officials, Colombo, February 2006. According to one diplomatic source, the lawyer hired to defend the agreement in court never liaised with the Attorney General's lawyer who handled the case. "While peace secretariat officials really wanted a good case made and tried to work with the Attorney General's Department, they were given very little chance to work with them."
29 Interview with British diplomat, Colombo, February 2006.
30 Interview with Swedish diplomat, Colombo, February 2006. According to another aid agency official, "By the end, it's not clear that the LTTE really wanted P-TOMS to happen. They were sincerely behind it for the first few months, but slowly got more disgruntled." Interview, Colombo, February 2006.
31 Interview with TRO representatives, Colombo, February 2006. A diplomat close to the negotiation process made the same point: "If they can't agree on an administrative mechanism for humanitarian purposes, what hope is there for negotiating more explosive issues like power-sharing?" Interview with Swedish diplomat, Colombo February 2006.
32 The analysis in this section of the chapter is particularly indebted to Grewal 2006.
33 There were also in many cases significant inequities in the treatment of tsunami IDPs within the same districts and ethnicities. While these differences were not always the result of deliberate ethnic or regional discrimination, they were nonetheless often interpreted as being so by those who saw others elsewhere getting more or better relief than they did.
34 In the opinion of one UN official more than a year after the tsunami struck, "There does

seem to be clear discrimination between the war-affected and the tsunami-displaced. These are not just effects of lack of coordination." Interview with UNOCHA official, Trincomalee, February 2006.

35 Interview with international donor agency official, Colombo, February 2006.

36 Also important was the relative paucity of skilled labour throughout the north and east, and the significantly higher costs to employ those who were available to buy or bring in supplies. Aid worker interviews, Trincomalee and Batticaloa February 2006.

37 Interview with Norwegian Refugee Council staff member, Trincomalee, February 2006.

38 Interview, Kattankudy, Batticaloa District, February 2006.

39 Interview with UNOCHA official, Trincomalee, February 2006.

40 Interview with Norwegian Refugee Council staff member, Trincomalee, February 2006.

41 President Kumaratunga's decision in early 2005 to consolidate control of tsunami relief through the Task Force for the Reconstruction of the Nation [TAFREN] undermined what little scope for local initiative there might have been. After the election of Mahinda Rajapaksa in November 2005, TAFREN was replaced by the Reconstruction and Development Agency [RADA].

41 "The Mutur Divisional Secretary is Muslim and it's very clear he's less interested in Tamil and uncleared [LTTE] areas. There's less data available on Mutur East and LTTE areas because they're less interested in getting it." Interview, ZOA Refugee Care staff member, Trincomalee, February 2006.

43 Interview with UNOCHA official, Trincomalee, February 2006.

44 There were no equivalent figures for Tamils in the north and east. Eventually, a few well-connected Muslim politicians were able to channel significant funds to east coast towns, but only after years of delay.

45 Mangala Samaraweera was at the time of the tsunami a powerful minister elected from the southern town of Matara and a close advisor to President Kumaratunga.

46 One diplomat explained it from another angle: "I don't think the government was actively pushing NGOs or aid deliverers to LTTE-controlled areas – as they were in the south." Interview with Swedish diplomat, Colombo, February 2006.

47 A police investigation into the missing money was ruled illegal by the Supreme Court in a decision that many thought was part of the complicated political dance that eventually saw Rajapaksa elected as President (BBC 2005a).

48 The Government of Sri Lanka's current (August 2009) estimate of external funding committed to tsunami aid is US $3.4 billion, with US $1.4 billion already expended (http://edims.mpi.gov.lk/portal/). Speaking in February 2006, one donor who closely tracked money for tsunami relief explained it was "impossible to keep track of all the private money ... No one knows what happened or what's going on." Interview with Swedish diplomat, Colombo, February 2006.

49 Interview with UNOCHA official, Trincomalee, February 2006.

50 Interview with Sunil Bastian, International Centre for Ethnic Studies, Colombo, February 2006.

51 Interview with Swedish diplomat, Colombo, February 2006.

52 Most donors and aid officials at the time argued that the unequal distribution of aid was not due to a clear design to discriminate against the northeast but was "more neglect than discrimination." Interview with official of the Asian Development Bank, Colombo, February 2006.

53 In the words of one aid official, "Many people in the northeast feel they only got what they did because the south was also damaged." Interview with British diplomat, Colombo, February 2006.

54 For detailed analyses of Sri Lanka's human rights crisis under the Rajapaksa administration, see the reports of the University Teachers for Human Rights (UTHR), available online at www.uthr.org.

55 The United States ended most forms of military cooperation with Sri Lanka in 2007 and 2008. In 2007 it effectively cancelled hundreds of millions of dollars of economic assistance under the Millenium Challenge program. A number of European countries reduced or ended development assistance to Sri Lanka during the Rajapaksa administration. Following a 2009 European Commission investigation that found Sri Lanka had failed to implement a number of human rights agreements, the European Union is expected in 2010 to end Sri Lanka's eligibility for trade preferences under the "GSP+" system of tariff reductions.

56 Anywhere from 7,000 to 20,000 civilians – virtually all of them Tamil – were killed in the final three months of fighting in the Northern Province in early 2009. See UTHR 2009 and Crashaw 2009.

57 The limits of international aid in promoting peace was one of the major claims of Goodhand and Klem 2005.

2 Conflict, coastal vulnerability, and resiliency in tsunami-affected communities of Sri Lanka

Randall Kuhn

Introduction

What can a quantitative analysis of pre- and post-tsunami social indicators tell us about the broader regional and ethnic dimensions of the Sri Lankan tsunami recovery process? Recent years have seen a more systematic effort to quantify disasters, relief efforts, and paths to recovery. Indeed, when the humanitarian community set out to establish clear humanitarian guidelines and responsibilities under the Sphere Project and its Humanitarian Charter and Minimum Standards in Disaster Response, a major element was the application of specific measurement criteria, evidence-based standards, and tools for evaluation of disaster relief efforts (Sphere 2004). Yet there remains a disconnection between the quantitative and qualitative approaches. Quantitative statistics are typically analyzed only at a very high level, which in Sri Lanka typically entails taking the district, with a population of around 300,000 people, as the primary unit of analysis. Qualitative needs assessments and ethnographies usually take the individual, family, or neighborhood as the unit of analysis and one or perhaps a small number of villages as the scale of analysis. Donor-driven ethnographies are typically aimed at understanding local needs or progress as representative of a larger context (for instance the district) rather than addressing differences between a number of localities. Furthermore, donor-driven analysis often focuses on local needs rather than on capabilities or resiliencies.

In light of these gaps, the multidisciplinary Sri Lanka tsunami project described in the Introduction to this volume included a quantitative study designed to bridge the micro and macro levels. The author assembled a quantitative database linking publicly available and newly collected data on population, tsunami impact, and tsunami relief and recovery. Donor-driven analyses of Sri Lanka have been done at the provincial level (Sri Lanka has eight provinces, four of which were tsunami-affected) and the district level (Sri Lanka has 25 districts, 12 of which were tsunami-affected). The current analysis captures the two lowest levels of administrative organization. Below the district is the Divisional Secretariat (DS) Division, with 41 out of a total 325 affected. At the lowest level of organization, typically containing about 1,000 people is the Grama Niladari (GN) Division, literally meaning "Village Headman," with 663 affected out of about 14,000. The study focused on a comparison of 429 affected and 782 unaffected GNs in the five most heavily affected districts: Ampara and Batticaloa in the mostly Tamil and Muslim Eastern Province, and Galle, Matara, and Hambantota in the majority Sinhalese Southern Province. More in-depth surveys were conducted with 146 affected and unaffected GNs.

Data were gathered to address antecedents, recovery efforts, and outcomes of the tsunami in light of the ongoing civil conflict between the majority Sinhalese and minority Tamil population, as well as Sri Lanka's history of greater government support to Sinhalese-dominated areas versus those populated by Tamils or Muslims. Data collection was carried out with the approval of the Sri Lankan Ministry of Public Administration and Home Affairs. Data were collected by a team of four researchers (one Sinhala, one Tamil, one Muslim, and one American Fulbright scholar with strong Sinhala language abilities) between July and December 2006. The author spent one month of the data collection period in Sri Lanka, taking the lead on the collection of GN-wise statistical information from DS offices (including tsunami damage), design and pre-testing of GN survey instruments, and selection of GNs for inclusion in the survey. The dataset also incorporates a range of publicly available population, damage, and recovery data.

The demographic study was designed to produce broader statistical results that would contextualize key ethnographic findings from Tamil (McGilvray, Lawrence, and Gaasbeek) and Sinhalese (Gamburd) communities, while local ethnographic studies would reveal specific causal factors that contributed to the quantitative findings. The key study hypothesis anticipated regional or ethnic differences in post-tsunami recovery and welfare between the Sinhala-majority Southern Province and the Tamil-speaking (both ethnic Muslim and Tamil) Eastern Province.

The findings of this data collection project are illustrative of a more complex reality reflecting the unique tripartite dimension of Sri Lankan society, the unprecedented scale of foreign assistance to the country, and the complexities of coastal ecosystems, as well as the fundamental gap between Sinhalese-dominated areas of southern Sri Lanka and minority areas in the east. They illustrate key ways in which conflict and disaster interact to exact a considerable toll on minority communities. Yet basic health and educational standards thus far remain robust despite the conflict and tsunami impact. Post-tsunami foreign assistance flows reflect a distinct bias towards the majority Sinhalese community, yet it is not at all clear that excess funds have really addressed the basic human needs of affected Sinhalese communities.

Ultimately, tests of an ethnic/regional differential hypothesis were complicated by important factors that will constitute the bulk of this chapter. First, the complexity of pre-existing socioeconomic differentials among affected and unaffected communities across the three ethnic groups undermined the assumptions of a simple pre-post experimental design. Second, the magnitude of the international post-tsunami relief effort fundamentally altered the nature of the study, swamping the role of community-level factors while introducing new sources of ethnic differential. With these caveats in mind, this chapter describes basic ethnic and community variations in objective and perceived indicators of tsunami recovery. It concludes with comments on the relevance of these findings for Sri Lanka's recovery process and for future community analysis of disaster recovery.

Ethnicity, conflict, and recovery

It is by now conventional wisdom that the global response to the Indian Ocean tsunami of 26 December 2004 was unprecedented in its scale and complexity. Foreign governments, charities, and private donors allocated and delivered more financial and logistical assistance than in almost any natural disaster to date. Donors became directly involved in service delivery and reconstruction in unprecedented ways, most notably in housing reconstruction.

In the aftermath of the aid-fueled conflicts of the 1990s in places such as Rwanda and Sudan, considerable concern was voiced about the role of foreign donors in supporting discrimination against minority groups, in promoting insurgency and insecurity, or in assisting military build-ups (Gasper 1999; Le Billon 2000; Cliffe and Luckham 2000; Fox 2001; Barnett 2005). Of particular concern has been the increasing tendency for modern humanitarian operations to span the continuum from emergency relief to long-term political and economic development (Fox 2001; Goyder, et al. 2006). Whereas the former activity can be carried out in a largely apolitical fashion, the latter can more readily be co-opted to reflect the political agendas of geopolitical powers and local political elites (Buchanan-Smith and Maxwell 1994; Weiss 1999; Easterly 2002; Hillhorst 2002; Freeman 2004). The formalization of this shift in the Sphere standards for humanitarian intervention raised considerable controversy among donors and implementers (Sphere 2004; Tong 2004). As will be demonstrated in this chapter, a great majority of the post-tsunami assistance provided to Sri Lanka, even in the early relief stages, crossed into the development sector with political consequences, whether this was intended or not (Houghton 2007; Telford and Cosgrave 2007).

Sphere also placed an unprecedented emphasis on accountability and measurement in humanitarian operations. This has encouraged creative and innovative analyses of the conduct, effectiveness, and ethics of aid delivery (Benini, et al. 2008; Fengler, et al. 2008). It is hoped that the analysis presented here will advance this scholarly process by reconciling the regional patterns of tsunami devastation against the financial accounts of foreign donor agencies. A number of potential pathways could explain regional differences in foreign assistance. First, conflict may obstruct the delivery of post-disaster assistance to affected areas (Slim 1997; White and Cliffe 2000). Second, donors may eschew areas under the immediate control of insurgent groups (Smillie and Minear 2003; Uvin 1998). Third, the government may divert assistance away from areas affected by conflict or areas populated by minority groups (Macrae, et al. 1997; Smilie 2001). This analysis explores regional patterns and their possible causes in Sri Lanka's tsunami-affected areas.

Humanitarian assistance may also disproportionately accrue to privileged or dominant population groups for logistical reasons that, while still problematic for operational efficacy, do not imply politically motivated bias or manipulation. For example, areas populated by dominant ethnic groups may be characterized by higher levels of development and higher wages and prices, thus perhaps justifying greater investment (Morris and Wodon 2003). Politically dominant areas may also happen to be more accessible to points of entry for finance, materials, and relief personnel, a situation often referred to as "tarmac bias" (Waters 2001; Benini, *et al.* 2008).

The environmental justice literature also highlights how vulnerable groups often bear the heaviest burden of disaster, particularly under conditions of political or military conflict (Blaikie and Brookfield 1987; Peet and Watts 2004; Bryant and Bailey 1997; Peluso and Watts 2001; Bohle and Fünfgeld 2007). It is important, however, to clarify whether disadvantaged groups were hit hardest by a disaster because they happened to live in a vulnerable area, or because systematic processes of exclusion placed them there. These issues are particularly complicated in the context of coastal ecosystems. Depending on industrial mix, rates of inequality, migration, and topographical characteristics, coastal areas can either be among the most wealthy residential areas or among the poorest, or they may be largely uninhabited industrial or ecological protection zones. Whether pre-existing differences are the result of systematic or random forces, this study aims to measure variations in post-tsunami community outcomes while accounting for pre-existing variations in community well-being.

Conflict, coastal vulnerability, and resiliency in Sri Lanka

In 2002, Sri Lanka's population composition by ethnicity/nationality was 74 percent Sinhalese (primarily Buddhist), 18 percent Tamil (primarily Hindu), and 7 percent Muslim (Department of Census and Statistics 2001). The Sinhalese, traditionally residing in the west and south of the country, have dominated Sri Lanka's political and economic life since the country gained independence in 1948. Tamils, living predominately in the North and East, have faced considerable discrimination as a result of physical and social isolation, government policies aimed at promoting the Sinhalese language and population, and civil conflict (de Silva 1997). Yet Tamils also continue a legacy of high educational and occupational attainment dating back to the colonial era (Bush 1993). The Muslim population, typically Tamil-speaking but ethnically distinct from Tamils, have fared better than Tamils on most living standards indicators.

Each of Sri Lanka's major ethnic groups resides in large numbers near the coastline, yet the quality of their existence and their reasons for living in these areas is conditioned by the local topography, by political and economic forces, and most of all by the ongoing ethno-nationalist conflict (Peebles 1990; Bastian 1999; Dunham and Jayasuriya 2001; Korf and Engel 2006; Korf 2005). All tsunami-affected regions of the Southern Province share a similar demographic makeup, with a large Sinhalese majority and pockets of Muslims in the cities, and a similar ecology: a moist, flat, tropical coastline. Yet there are important differences, most notably a significant political division between administrative districts. Galle District traditionally supports the opposition United National Party, while Hambantota and Matara Districts are the home base of the ruling Sri Lankan Freedom Party as well as the ultra-nationalist Janatha Vimukhti Peramuna (JVP). For instance, in the 2001 election, JVP received 21 percent of votes in Hambantota, 13 percent in Matara, and 11 percent in the rest of Southern and Western Province compared to between 4 percent and 9 percent in southern areas away from the coast (Department of Elections 2009). Economic differences exist as well, with Galle's economy drawing considerable hard currency income from tourism and overseas remittances.

Further complexity shapes the ethnic and political fabric of the Eastern Province. Ampara and Batticaloa Districts, two areas of focus in this study, both sit in Sri Lanka's dry zone directly facing the Indian Ocean to the east, the direction from which the tsunami originated. Both have sizable Tamil and Muslim populations. Both have been affected by the ongoing conflict between the government and the LTTE. Yet considerable differences and occasional animosity exist between the Tamil and Muslim communities.

More recently, these differences have been reinforced by an ongoing administrative reorganization of Tamils and Muslims into separate divisions within each district and also increasingly into separate districts, with Ampara seen by many Muslim leaders as a Muslim stronghold and Batticaloa as a place for the Tamils (Routray and Singh 2007). While the higher intensity of armed conflict in Batticaloa District has created considerable hardship for both groups, and frequent attacks on the Muslim population, the conflict has had a more moderate effect in Ampara. Major government water schemes such as the Gal Oya and Mahaveli, resulting in the large-scale settlement of Sinhala people in the Eastern Province, have increasingly been utilized as a wedge between the Tamil and Muslim communities (Peebles 1990; Bastian 1999; Dunham and Jayasuriya 2001; Korf and Silva 2003; Korf and Engel 2006). These conditions form the background for the current demographic investigation.

Assessing tsunami impact

The tsunami affected each of Sri Lanka's 14 coastal districts. Figure 2.1 depicts the regional pattern of damage in terms of the official death toll, based on police reports, and the number of homes destroyed according to the Department of Census and Statistics (DCS). The impact was felt first and, by most measures most severely, in areas to the east that directly faced the source of the wave in Sumatra. Total death tolls and housing damage were highest in the mixed Tamil and Muslim regions of Eastern Province, particularly the Muslim-dominated coastal region of Ampara and Tamil-dominated Batticaloa, as shown in Figure 2.1. Rates of death and destruction were even higher in these areas, which are far less densely populated than the south. The toll of death and destruction was also quite high in the Northern Province, particularly the LTTE-controlled districts of Mullaitivu and Kilinochchi, though data from these areas is less verifiable. Although the wave hit the southern districts less directly, their higher population densities nonetheless resulted in a substantial number of victims, particularly in Galle and Hambantota District. Each of these areas has a substantial Sinhala majority, though areas most closely abutting the coast were often heavily populated with Muslims. Areas on the west coast were far less affected, particularly the lightly populated Puttalam District north of Colombo. The official death toll was 31,000, with around one million people (5 percent of the total population) directly affected by the tsunami and 180,000 (about 1 percent of the population) displaced temporarily or permanently. This study focuses on five heavily-affected districts in the Southern and Eastern Provinces.

The study employs a research design in which the tsunami is taken as a random shock simultaneously affecting multiple locations and ethnic communities. It seeks to measure differential changes in social indicators before and after the tsunami in Tamil, Muslim, and Sinhalese communities, while looking also at other co-variants relating to community efficacy and organization. This design has a number of inferential limitations, the first being the difficulty of identifying meaningful markers of community distinction that could be measured with equal precision both before and after the tsunami. Second are confounding forces that vary across region but have little to do with the ethnic variations of interest in the study. For example, eastern areas, home to most of the Tamils and Muslims in the study, lie in a sparsely populated dry zone, while the largely Sinhalese southern areas resembled urban areas in many ways. Eastern communities themselves differ from one another in the extent of conflict exposure.

Two other factors also limited the viability of the original study design and the success of the data collection. First was the sheer magnitude of foreign donor response, which extended into even the most isolated areas of the island. Beyond its magnitude, the foreign response was notable for its complexity. In particular,

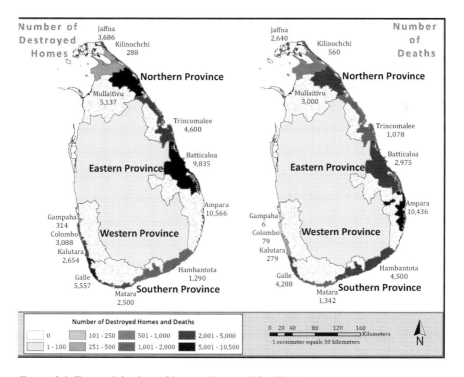

Figure 2.1 Tsunami deaths and homes destroyed, by district.

the housing reconstruction program, possibly the most intricate in the history of humanitarian assistance, included a complicated mix of finance mechanisms. Some homes were rebuilt by owners themselves using US $2,500 in phased transfers from the government, with donor support.[1] Others, particularly those originating from inside a coastal protection buffer zone (initially 100m or closer in the South and 200m or closer in the East, then later reduced), had their homes built through direct donor involvement with no government fund transfers. Between these two extremes lay an array of hybrids, including owner-built homes with co-financing or top-up transfers from donors, donor-built homes that required owners to sign over their government housing grants, and donor-built homes for which victims were also able to keep their US $2,500 grants from the government. These latter arrangements were most typical during Phase II of housing reconstruction, which began in July 2006 when the buffer zone was narrowed to 35–60 meters in the south and 65–125 meters in the east. The scale and complexity of housing assistance was likely to outweigh the impact of local cultural and community factors, a key interest of our study, on subsequent outcomes. The scale of district-level differentials in donor assistance is described below in the section on post-tsunami response.

A final confounding force was the reemergence of the ethnic conflict soon after this study began. On 15 July 2005, the Sri Lanka Supreme Court ruled key provisions of the government's proposed Post-Tsunami Operational Management Structure (P-TOMS) to be unconstitutional, setting the stage for a new round of conflict over tsunami assistance (see Keenan, this volume). The election in November 2005 of Mahinda Rajapakse as President was followed by further escalation in tension. Military activity increased considerably, particularly in Trincomalee and Batticaloa Districts in the Eastern Province, each of which has been the site of government recovery of territory, coupled with sustained humanitarian crises. It is estimated that 21,000 people died in the conflict between the time of the tsunami and December 2008 (SATP 2009). In some areas in the east, particularly Batticaloa District, the post-tsunami recovery might have been affected by renewed conflict.

Results of the community study: facts on the ground

The study design necessitated the availability of comparable socioeconomic indicators from before and after the tsunami. Given the absence of pre-existing individual or household surveys with adequate sample sizes, the study focused on the community level of analysis. The primary unit of analysis was the Grama Niladari (GN) division, the smallest unit of public administration. Under Sri Lanka's highly integrated and effective system of local data collection, GNs are neighborhood civil servants (called "village headmen" in colonial days, and "Grama Sevakas" until recently), responsible for maintaining and reporting local data on population distribution, household living standards (water/sanitation, electricity, labor, welfare program participation, etc.) and community economic, social, and educational institutions. They also maintain an election registry, which requires the tracking of all deaths of residents occurring to residents age 18 and over. For clarity, the administrative unit is referred to as "GN" while the officer in charge of the GN is referred to as the "Headman."

To capture greater between-community diversity within each locality and to be broadly comparable to the communities of interest in qualitative chapters (see Gamburd, Lawrence, McGilvray), communities were sampled in Galle, Matara, and Hambantota Districts of Southern Province (predominately Sinhala with small Malay Muslim minorities) and Ampara and Batticaloa Districts in Eastern Province (each having a mix of Tamil and Muslim populations). These districts accounted for about two-thirds of all deaths and homes destroyed in the tsunami. The ethnic population distribution of affected DS divisions is depicted in Table 2.1. Affected areas of Southern Province are overwhelmingly Sinhalese, with a Muslim minority typically living in close proximity to the coast. Ampara District is two-thirds Muslim, with a one-third Tamil minority and a small number of Sinhalese. Batticaloa district was 82 percent Tamil, with a 15 percent Muslim minority and almost no Sinhalese population.

Department of Census and Statistics (DCS) estimates of GN-level housing damage provide a starting point for the study. DCS identified affected Divisional Secretariat (DS) divisions (i.e. sub-districts), including almost all those abutting the coast (DCS 2001). DCS then assessed damage at the GN level. DCS data are used to construct GN-specific estimates of housing damage and to identify tsunami-affected GNs for the survey described below. Measurement of other important variables such as deaths was hampered by the fact that DCS only surveyed families remaining in the GN, thereby excluding those families that were displaced or in which all members perished.

Population statistics were gathered for affected and unaffected GNs in coastal divisions of the five study districts. Initial data came from the 2001 Sri Lanka Population Census, which did not include Batticaloa (DCS 2001, 2005). All data for Batticaloa and GN-level ethnic distributions (not included in 2001 public release) came from Divisional Resource Profiles maintained by DS offices. Further estimates of local population distribution came from the community survey and from archival research on community history.

The author worked with a team of four fieldworkers to conduct a survey of 146 GNs evenly divided between affected and unaffected communities in Southern and Eastern Province. The sample was designed to compare a representative cross-section of highly-affected areas with significant Sinhala, Tamil, and Muslim populations. Affected GNs were identified using a random sampling methodology with weights to favor the sampling of heavily-affected communities (measured by the proportion of homes destroyed). Unaffected GNs were sampled at random to closely match the number of affected GNs surveyed in the same DS division. Surveys were authorized by the Sri Lanka Ministry of Public Administration and Home Affairs. Headmen shared administrative data on population, household living standards (e.g. water, electricity, housing quality), and community resources for 2004 and 2005. When administrative data were not available (because it had not been collected or was lost in the tsunami), fieldworkers asked the headmen to estimate these figures. Headmen reported adult deaths for 2004, 2005, and 2006.

Table 2.1 Ethnic population distribution of coastal DS Divisions for study districts

	Sinhala	Tamil	Muslim	Total*
Ampara	10,795	101,961	201,360	314,116
	3%	32%	64%	
Batticaloa	5,813	260,596	58,831	330,998
	2%	79%	18%	
Galle	425,557	251	44,526	470,334
	90%	0%	9%	
Hambantota	235,576	571	13,966	250,107
	94%	0%	6%	
Matara	262,474	632	12,357	275,542
	95%	0%	4%	
Total	940,215	364,011	331,040	1,641,097
	57%	22%	20%	

*Totals include small numbers of other ethnic groups.

In tsunami-affected areas they also estimated the scale of tsunami damage to local health and educational facilities, the scale of tsunami relief efforts, and the extent of recovery. Interviews were conducted in the Headman's preferred language. It is important to note that survey data are only used for results on community living standards (Tables 2.4, 2.5, and 2.7) and on aid worker presence (Figure 2.2). Other results are based on all GNs in the districts of interest.

Table 2.1 describes the distribution by district and ethnicity of homes judged by DCS to be destroyed or rendered completely unusable during the tsunami. As expected, in the Southern Province Muslims were overrepresented among tsunami victims, suffering for instance 25 percent of home destruction in Hambantota while only contributing 6 percent of the coastal population.[2] Significantly, Tamils were somewhat overrepresented among destroyed homes in both Ampara and Batticaloa districts. Although the tsunami crisis in Ampara has been depicted by many as a Muslim crisis, owing to the large Muslim majority and the tendency for Muslims to dwell near the coast, observed housing impact statistics suggest that Tamils, comprising only 31 percent of the population of Ampara's coastal divisions, suffered 46 percent of home destruction. Muslims, while 66 percent of the population, suffered only 53 percent of the homes destroyed. Similarly in Batticaloa, while Muslims comprised 18 percent of the population, they suffered only about 8 percent of the lost homes.

Table 2.1 defines four groups that faced the greatest tsunami impact in the study districts and that constitute the basis for the study. Sinhalese communities in Southern Province suffered 7,072 destroyed homes, or 24 percent of the total for the five districts.[3] Second, Muslims in Ampara District accounted for 5,639 homes, or 19 percent of the total. Third, the Tamil minority in Ampara experienced a disproportionate share of the damage, accounting for 4,895, or 17 percent, of all homes destroyed. Finally, Tamil communities in Batticaloa district lost 8,835, or 30 percent, of all homes. The study will primarily compare outcomes for these three conflict-affected eastern groups in comparison to the largely Sinhalese reference group in the Southern Province.

For each study group Table 2.2 characterizes the total number of tsunami-affected GNs, their aggregate population size, and the tsunami housing impact. Although the total number and cumulative size of affected communities in Southern Province was quite large (about half of the total), the average Southern Province tsunami-affected GN lost only 36 homes, or 12 percent of the total. By comparison, in Ampara affected Muslim GNs lost 20 percent of all homes (71 per affected GN) while Tamil GNs lost 40 percent of all homes (107 per GN). In Tamil parts of Batticaloa, 25 percent of all homes in affected GNs were lost, with the considerably larger size of GNs resulting in 110 destroyed homes per affected GN. Although the Southern Province communities accounted for half of our total survey population, they accounted for only 28 percent of lost homes.

Table 2.3 describes pre-existing differences between affected communities among the four study groups, dividing affected GNs into those that are heavily affected (meaning greater than 50 percent of all homes were destroyed) or moderately affected. Victims from Eastern Province, particularly Tamils, were far more likely to reside in heavily affected communities. In such communities the mechanisms of inter-household support and assistance would likely be less effective since all of one's neighbors – including in many cases matrilocally clustered married sisters – would be in similarly dire straits (see McGilvray and Lawrence this volume for ethnographic examples). Only 41 percent of Sinhalese victims came from heavily affected communities, largely in Hambantota and Hikkaduwa. By contrast, about 80 percent of those Ampara Tamils who lost their homes came from communities where more than half of their neighbors also lost their homes. Muslims in Ampara (57 percent) and Tamils in Batticaloa (65 percent) had an intermediate level of concentration in heavily affected communities.

Although Ampara's tsunami victims were divided almost evenly among Tamil and Muslim, more than two thirds of those losing their homes in moderately affected communities were Muslim (2,268 Muslim versus 1,056 Tamil), while 58 percent of those losing their homes in heavily affected communities were Tamil (4,206 Tamil versus 3,029 Muslim). A number of possible explanations explain this pattern. First, it is possible that Tamils lived nearer to the coast or in more vulnerable coastal areas. It is also possible that Muslim communities lived in similar areas but had better housing or flood control. Cursory observation of coastal areas of Ampara offer support for both possibilities.

With respect to residential patterns, a significant number of Tamils lived in close proximity to the coast, often situated between a coastal lagoon and the ocean. This includes Tamil villages such as Sinna Muhathuwaram (in the Akkaraipattu area);

Table 2.2 Characteristics and tsunami impact for key study groups

	GNs	Population	Households	Homes Destroyed	Percent Destroyed	Homes Destroyed per GN
Southern Province	225	317,631	68,473	8,011	12%	36
Ampara Muslim	75	116,472	26,807	5,297	20%	71
Ampara Tamil	49	54,599	13,232	5,262	40%	107
Batticaloa	80	127,182	33,240	8,675	26%	108
Total	429	615,884	141,752	27,245	19%	64

Table 2.3 Extent of tsunami housing damage, by study group and severity of impact

	Moderate Damage			Heavy Damage		
	Households	Homes Destroyed	% Destroyed	Households	Homes Destroyed	% Destroyed
Southern Province	62,091	4,765	8%	6,382	3,246	51%
Ampara Muslim	20,830	2,268	11%	5,977	3,029	51%
Ampara Tamil	7,192	1,056	15%	6,040	4,206	70%
Batticaloa	24,861	3,071	12%	8,379	5,604	67%
Total		11,160			16,085	

Thampaddai and Tambiluvil (in Tirukkovil Division), and the Methodist village of Komari (in Pottuvil Divison), which sat perched on a particularly narrow cause-way and lost 100 percent of homes. In contrast, large Muslim population centers such as Akkaraipattu are largely built away from the coast, though some heavily affected Muslim fishing communities such as Maruthamunai had expanded along the coast. It is unclear whether Tamil proximity to the coast reflected systematic vulnerability or displacement from more ecologically secure areas. Few in the area would have based residential decisions explicitly on tsunami risks, which were not widely understood before the event. But factors predisposing areas to ecological vulnerability were not unrelated to those factors that would also predict vulner-ability to tropical cyclones, coastal erosion, flooding, and withholding of upstream water resources.

The results of a survey conducted in 146 tsunami-affected GNs in Southern and Eastern Province shed light on the socioeconomic disadvantage of the tsunami-affected areas of Eastern Province, and Tamil areas in particular. GNs shared pre-tsunami records on the proportion of households having an indoor water tap, a flush toilet, cement or block wall construction, natural gas or electric cooking facilities, or an electric lighting source.[4] Table 2.4 shows the disparities among the study groups, looking at both the affected and unaffected communities combined, prior to the tsunami. Southern Province ranked highest on indoor water taps, flush toilets, and electric lighting sources. While 67 percent of Southern Province communities had an indoor water source, only 42 percent of Ampara Muslims, 20 percent of Ampara Tamils, and 14 percent of Batticaloa Tamils had this facility. In terms of brick or concrete wall construction and modern cooking facilities, Southern Province and Ampara Muslims had comparable levels well ahead of those experienced by Tamils in Ampara and Batticaloa. Of the five indicators, Ampara Tamils ranked lowest on all but indoor water taps, for which Batticaloa was lowest. These indicators suggest significant pre-tsunami differences in household infrastructure between the different study communities.

The divergence in pre-tsunami living standards of the study groups is summarized in the living standards index (LSI) shown in the last column. As all five living standards measures are highly concordant, a single index was constructed using a latent variable analysis. LSI thus measures a community's standard deviation from the combined living standards of the average community on all dimensions. For example, the mean community with an LSI score of 0 saw 36 percent of households with gas or electric cooking, 84 percent with flush toilets, 92 percent with concrete walls, and 52 percent with indoor water. This compares to 72 percent, 93 percent, 94 percent, and 77 percent respectively for communities one standard deviation above the mean (+1 LSI) and 15 percent, 70 percent, 84 percent, and 24 percent for communities with a −1 LSI. The LSI score demonstrates a clear ordering among the four study groups. Southern Province communities had an LSI score of 0.45 standard deviations above the mean, meaning that the average community was in

Table 2.4 Community indicators of household living standards prior to tsunami, by study group

	Indoor Water Tap	Flush Toilet	Cement or Block Walls	Cooking gas/ electric	Lighting source electric	Living Standards Index
Southern Province	67%	84%	89%	46%	84%	0.45
Ampara Muslim	42%	73%	93%	46%	67%	0.07
Ampara Tamil	20%	62%	61%	14%	42%	−0.90
Batticaloa	14%	71%	74%	24%	56%	−0.62
Total	47%	76%	83%	38%	71%	0.00

about the 67th percentile of living standards. Ampara Muslims were just about average at 0.07. Batticaloa LSI was –0.62, meaning that the typical community was in about the 27th percentile nationally. Ampara Tamils worst off at –0.90, meaning they were in about the 18th percentile nationally.

With a single LSI measure in place, it is possible to look at the selectivity, or patterns of pre-tsunami difference, between tsunami-affected communities in the four study groups. Table 2.5 demonstrates a common pattern of selectivity in both Southern Province and among Ampara Tamils whereby moderately affected communities display higher living standards than both unaffected and heavily affected communities. This pattern fits with a typical understanding of coastal vulnerability patterns: while those who are better off might choose to live near the coast for improved access to trade and roads, highly vulnerable areas closest to major bodies of water as well as isolated inland sites with few amenities might be avoided. Nonetheless, even comparatively well off Ampara Tamils in moderately affected communities had lower LSI than the worst off Southern Province or Ampara Muslim communities. Affected and unaffected communities in Batticaloa had lower living standards than all categories of Southern Province or Ampara Muslim community. Interestingly, among Ampara Muslim communities, the heavily affected communities were in fact the best off.

Taken together, LSI patterns for Ampara Muslims and Tamils indicate considerable population sorting with respect to coastal vulnerability, though the specific demographic mechanisms underlying this risk (in-migration, out-migration, or fertility) have not yet been identified. Tamils living in moderately affected communities, which are presumably the most desirable communities located near the coast, display a relatively small LSI disadvantage relative to Muslims (-0.46 versus 0.05), equivalent to the difference between the 50th and 32nd percentile of the living standards distribution. But among the hardest-hit communities, the typical Tamil community was in the 17th percentile of living standards, compared to the 67th percentile for Muslims (-0.95 Tamil LSI vs. 0.44 Muslim).

Table 2.5 Community living standards prior to tsunami, by study group and severity of impact

Study Group	Unaffected	Moderately Affected	Heavily Affected	Total
Southern Province	0.12	0.72	0.45	0.45
Ampara Muslim	0.03	0.05	0.44	0.07
Ampara Tamil	–1.19	–0.46	–0.95	–0.90
Batticaloa	–0.66	–0.62	–0.48	–0.62
Total	–0.19	0.23	–0.30	0.00

Post-tsunami response

Analysis of post-tsunami response can focus on a number of outcomes including expenditure, recovery achievement, or social welfare outcomes. Research emerging from this project has demonstrated substantial province-level differentials in post-tsunami financial assistance from foreign donors and related these to housing reconstruction outcomes (Kuhn 2008). Levels of donor assistance per affected population (accounting for total affected population, death toll, and housing destruction) were markedly higher in Southern Province than Eastern Province. Aid allocations in Northern Province, even in areas controlled by LTTE, were also higher than in Eastern Province.

Table 2.6 depicts donor assistance flows by district for the five districts of interest in this chapter (Development Assistance Database 2008). These data cannot easily be disaggregated by ethnic group. Nevertheless, the data indicate substantial variations in the level of financial influx. The first column repeats the total number of homes destroyed in each district from Table 2.1. The next two columns characterize donor commitment in total and relative to the number of homes destroyed. Total aid per home destroyed was similar in Ampara, Batticaloa, and Galle (about US $30,000 per home destroyed) but substantially higher in Matara (US $71,000) and Hambantota (US $141,000).

Relating total aid commitments to destroyed homes could obscure substantial non-housing impacts in affected areas, for instance the extraordinarily high death toll in Hambantota, so the next columns restrict foreign assistance flows to those coded as relating to the housing sub-sector. The higher commitment to Matara and Hambantota persists, with a total commitment amounting to more than US $25,000 per destroyed home in Hambantota and almost US $14,000 in Matara. By comparison, the average donor housing commitment was US $5,060 per home in Ampara and US $6,262 in Batticaloa. Galle represented an intermediate commitment of US $7,612.

Data on observed expenditures as of October 2007 offer an even more striking result. More than three-quarters of the total aid commitment to Hambantota had been expended, compared to about half in Ampara and Batticaloa and a bit more than half in Galle and Matara. It is unclear whether the failure to expend committed dollars in Eastern Province resulted from the ongoing conflict or from a lack of institutional commitment. Whatever the reasons, the housing expenditure per destroyed home was more than six times higher in Hambantota (US $19,185) than in Ampara (US $2,613) and Batticaloa (US $2,949). Although Galle District (US $4,578) received less than one-fourth the average commitment per destroyed home as Hambantota, it nonetheless received about 50 percent more than Ampara or Batticaloa. This data indicates significant regional disparities in aid distribution (confirmed also by Silva 2009: 70). In such an ethnically charged context, these disparities have high potential for political ramifications.

Such high-level evidence of differential responses does not identify variations within district or the conversion of funding into measurable impacts. If better-off areas also have higher labor or materials costs, then fewer houses might be built

Table 2.6 Donor financial commitments in relation to homes destroyed, by district

District	Total Commitment			Housing Commitment			Housing Expenditure	
	Homes Destroyed	Total (US $millions)	Dollars per Home	Total (US $millions)	Dollars per Home	Total (US $millions)	Dollars per Home	
Ampara	10,553	369	34,966	53	5,060	28	2,613
Batticaloa	9,630	263	27,310	60	6,262	28	2,949
Galle	5,544	184	33,189	42	7,612	25	4,578
Hambantota	1,288	182	141,304	33	25,388	25	19,185
Matara	2,398	171	71,309	34	13,970	18	7,611

for the same cost. Although financial assistance cannot be disaggregated to the GN level, the GN survey incorporated a subjective measure of relief activity: the presence of individuals conducting relief work. GNs were asked to report the number of aid workers whom they had seen in their community during the tsunami relief effort during the 2005 calendar year for three categories of worker: people from the local community, people from elsewhere in Sri Lanka, and people from outside the country. This data showed a high degree of consistency by study group and degree of tsunami damage, and a strong correlation with objective measures of impact such as housing recovery, suggesting that comparisons of relief worker presence across GN are indicative of relief effort.

Figure 2.2 depicts the presence of relief workers by study group and tsunami impact for heavily and moderately affected communities. Heavily affected communities saw only slightly greater numbers of relief workers than moderately affected ones, perhaps because every affected community requires a basic relief infrastructure that is not wholly proportionate to tsunami impact. More significantly, Southern Province saw about twice as many relief workers as other areas, about 86 for moderately affected and 121 for heavily affected communities, even though a typical affected community in Southern Province lost few households, a smaller proportion of households, and had less preexisting vulnerability than typical Eastern Province communities (see Table 2.2). Levels of relief worker contact were considerably lower among the three Eastern Province groups, with between-group variation in accordance with the average level of tsunami impact: highest among Ampara Tamils, then Batticaloa Tamils, then Ampara Muslims.

Differences in the presence of Sri Lankan and international aid workers are also notable. International aid worker sightings offer considerable evidence of tarmac bias, the tendency for international aid workers to visit places that are convenient. In Southern Province, the average moderately affected community received 12 international workers on average, while the average heavily affected community received 42. A closer look at the data reveals a more obvious pattern whereby two heavily affected communities in the tourist area of Balapitiya saw 95 international workers on average, while two moderately affected communities received 45 international workers. Five heavily affected communities in war torn Batticaloa District saw a single aid worker between them, though moderately affected communities in Batticaloa saw six on average. This data indicates substantial regional variation in local, national, and international relief activities. Here again, differential administration of aid could have political causes or ramifications.

Housing construction

High-level variations in financial assistance and low-level variations in the presence of relief workers are also reflected in the accomplishments of the housing program, which constituted by far the most significant relief activity carried out by local and international agencies. Figure 2.3 compares the assessed housing damage shown above to the progress of the donor- and owner-driven housing reconstruction programs as of October 2006, almost two years after the tsunami occurred.[5] It

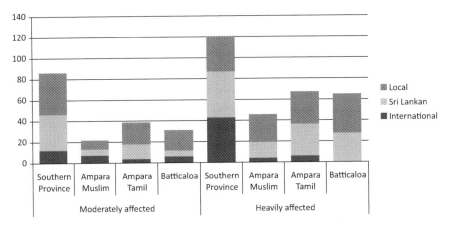

Figure 2.2 Reported sightings of relief workers, by study group, severity of impact, and area of origin, 2005.

is important to note that the ratio of completed homes to destroyed homes cannot be reliably interpreted as a proportion, since those who lost their homes and those who received homes might not be the same people. In reality, the number of homes proposed for construction as of October 2006 amounted to about 140 percent of the total number of destroyed homes nationally.[6]

This unexpected outcome results first from the intention to relocate even residents of partially damaged or undamaged homes lying within coastal buffer zones between 35 and 60 meters from the sea in Southern Province and between 65 and 125 meters in Eastern Province. It also stems from the need to sign extra MoUs to ensure that a sufficient number of homes are built, as well as a tendency to build too many homes in some places.

Relative to the total number of destroyed homes, the shaded segments of the bars indicate homes completed through the donor-driven program, those completed through the owner-driven program, and those remaining to be built. In Southern Province, the number of completed homes was 99 percent of the number of destroyed homes, with a sizable majority (70 percent) built directly by donors. By comparison, the number of completed homes was only 20 percent of the total for Ampara Muslims and 19 percent for Ampara Tamils. In the Ampara Tamil GNs, a bigger proportion of completed homes was built directly by donors. In Batticaloa, the number of completed homes was slightly higher, at 30 percent of the total burden of destroyed homes, on the strength of a highly effective homeowner-driven housing program in Batticaloa Town. These differences could be explained not only through political favoritism but also through tarmac bias, distance from the capital, and construction difficulties caused by the increase in the ethnic conflict.

A comparison of differential housing construction rates in Southern Province better illustrates the extent of politically-motivated aid distribution, since no tsunami-affected district was affected by the fighting. Figure 2.4 separates the

Southern Province housing results into the three affected districts of Hambantota, Matara, and Galle. It is also important to note that Galle is considerably closer to Colombo, and presumably is favored by tarmac bias. In Hambantota, where President Rajapakse spent his formative years, more than 5,000 homes were being built to replace 1,290 that had been destroyed; more than 4,000 had already been completed by October 2006. In neighboring Matara the intended and completed number of homes matches the number of destroyed homes, but this still does not reflect a simple reality. The owner-driven program for homesites that had been reclassified from the prohibited coastal buffer zone to permitted building sites included 469 homes, none of which had been completed, while the donor driven program for people still classified in the buffer zone had already produced more than the necessary number of homes.

Finally, in Galle District in 2006, a significant number of homes had been planned but very few had been completed. Since the majority of destroyed homes were in the buffer zone, Galle was highly dependent on donor-driven housing progress. While progress in the donor-driven program was accelerating, these people had already spent two years in transitional shelters or other temporary living arrangements. Only the popular tourist areas of Hikkaduwa and Balapitiya had seen even a slight majority of donor-driven houses completed (about 60 percent). Other areas had performed worse (e.g. 11 percent in Ambalangoda, 30 percent in Galle Town, 13 percent in Habaraduwa). Participants in the Galle owner-driven program also experienced much slower progress in comparison to Hambantota and Matara. In Hikkaduwa, only 16 percent of participants in the owner-driven program had received full compensation. Other areas of Galle District saw more rapid progress in the owner-driven program compared to the donor-driven program (e.g. 58 percent in Balapitiya, 56 percent in Galle), but progress was still considerably slower than in Hambantota or Matara. More importantly, a majority of affected households were not eligible for the owner-driven program as a result

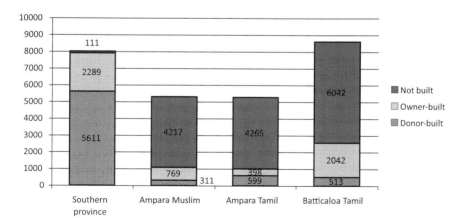

Figure 2.3 Progress of housing reconstruction as of October 2006, relative to stock of destroyed homes, by study group.

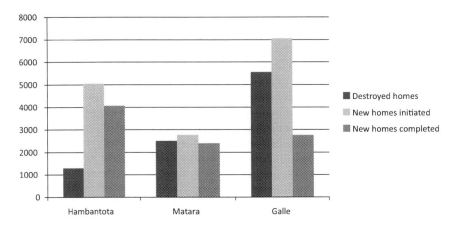

Figure 2.4 Housing plans and progress relative to housing damage as at October 2006, by district, Southern Province.

of living in the buffer zone. In light of the results in other chapters, it seems clear that politics played a role in the distribution of houses between the three districts in the Southern Province.

Finally, it is worth considering the relationship between coastal vulnerability and the pace of housing reconstruction. While complete GN-specific housing progress records could not be constructed for Southern Province, Table 2.7 describes the ratio of completed homes to destroyed homes for the three Eastern Province study groups, by level of tsunami impact (for all GNs) and by the Living Standards Index (for the surveyed GNs). The imposition of the coastal buffer zone had a devastating effect on the pace of housing reconstruction in heavily affected communities where it would have been difficult to rebuild in any case. In all cases the rate of home construction was three times higher in moderately affected communities compared to heavily affected communities. In Batticaloa where the owner-driven program was so effective, 71 percent of homes in moderately affected communities had been rebuilt by October 2006 compared to only 11 percent in heavily affected communities. In Ampara, the burden of slow housing reconstruction in heavily affected GNs had a disproportionate effect on Tamils, who were overrepresented in heavily affected communities where only 6 percent of homes had been rebuilt after two years.

The second set of results in Table 2.7 illustrates the burden of the housing reconstruction program on the poor, particularly poor Tamils living in Ampara. Coastal Tamil communities in Ampara bore a triple burden given their preexisting disadvantages (see Table 2.5), their more comprehensive tsunami losses (see Tables 2.2 and 2.3), and the housing reconstruction deficit. Low LSI Ampara Tamil communities had a reconstruction rate of 4 percent, compared to 6 percent for middle and 15 percent for high LSI communities.[7] In summary, the data presented here indicate significant regional and ethnic variation in relief and recovery operations.

Post-tsunami exam scores

A final study goal was to assess the differential impact of the tsunami on measurable human welfare outcomes. One outcome of great importance in the lives of young people in Sri Lanka is the nationwide Grade 5 scholarship examination. The exam provides an objective measure of community academic achievement, and holds considerable consequences for future progress. Children passing the scholarship exam are eligible for admission to competitive national schools. Those from poor households are also eligible for scholarship funding from government, corporate, and non-profit sources. The exam measures academic achievement, not basic aptitude, in mathematics and the student's primary language (World Bank 2008). It therefore offers some indication of children's knowledge acquisition, retention, and test performance in the year before and after the tsunami.

Exam results were gathered from the National Department of Examinations for all schools in the five districts of interest, including divisions farther away from the ocean. The results of exams taken in August 2004, just before the tsunami, and August 2005, the year immediately following the tsunami were selected for analysis. Because it is difficult to link individual schools and GNs, the source of variation is the amount of tsunami damage in the DS division of which the GN division is a part.[8] Separate results for the different study groups in Eastern Province are not presented due to sample size limitations. The total sample includes 1,076 schools in Southern Province (with 37,692 applicants in 2004, and 35,373 in 2005) and 685 in Eastern Province (12,041 applicants in 2004, 12,351 in 2005).

Figure 2.5 summarizes changes in test outcomes from 2004 to 2005 for schools in unaffected, moderately affected, and heavily affected divisions of Southern and Eastern Province. Before and after the tsunami, qualification rates were higher in Southern Province (7.1 percent) than in Eastern Province, (5.6 percent). In both areas, qualification rates were highest in moderately affected DSs, then in heavily affected, and lowest in unaffected. Between 2004 and 2005, the qualification rate rose slightly in unaffected areas (5.8 percent to 6.2 percent) and declined only slightly in moderately affected DSs (9.5 percent to 9.4 percent), but declined substantially in heavily affected DSs from 7.8 percent to 6.9 percent, or a 13 percent drop. Since the number taking the test also declined slightly in affected areas, the actual number of qualifiers was reduced by 60 in moderately affected areas, or a

Table 2.7 Housing reconstruction ratios for Eastern Province, by tsunami impact and community living standards

	Moderately Affected	Heavily Affected	Low LSI	Medium LSI	High LSI
Ampara Muslim	26%	9%	14%	9%	38%
Ampara Tamil	18%	6%	4%	6%	15%
Batticaloa	71%	11%	31%	18%	55%

7.5 percent reduction, and by 100 students in heavily affected areas, or a 15.4 percent reduction. The greatest declines were seen in economically advanced urban areas, including some of the largest recipients of post-tsunami assistance. Tangalle division lost 62 qualifiers, or a 27 percent drop, Matara Four Gravets (Matara City) lost 60 for a 19 percent drop, and Hikkaduwa lost 36, for a 50 percent drop.

In contrast, both attendance and qualification rates remained relatively stable in all parts of Eastern Province.[9] Pass rates dropped slightly in unaffected (4.1 percent to 3.9 percent) and moderately affected DSs (7.4 percent to 7.2 percent) but actually rose slightly in heavily affected areas, from 5.3 percent to 5.5 percent. The over-all number of qualifiers did not decline in any part of Eastern Province, including a small but still surprising 4 percent increase in the heavily affected areas.

It is difficult to reconcile these changes in academic achievement with the broader context of tsunami impact and relief, but a few caveats are worth mentioning. First, exams were taken only 8 months after the tsunami, so results may not reflect recovery so much as immediate impact. Students in tsunami-affected areas of Southern Province, having a history of high qualification rates, also had more room to lose ground. Many of the worst hit Tamil areas of Eastern Province had almost no qualifiers in either 2004 or 2005, and thus little room for decline. Yet qualification rates remained stable even in high-achieving, heavily affected parts of Ampara and Batticaloa. For at least this one human welfare outcome, the results do not reinforce inequities observed in terms of preexisting vulnerability, financial commitment, aid worker presence, or housing reconstruction.

Conclusions

While a complete assessment of the impacts of the tsunami and its complex reconstruction process is yet to come, this inter-regional and inter-ethnic study of grassroots statistical data suggests that a micro-demographic approach can pose new questions and yield new insights for multidisciplinary post-disaster research. This sprawling comparison of tsunami-affected communities before, during, and after the tsunami has attempted to place the disaster into a local and regional context of selective political opportunism, population movements, and socioeconomic disadvantage, all in some ways connected to the island's ongoing civil conflict.

On the day of the tsunami, striking regional variations in the coastal vulnerability and tsunami impact largely reflected the cleavages of Sri Lanka's ongoing civil conflict. Tamil and Muslim areas in the east showed substantially higher concentrations of tsunami damage and lower living standards than Sinhala-majority areas of the South. Variations within the east are illustrative of the more immediate connections between conflict and ecological vulnerability. As in many areas of the developing world, in Sri Lanka traditional areas of high settlement density tend to be situated a moderate distance from the coastline, enabling access to coastal economic opportunities and amenities without exposure to coastal disaster risks. Throughout the developing world rapid population growth and movement have led to the formation of new settlements in areas nearer or farther from the coast, typically by vulnerable, low status populations. In eastern Sri Lanka, several aspects

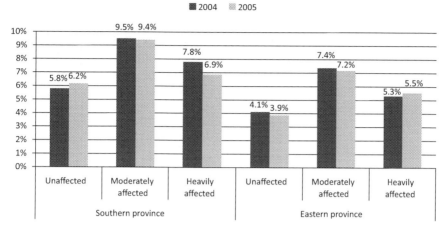

Figure 2.5 Annual change in number of students qualifying for scholarship on Grade V exam, by province and severity of impact, 2004–2005.

of the ongoing conflict – including Sinhalese settlements, LTTE guerilla camps, and military closures – have restricted inland settlement opportunities. Although this paper does not document these movements, it does document the considerable concentration of Tamil communities, particularly in areas of Muslim- and Sinhala-dominated Ampara District, in vulnerable coastal settings, typically with water on all sides. Such communities also showed deep pre-existing socioeconomic disadvantages in comparison to less affected Tamil communities and to similarly affected Muslim ones.

In the aftermath of the tsunami, foreign assistance efforts placed considerable emphasis on the less heavily affected communities in Southern Province, seemingly at the expense of more vulnerable, more heavily affected areas of Eastern Province. This was visible in levels of foreign financial assistance, in local perceptions of aid worker presence on the ground, and in the pace of housing reconstruction. The challenging context of disaster recovery in a conflict-affected environment was reflected in the politics of the coastal buffer zone, which was initially set to 200 meters in the east versus 100 meters in the south, leading to observable deficits in housing progress and widespread perceptions of bias. In Southern Province, the largely donor-driven housing program in Hambantota and Matara Districts offered a means of expressing favoritism not merely vis-à-vis the east, but also in comparison to neighboring Galle District. This favoritism is clearly not ethnic in nature, but rather fits with a general pattern of political party-based distribution of entitlements in Sinhalese areas of Sri Lanka: areas such as Hambantota that are supportive of the current ruling party received substantially greater support than opposition-led areas such as Galle. While the scale or effectiveness of relief efforts did not vary substantially between the Muslim and Tamil communities of Eastern

Province, the distribution of relief did not take into account the greater level of vulnerability among Tamil affected communities.

In a separate paper, the excess tsunami impact in the northeast was combined with the excess tsunami relief to estimate that the tsunami constituted about US $500 million in excess net losses for the east and north compared to the south (Kuhn 2009). This included a rather conservative assessment of the value of a lost life at US $50,000, but the tsunami would have constituted a considerable net transfer from northeast to southwest under any assumptions. This deficit must surely create a perception of grievance within the Tamil and Muslim communities. It is also possible that the greater net impact on the Tamil community contributed to the government's decision to increase defense spending in an effort to defeat the Tamils on the battlefield, an effort that led to the return of the entire island to government control in 2009.

While this study documents significant conflict-related variations in prior vulnerability and subsequent relief activity, it was not able to link these with welfare outcomes. In the context of the current chapter, for instance, it remains unclear whether the extra aid and homes poured into Hambantota actually generated a welfare benefit. It is unclear who received these new houses, whether unaffected families received them, and whether the homes were of satisfactory quality. Certainly visual and anecdotal evidence would cause one to question the merits of the extra homes in Hambantota, which are situated in a dry interior area 14km from the city centre and the coastal livelihoods of many affected communities. Analysis of children's scholarship exam scores suggested a pattern of deterioration among affected Sinhalese communities and resiliency among Eastern Province Tamil and Muslim communities. Further research is needed to link variations in financial assistance and relief effort with measurable variations in welfare. For a society as fragmented and troubled as Sri Lanka's, however, any perception of bias, whether based on intentions, allocations, or outcomes, may only add to the grievances that have been accumulating for decades.

Notes

1 Housing reconstruction payments were paid in four installments: an initial payment, one for completion of the foundation, one for the walls, and one for the roof.
2 It should be noted that exact estimates of home damage by ethnicity are somewhat less reliable in Southern Province due to the unavailability of detailed ethnic composition data for all areas.
3 Although Muslims in Southern Province are an interesting study population in their own right, they accounted for only 4 percent of the total homes destroyed in the study and are excluded.
4 "Indoor water tap" refers to the presence of a municipal water source, indicating the availability of water and the time and labor required to draw water. Shorter travel distances would also tend to reduce the risks of external contamination of the water in unsanitary containers or due to temporary storage indoors. "Flush toilet" refers to any toilet that uses a powerful, mechanical force enabling the immediate separation of waste from proximity to humans.
5 By October 2008 virtually all permanent housing projects had been completed, but it

is the analysis of this data from 2006 that reveals the differential patterns of tsunami reconstruction in the regions and ethnic communities that form the basis of our study.

6 "Initiation of house construction" means either that the owner had registered for reimbursement from the owner-driven housing program or a Memorandum of Understanding (MoU) had been signed for a donor to build a house.

7 It should be noted that no data source accounts for houses that were built without donor assistance.

8 Because DS divisions are much larger and extend farther inland in Southern Province, the cut-off for a heavily affected district there was 5 percent of all homes destroyed, whereas the cut-off in Eastern Province was 15 percent of all homes. The reported relationships also hold when a continuous measure of DS-level housing damage is correlated with exam outcomes.

9 Some of this pattern may be explained by the fact that the minimum qualification score was reduced considerably for Ampara District, from 126 to 118, and in Batticaloa District, from 128 to 124. In Galle and Matara, the minimum score was reduced only from 133 to 132, while in Hambantota it rose from 130 to 131. All changes in minimum qualification score were consistent within District, and thus should have resulted in equal changes in qualification rates in tsunami-affected and unaffected areas. Since these results reflect tsunami-related differences in the relative change from 2004 to 2005, changes in scoring criterion should not obviously affect the results.

3 The golden wave
Discourses on the equitable distribution of tsunami aid on Sri Lanka's southwest coast

Michele R. Gamburd

Introduction

The Indian Ocean Tsunami of 26 December 2004 devastated 70 percent of Sri Lanka's coastline. Due to the southwest coast's proximity to the nation's capital, its high visibility as a foreign tourist zone with luxury hotels, and its political clout at the national level as a Sinhala-majority area, the Southern Province was quickly and deeply inundated by a "golden wave" of aid. In this chapter, I report on events that took place within a year after the tsunami in the predominantly Sinhala Buddhist area between Aluthgama and Ambalangoda in Galle District on the southwest coast of the island. I focus specifically on the relationship between institutional policies, interpersonal status dynamics, and individual identities as they played out against the backdrop of the tsunami and the subsequent windfall of disaster relief aid.

"Disaster," write Susanna Hoffman and Anthony Oliver-Smith, "draws a researcher as close to basic elements of culture and society as ever found" (1999: 11). In the aftermath of the tsunami, people focused not only on basic physical needs for sustenance and shelter, but also on social needs for status and respectability. The disaster revealed not only the fundamentals of material culture and political economic dynamics, but also the backbone of class stratification, caste hierarchies, and ethnic and religious identity structures.

The post-disaster administration of aid presents a key juncture in the relationship between the citizen and structures of governance. I explore this relationship through stories I gathered in southwestern Sri Lanka about entitlement and dishonesty in the relief and recovery operations. In particular, I consider the strategic and performative subtexts underlying frequently heard statements like "We didn't receive anything." After immediate survival needs were met, discussions increasingly touched on issues of ethics, equity, and entitlement. My analysis reveals class and caste-based patterns in the accusations of immorality and favoritism that followed the distribution of aid. I also explore the crafting of ethnic identity in evaluations of the relief and recovery operations that unfolded against the politically charged backdrop of Sri Lanka's ongoing civil war.

Narratives and identity

"People will probably always assume their leaders are corrupt, even if they are as clean as a whistle," contends Sian Lazar (2005: 220). Lazar urges scholars to examine accusations of corruption with a critical eye; he suggests that allegations may report what is, but can also warn against what might be. In short, relating a narrative about corruption is a highly political social action.

When people talk about entitlement, immorality, and corruption, they simultaneously craft their own identity as moral agents. Narratives about misappropriation and corruption often contain stock characters – an immoral villain, a victim, and a hero (Sampson 2005: 111). The villains extort bribes from the helpless and plunder public coffers; the victims face partial, unresponsive, and exploitative bureaucrats; and heroic whistleblowers step in to defend the downtrodden and uphold the system. "The accusers position themselves as morally righteous, and the accused are variously branded as 'outsiders' [or] 'chaotic' others" who distort and destroy public order (Zinn 2005: 233). Discussions of entitlement and corruption thus present ample opportunities for the narrative crafting of self and others within a wider system of governance.

During my research in south-western Sri Lanka, I heard multiple discussions about the morality of distributing tsunami relief aid. Donors (including private citizens, the state, and non-governmental organizations (NGOs)), distributed goods in person and through public officials, NGO workers, and local intermediaries. Many of my interlocutors discussed the handling of relief and recovery operations. They critiqued not only the work of people in official positions, but also the actions of fellow villagers, friends, and neighbors. I argue here for the importance of analyzing the performative, agentive functions of these critiques (Ortner 2006). In particular, I suggest that engaging in discussions about entitlement and debates about morality are strategic actions. Analysis of these discourses reveals the micropolitics of status negotiations across a series of identities.

In the disruption following the Indian Ocean Tsunami, people struggled to reassert or challenge prior social hierarchies. The data presented here suggest that as tsunami-affected individuals and their fellow citizens discussed aid distribution, they engaged in self-making activities vis-à-vis each other, their would-be beneficiaries, and their government representatives. In the process, they both reproduced and transformed existing hierarchies within a variety of identity categories. Sri Lanka's long-standing ethnic conflict has actualized Sinhala, Tamil, and Muslim ethnic identities as collectivities with a sense of solidarity between members and a strong sentiment of antipathy to outsiders (Brubaker and Cooper 2000: 19). At the same time, entrenched local power struggles unfold over caste and class statuses. My goal in this chapter is to explore the local and national renegotiation of social standings in the aftermath of the tsunami.

I set the context by discussing a variety of relief activities provided for tsunami-affected families. Analyzing discussions about entitlement, I examine claims to status based on class and caste-based criteria. Specifically, I consider the moral evaluation of people who took what they did not deserve, or who did not take what they were entitled to receive. I also examine how government administrators used the same criteria and systems of logic to position themselves as moral agents and to defend themselves against the accusations of corruption that circulated freely after the tsunami. Finally, I consider how discussions of entitlement affect understandings of national sovereignty and ethnicity by examining political wrangling about the Post-Tsunami Operational Management Structure (P-TOMS) and the re-envisioning of an old historical legend about the Sinhala cultural heroine Vihara Maha Devi.

Research design and methodology

As a cultural anthropologist, I have done ethnographic fieldwork in the Sinhala village I call Naeaegama since 1992[1]. My family connections to this village go back to 1968, when my mother, Geraldine Gamburd, began research for her doctoral dissertation in the same location. Together, we have gathered forty years of longitudinal data about the village and its surroundings. Naeaegama is located a mile from the beach. At this location on the southwest coast, the seawater came only a half mile inland. None of the village houses was damaged, but two villagers died in the tsunami. Living so close to the ocean, Naeaegama residents were on the frontlines of the initial relief effort, hosting in their homes and at the Buddhist temple the many friends, relatives, and acquaintances who fled from the waves. Area people were keen observers and integral participants in the relief and recovery activities that followed the disaster.

I spent a month in Naeaegama in November 2004, missing the tsunami by three weeks. When I returned in July 2005, tsunami issues completely superseded my original research agenda. One simply could not study anything else. As Hoffman and Oliver-Smith assert: "Disasters are emphatic and all-absorbing occurrences ... No social scientist in proximity could ignore the turbulence disasters ignite" (1999: 7). I spent 10 weeks in the Aluthgama – Ambalangoda area in 2005 and returned for another four and a half months in April 2006. I conducted 60 interviews and informal focus groups in Naeaegama and the surrounding area in 2005, with follow-up interviews and site visits in 2006. I interviewed a wide range of individuals, all of whom still recalled vividly the immediate events of the tsunami. My interviews contained hair-raising stories from people caught in the angry water, as well as heart-wrenching narratives of people who visited all the area refugee camps and searched among hundreds of bodies to find their loved ones.

By July 2005, relief and recovery efforts had moved to interim and longer-term measures, and people discussed both the tsunami and its aftermath. In addition to speaking with villagers, I performed a series of targeted interviews in the Aluthgama-Ambalangoda area. To find out about camps set up for tsunami-affected people, I spoke with the chief monks at three local Buddhist temples and the pastor of an area church that hosted crowds of people fleeing the shoreline. My informants include four Samurdhi Niyamakas (poverty alleviation program workers, hence SNs), two Grama Niladharis (village-level government administrators, hence GNs), and a representative from the Balapitiya District Secretariat (DS), all of whom administered government aid and two of whom helped run camps in the immediate aftermath of the tsunami. I visited two areas with temporary shelters (one a tsunami-affected village where owners were rebuilding on their own land, the other a camp for people who had lived within the 100 meter exclusion zone and awaited new houses elsewhere). I also interviewed four local intermediaries who distributed money, goods, and (later) houses from international donors. In addition, I spoke with stakeholders about damage to local tourist hotels, garment factories, and the fishing industry, and learned about the tsunami's effects on other sectors, such as construction. This chapter draws mainly on data collected between July and September 2005; by 2006, the tsunami was basically "over" on the southwest coast, save for a few displaced individuals still waiting in camps for permanent shelter.

Relief activities

The Sri Lankan government's post-tsunami distribution of aid raised moral and legal concerns among Naeaegama residents. This sort of concern is not unique to Sri Lanka; indeed, disasters often raise such questions about governance. Disasters simultaneously increase citizens' needs and decrease the ability of governments and other institutions to meet those needs. Le Billon and Waizenegger write, "External assistance can help local authorities in this regard, but windfalls in relief and reconstruction aid can also increase the risk of (perceived) fraud, corruption, mismanagement and dispossession by the government and its cronies, aggravating the plight of the most vulnerable and grievances against authorities" (2007: 414). Despite what some observers deem to have been a highly successful relief and recovery operation (see Gasbeek, this volume), the government of Sri Lanka nonetheless met with embarrassing criticism of its handling of the disaster (see for example Sarvananthan and Sanjeewanie 2008: 345; Frerks and Keenan, this volume).

Complex political dynamics shadowed the distribution of aid, and criticism and suspicions over the abuse of aid money ran rampant. As the immediate crisis ebbed, government officials and international donors took over the administration of aid from the religious institutions, local organizations, and private citizens who met displaced people's initial needs. In July 2005, I spoke with Ashok and Janaka, two SNs from the Naeaegama area who had worked in tsunami-affected areas during the height of the administrative logjam. Ashok and Janaka noted that the first rush of aid (food, clothing, household items) was distributed generously but not selectively. Ashok asserted, "Individual people were bringing help to the temples. So they were sometimes giving aid to people who had never seen the tsunami." Janaka agreed, "There was a lack of officials to help these individuals. So they would just give aid to whoever was in the queue. They were distributing without knowledge of who was who." It took a few days for the government to organize the distribution of aid, particularly because many of the relevant officials had themselves been affected by the tsunami.

I spoke in 2005 with four SNs and an official at the Balapitiya Divisional Secretariat (DS) who described the compendium of aid offered by the government.

In tsunami-affected divisions, the GNs, helped by the SNs, took a census to find out which families had been affected, asking who had died, what buildings had been destroyed, what jobs, livelihoods, and property had been lost. Through the DS offices, the government gave SL Rs. 15,000 (US $150 at the time) as death compensation to the deceased person's relatives. Because many bodies were washed out to sea and numerous others were buried in mass graves, local areas formed committees headed by the GN to issue death certificates for genuine losses.

Through the poverty alleviation program Samurdhi, the government also issued a ration card for cash and food items. Each member of a tsunami-affected family received SL Rs. 375 a week (SL Rs. 200 in cash from the Samurdhi Bank and SL Rs. 175 in goods from the government cooperative store). The government printed the ration cards according to the GN reports. Some troubles arose over which families deserved this aid.

For tsunami-affected households, the government also provided SL Rs. 2500 for household goods such as pots and pans. In addition, based on GN reports, they paid SL Rs. 5000 a month through the People's Bank for 2–3 months to people who had lost stable jobs due to the tsunami. (Hotel workers, shop owners, and fishermen qualified for this aid, but only if they had no income during the period.) Government aid, though welcome, generated a flurry of confusion and complicated paperwork.

Housing: owner-built houses, new schemes, and the 100 meter buffer zone

The government provided compensation for houses that were damaged or destroyed. Compensation went to home owners, not to renters, and no one received anything for damaged household items. The local GN and a Technical Officer (TO) surveyed the damaged houses. The government provided SL Rs. 250,000 for destroyed houses and SL Rs. 100,000 for damaged houses. People who had no damage did not receive compensation money, even if the tsunami water entered the house. Compensation came in installments. By July 2005, people with partially damaged houses had received SL Rs. 50,000 and those with fully damaged houses had received SL Rs. 100,000. People had to show that they had used the first installment of money to repair their house before they received another installment.

By August 2006, many houses had been built or rebuilt on owners' existing land. Victor, a community leader in a beachside community near Naeaegama, reported that in his village, most of the houses were under construction. He pointed out the 500 square foot house built with the SL Rs. 250,000 [US $2,500] provided by the government and compared it with the much larger house of one of his neighbors, who had put together house-construction money from various sources. He said, "This neighbor got SL Rs. 250,000 from the government. Then someone who had a private shipping company gave SL Rs. 300,000. The aid organization CHF[2] gave SL Rs. 600,000. And, because the husband works at the Triton Hotel, the Aitken Spence Company gave him SL Rs. 200,000. So this man received SL Rs. 1,350,000 [US $13,500] total and has made a two-story house!" But not all homeowners were so lucky.

Much controversy developed regarding rebuilding close to the beach. Immediately after the tsunami, the government proposed boundaries within which no rebuilding could occur. These exclusion zones were to protect beach ecologies as well as to keep people from rebuilding in areas prone to damage from future tsunamis. Soon, however, tourist hotels received exemption from these boundary rules (Gunawardena 2008). The fishing community also made clear their need to have access to beachfront property. As fears of another tsunami subsided, beachside homeowners also asserted their rights to return. As pressures mounted, the exclusion zone shrank. By July 2005 on the southwest coast the boundary stood at the 100 meter mark; by 2006 it was a mere 35 meters in many areas.

For people who had had houses within the remaining exclusion zone, the government promised alternative land (provided by the government) and a new house (constructed by national and international donors). In July 2005, I interviewed Rani, an official at the Balapitiya DS office. She said that there were 713 fully damaged houses in the Balapitiya area. The Urban Development Authority, the Divisional Secretariat, and the Housing Ministry were working together to find land and coordinate donor construction. "But they can't make all these houses at the same time. There are 713 houses to make just in Balapitiya. For the whole island, the Housing Authority usually makes only 100–200 a year!" She felt that it would take one or two years to replace the destroyed homes with new 500 square foot houses.

Despite ample access to construction funds, the government faced many difficulties in obtaining suitable land, and in mid 2005, most people who had lived within the exclusion zone still occupied temporary shelters. My research associate Siri asserted, "The government says that they will give them land and put up houses, but my beard will be three feet long before that happens. So people are fed up." Government servants agreed with this assessment. Ashok, one of the SNs introduced above, said "I can't like all of the way things were done. For example, the people who were living within the 100 meter boundary are still in temporary houses in the interior. If the project had been done correctly, they would have been settled permanently by now. The government should have looked after the people whose houses were fully destroyed first. They should have started their efforts in a different order. They have helped the people whose houses were half damaged and they are now fully restored, while a lot of people who lost everything are still in plank houses." As regulations surrounding the exclusion zone shifted and changed, people who had lived within the 100 meter boundary began to reconstruct their homes. They received no government money to rebuild, but government officials took no action to stop the construction.

In July 2006, a year after our first interview, I again spoke briefly with Rani at the Balapitiya DS. She said she had spent the intervening year doing nothing but tsunami-related work. She reported that their office was currently paying the last installments of money to people who were rebuilding their own homes. In addition, most people who had lived within the exclusion zone had received new houses.

Despite the provision of new homes, some people still remained in temporary shelters, particularly members of families too large to fit into the donor-built

500-square-foot houses. The government was giving only one house for each house that had been destroyed, no matter how many families had lived in the original house. She asserted that all the families that deserved houses would receive them. Some people remained in the temporary shelters because they had no other place to go, and some remained because they hoped that if they stayed long enough, someone would build them a home. "They are hoping and hoping and waiting and living in the camp," said Rani. Indeed, as early as mid 2005, some people living in refugee camps were not eligible for new houses but were staying at the camps anyway. For example, a middle-aged woman from the Naeaegama area, Udani-nona, had nowhere else to live, and a government official told her to go to a nearby camp. She did not receive government aid but she did get the goods that foreign donors distributed. During an interview, she noted that some of her neighbors at the camp had lived on the beachside in rented houses. Although the government had no intention of providing new housing for renters, her neighbors said that they would not leave until they got a house. As eligible people went to new or rebuilt homes, the camps filled with less entitled residents.

Some of the new homes had serious drawbacks. Potential residents often found the new housing locations unsuitable or undesirable. In addition, many schemes suffered from substandard construction. In 2006, the newspapers carried a number of stories about cheating subcontractors and unlivable homes. Many Naeaegama area residents felt that the people who live within the exclusion zone, who had been neither high nor dry during the tsunami, were left (figuratively) high and dry in the resettlement process. These deserving citizens had not received their due benefits from the state.

In 2005 and 2006, opinions in the Naeaegama area varied about how well the government had handled the disaster. My observations, confirmed in several interviews, suggest that political allegiance flavored opinions. People in the political opposition often suggested that the government had done "nothing," or, worse, had distributed aid along party lines. One supporter of the opposition insisted that some people in his area had gotten housing compensation although they had no damage from the tsunami, and that other people with fully damaged houses received no aid because they were from the wrong political party. "You had to bribe people to get what you deserved," he insisted. In contrast, government employees (whatever their party) and those who supported the party in power felt that the government had done more than enough and that the critics were "beggars and liars." Renoza, a Muslim SN, remarked, "No matter how much [you/the government] gave, [they say that you/the government] didn't give [anything] (*Kochara dunnat, dunne naeae.*)" Rani at the DS office echoed the sentiment. These discussions reveal an issue of great local interest: the fairness and equity of the distribution of aid. They also reveal the strategic and performative nature of narratives about gift givers and recipients.

The golden wave: status dynamics and the distribution of aid

Immediately following the tsunami, Naeaegama villagers reported a prevailing sense of generosity, equality, and open-hearted community spirit ("communitas" in the lingo of Victor Turner (1974)). Shortly thereafter a reassertion followed of self-interest and social hierarchy.

In mid-2005, I heard many stories about entitlement and inequity. One genre consisted of stories about people who got more than their fair share of aid, or undeserving people who schemed to get handouts. A second genre consisted of stories about people distributing aid who creamed off materials to give to their friends, families, and political connections, and government officials who collected bribes in exchange for favors or (worse) for doing their assigned jobs. But self-interest was not the only source of inequity, as revealed in a third common story pattern. My interviewees felt that local government and non-governmental authorities knew who was who but often administered aid according to unfair priorities. In contrast, they felt that foreigners had no idea who had gotten caught in the tsunami; instead, for several weeks they administered aid by parking lorries near the beach and handing things out to anyone who showed up. The foreigners' mode of distribution, while unbiased, was still not particularly fair. In this section, I examine the cultural patterns revealed in these narratives about entitlement and inequity. In particular, I consider what these stories reveal about identity strategies based on local class, and caste-based claims to status.

Undeserving people: cheating, sponging, and selling relief supplies

One common narrative structure consisted of stories about people who got more than their fair share of aid, either by cheating the system to get undeserved handouts or by being in the right place at the right time to receive a random distribution of aid. Narrators deemed these schemers to be morally inferior. They associated the receipt of aid with lower class status, as indexed by poverty or unseemly greed. They also associated receipt of aid with lower caste status, within the South Asian understanding of higher caste or politically central patrons as gift-givers and lower caste, marginal clients as recipients (Raheja 1990).[3] In both frames of reference, receiving handouts diminishes status.

Stories about undeserving people usually started by invoking their moral opposite, deserving tsunami-affected individuals whose every possession had disappeared in the tsunami. For example, my research associate Siri's neighbor Chandradasa illustrated the tragedy of the tsunami by saying, "Some people didn't even have a hearth left to make tea, and the water in the seaside wells was bad." With no water and no fire, people lacked the barest minimum for subsistence, symbolized by a cup of hot tea. Such people categorically and unquestionably deserved whatever aid they received. Then, unprompted, Chandradasa turned to the topic of undeserving people who profited from the tsunami: "It was indeed the people who didn't get caught in the tsunami who benefited [literally 'ate,' which has a derogatory overtone] a lot (*tsunami naeti minissu tamayi goDak kaeaeva*).

Those are the people who got a lot of aid." As an example, he mentioned several families from unaffected sections of the Naeaegama area who spent two weeks at the Naeaegama temple. A few people, for example those who were crippled, genuinely needed to stay safely in high places until all danger had passed. The rest, he felt, were just sponging. Siri agreed: "They were happy because they could eat for free and were getting handouts of clothing and money."

Sometimes social actors found themselves in the right place at the right time, when foreigners who knew little or nothing about the village area stopped by to distribute aid. Naeaegama narrators viewed these aid recipients with some disdain. For example, during an interview with Sarath, Siri said, "Anyone can grab tsunami aid if it's being distributed at the junction." Sarath laughed and agreed, then sketched out a darker version of the same event: "The lorry driver says that he dropped stuff off and people were happy, and that's enough [to satisfy the donors]. And if people tell a lorry to stop or they'll beat the driver up, why should he 'eat fist'? He can say he distributed the things in Balapitiya, and it's true. But about half of the tsunami stuff goes to the wrong people." Narrators implied that recipients of undeserved aid sometimes turned their goods into cash. For example, Siri reported that someone came to his gate trying to sell 110 packets of Nestomalt™ that Siri suspected had come from tsunami aid distributed at a temple in the nearby town of Urugasmanhandiya. Local narrators condemned people who passively accepted or actively demanded undeserved aid, or who sold gifts of food for cash.

The inequitable receipt of undeserved aid caused tensions. For example, one informant said that she had seen from the bus window that undeserving people from the Naeaegama area had lined up to receive tsunami aid in other villages. These undeserving folks, her friends and neighbors, all came from a relatively poor section of Naeaegama. "They get stuff and then they come home late at night with big bags of things on their shoulders. They bring rice, mosquito nets, and school books for their kids. But they never even saw the water from the tsunami. This is unfair. But if you say something to someone about it, it makes a grudge. Those people say, 'The government is giving this out for free, why shouldn't I take it!? You don't need to complain!'" This woman repeatedly emphasized that she and her family had not taken any aid they did not deserve. For example, she said that while she was walking on the main road, some people in a lorry had given her a large bag of goods. She had planned to keep the things, but her son was angry with her for taking it, saying "This is not ours." He put everything back in the bag and took it to the temple. Even though she condemned those who had profited unjustly from the disaster, this poor woman seemed jealous of the aid they received. In her description of her son's actions, pride in his assertion of gift-giver status mixed equally with exasperation at the loss of the goods.

In contrast to tales about undeserving others who got many goods for free, I observed, and a number of my informants also remarked, that many people claimed, "We didn't get anything." But a closer examination often revealed that some of these same people had indeed received amply. For example, the Naeaegama woman in the previous example had worked as a hotel maid. Early in our interview, she claimed that she had not received anything despite losing her job. Later she revealed that she had gotten for free from the hotel SL Rs. 30,000 [US $300] worth of used building materials (wooden doors, door frames, and window frames). On a similar theme, a local monk, Ananda Thero, related a humorous (and perhaps apocryphal) story about a man who claimed, "I didn't get anything." The man then showed a visitor his broken wardrobe – and opened the wardrobe door to reveal row upon row of powdered milk packets. The monk impatiently grumbled, "There is too much greed." Claiming not to have benefited from the tsunami may preserve a sense of social superiority, and acknowledging relief received may put some people out of the running to receive more.

In Naeaegama's densely populated village fishbowl, people watched each other with eagle eyes, examining and commenting on how various neighbors negotiated the aid environment. They spoke freely (and perhaps fictionally) about what others had taken, but when talking of their own actions, people often denied that they had received any aid. These statements doubtless reflect past events. But I speculate that these narrative tactics may also reflect two levels of strategy: strategy to get more aid from donors, and strategy to enhance individual and family standing within local logics of class and caste status. Within this social schema, the deserving, tsunami-affected poor are entitled to their fair share of aid. Those who take more than they deserve, particularly those who deserve nothing but take or (worse) demand aid, are morally condemned. In contrast, those who do not need or accept handouts have a higher social and moral status. As the following section illustrates, stating that one has passed up free goods is a powerful claim to economic security – and to a prestigious standing within local logics of caste and class status.

High status and the refusal of aid

Researchers who have spoken with tsunami-aid recipients in Sri Lanka report accusations of irregularities. Moonesinghe notes that some informants complained of political and religiously based favoritism; for example, one person said, "We have never received even a parcel of food" (2007: 59). Moonesinghe seems to take such assertions at face value. I here argue that an analysis of narrative strategies reveals a sophisticated politics underlying local discussions of receiving aid.

The status dynamics inherent in refusing handouts are clearly illustrated in the discussion of who accepted tsunami aid. While some undeserving people shamelessly took handouts, my informants suggested that deserving but respectable people refused to wait in line to ask for aid, even if they were entitled to it. For example, a Sinhala banker in his 30s whose house was inundated with seawater refused to eat at the refugee camp, perceiving the food as meant for those who were "less able" and "truly needed" it. He mentioned going to buy spices for one of the first meals at the camp established at a Balapitiya school, but made it clear that he did not eat there himself. This echoes village norms that suggest that only beggars eat food "from the temple" (or from other public charity events). The respectable people I spoke with emphasized what they had given after the tsunami, claiming (truly or not) to have received little or nothing themselves. Receiving charity is a blow to one's reputation; in contrast, giving augments one's status.

Local residents are acutely aware of the identity politics surrounding the receipt of aid. For example, a Muslim gentleman in Balapitiya suggested, "Government servants and teachers don't want to stand in long lines to get what they are entitled to. But those who stand in the queues get more." But even if people did not stand in line for goods, they did, according to another government worker, receive their due. Emphatically stating that all tsunami-affected people had benefited from government aid, this SN said, "Without a doubt the people who were badly hit by the tsunami have gotten help. The SNs go to their houses and give them the goods. Sometimes reputable people who had given to poor people before the tsunami don't want to wait in the queue for goods. If they don't come, the SN goes and gives the things to their house. These aren't necessarily rich people, but respectable people who are socially important and have been so for generations. They are embarrassed (*laejjayi*) to stand in line. So the SN goes and distributes to them, and then the next time they make an arrangement to have a servant or someone pick the goods up." In this case, relying on a servant allows aid recipients to save face in public, cushioning their respectable reputation.

The golden wave

The status dynamics of aid were crystallized in the scathing condemnation of people imagined to consider the tsunami as "golden water," "blessed water," or "a golden wave (*ratarang raellak*)" because they had profited from relief. The poor, whether deserving or (especially) undeserving, often occupied this category. A retired school teacher, Dayawansa, neatly categorized the population, saying, "If some family was living in a small shack, a tiny shelter, and now they are getting money, monthly aid, pay, donations, clothing, mosquito nets, good clothing, toys for their kids, bed sheets of the best fabric, and a new house, then they are happy! For other people the tsunami was the ultimate loss, because they lost their whole house, a good house, and what it's replaced with won't be as nice. If you didn't get any water in your house but you manage to get money or monthly compensation, ration cards, and donations from individual donors, then you could say it's a good thing." Similarly, the banker succinctly stated in English, "People who had nothing before the tsunami got the benefit. People who had something lost. What is given can't be compared to what they had. If someone was living in a hut with one plate, they got lucky. The people who didn't want to work hard didn't get so much money but they got a lot of other benefits. They would like to get this for their whole life." A Sinhala poem neatly captures these class dynamics. The poem (which I heard in several variations) states:

> The person who had, lost.
> The person who didn't have, gained.
>
> *Aeti minihaa naeti unaa*
> *Naeti minihaa aeti unaa*

In this logic, to claim that the provided relief does not measure up to what one has lost is to stake a claim to middle class status (*aeti minissu*, literally "people who have enough"). In contrast, those who benefited from the tsunami count as working class (*naeti minissu*, literally "people without").

During an interview with two young Naeaegama women who worked at a local garment factory, my research associate suggested that some people were calling for another tsunami. The young women, who had lost three co-workers in the waves, emphasized that no one whose loved ones had died would wish for another disaster. They temporarily refocused the discussion on human lives rather than material goods. Several government workers, however, acknowledged that some people had indeed benefited disproportionately, and cited government shortcomings as a reason.

Stories about corruption: government servants talk back

Speaking of the devastating earthquake that shook Peru in May 1970, Oliver-Smith notes, "The maldistribution of aid and the inefficiency of aid agencies over several years following the tragedy gave rise to the saying, 'First the earthquake, then the disaster'" (1999b: 86; see also Schuller 2008). This saying suggests that people perceived the problem not as the natural hazard but as the way it was handled – a critique, in short, not of the earthquake but of the inequality entrenched in post-colonial Peruvian social structure. After the tsunami, media coverage and local narratives abounded in Sri Lanka about incompetence and corruption. But government administrators told a different and more nuanced story. In this section, I examine what the discourse on corruption reveals about social status, citizenship, and morality.

Evidence suggests that despite the scale of the challenge and some disorganization and duplication of effort, most tsunami-affected individuals, particularly on Sri Lanka's southwest coast received a great deal of aid (see Gasbeek, Kuhn, this volume). Evidence related in this chapter shows the sensitivity of local people to the inequitable distribution of aid, particularly when undeserving people profited from the tsunami. I now turn to an analysis of narratives related by government servants, examining how they use this same calculus of entitlement and identity to refute accusations of improper behavior. In short, government servants portray themselves as moral, middle class actors and high status, authoritative patrons who give without receiving, simultaneously implying that those who voice accusations of corruption are immoral people who asked for what they did not deserve.

The inequitable distribution of goods created much ill will within communities, but may not have resulted from dishonest or corrupt intentions. Deepak, a Grama Niladhari in the Balapitiya area, said, "Within the first month the GNs got a list of rules to follow, but those needed to be stronger. If the rules had been stronger, then there would have been fewer of these 'golden wave' people. The strictness has to come from the GNs." In this statement, he implicitly acknowledged shortfalls in administrative policies. In his next statement, however, he implicitly shifted some of the blame: "But when we are strict, then there are complaints and threats." Other government officials voiced similar notions. For example, during an informal focus group with some Muslims in Balapitiya, a school teacher said, "After distributing, all the brotherhood disappeared. The brotherhood between Sinhalese and Muslims and the togetherness between families went down. The GNs were taking bribes and not doing a good job." Everyone present started talking at once in agreement or dissent. Someone muttered about "thieving work (*horu vaeDa*)." A discussion followed of how the meat shop owner had received a ration card but a man injured in the tsunami had not. But Renoza, a local SN, staunchly defended the local GN. She said, "It wasn't the GN's fault. They [villagers] came yelling for ration cards. The GN is very honest but he is afraid of the threats. If someone threatens him with a knife, he will give them a card. Now lots of people are writing lies [about the GN]." Both Deepak and Renoza blamed irregularities in aid distribution on threats issued by undeserving bullies.

Rani at the DS office in Balapitiya identified a similar pattern. She acknowledged the original lack of an overarching distribution plan. Then she said, "The stuff came in. The GNs made lists of the affected people. We set up places to distribute goods under GN instructions, fairly. But there were a lot of troubles between the GNs and the common people. The GNs didn't really have time to gather the right information. They just distributed aid 'whichever way' and from that the fights started. Everyone was saying he or she was tsunami-affected, both the people who had been affected and those who hadn't. The GNs had no time to get the real information. So there is still a grudge about that with the people. The GNs gave people a lot of stuff, but the story is that they didn't help the affected people. The GNs had a lot of work. They had to look after the refugee camps as well as doing their ordinary work with the other area people. It was a very difficult situation. The GNs were under a lot of pressure every day. One in [a nearby village] committed suicide. Some people called GNs 'thieves' to their faces and pasted accusations on posters on the streets. Some GNs retired under the pressure. [She gave several examples in the area.] People were scolding. But the GNs weren't bad; they just couldn't do the whole job. Outsiders came to help, but they didn't know the area and they couldn't really do the job right." In this narrative, Rani notes the challenges of distributing aid quickly and fairly, but emphasizes that false claims by undeserving individuals made a difficult situation even more complex.

In their narratives, local-level government officials pointed out how hard they had worked and how much they had distributed. For example, Deepak had two uprooted coconut trees and several feet of mud in his house. But on the day after the tsunami, he started work. "People were scared and angry, and they all wanted to talk with me. I started work at 7 AM and didn't get home again or get to eat until 10 PM!" Deepak also said that he was proud of the work he had done. He took care of his GN division and also administered a refugee camp. "No one died of hunger. We gave everything that we got, from both the government and from private and foreign donors. We gave everything as fairly as we could, under pressure." But Deepak's working conditions were not easy. He explained, "People who don't deserve stuff were demanding it from the GNs. When we didn't give it, they say we were holding out for a bribe. People would wait for me on the road and threaten me. They came with guns and knives, or they threatened to take me to the police or to file a court case. In those days I had no security. It would have been better if I had a motorcycle [to escape fast from trouble] or a hand phone [to call for help] or some backup. But I didn't have those. I was peddling around alone on my bicycle. I was afraid for my life and fed up with the job. The GNs who were old enough just retired, and others quit! But there was no other job for me at the time, so I went on. The tsunami came and disturbed things for one day. But for the GNs, every day after that was like a flood of work and fear. There were always demands and threats." At the end of our interview, Deepak noted, "Telling all this is like reliving a bad dream."

The SN Renoza summed up the post-tsunami aid distribution situation in three words: bitterness, greed, and jealousy. She paraphrased her interlocutors, saying "'If someone across the street gets something, I want it too. If an NGO is giving something, I also need it. If you give something to a daughter, you have to give it to the aunt, too.' Houses have broken up about this, with brother fighting with brother."

In the social sketches above, government administers portray themselves as doing the best they could within a difficult situation. While administering to the deserving middle class people (*aeti minissu*) unwilling to accept aid in public and to the tsunami-affected poor (*naeti minissu*) who deserved aid, GNs and SNs also came into contact with individuals whose moral compass had been overcome by greed, jealousy, and an expanding sense of entitlement. The narratives I heard from government officials emphasized bullying interactions with hostile clients, rather than the possibility of less threatening but equally persuasive exchanges requesting favors due to political patronage, caste alliances, or family connections. In their narratives, the government workers alleged that a group of angry citizens resorted to damaging upstanding officials' reputations and threatening them with bodily harm in order to get things that they did not deserve. Through this rhetorical move, the government officials asserted their own respectability by discussing their centrality and authority indexed by their selfless distribution of goods – all important aspects of status within caste-based logic. They simultaneously used their alleged accusers' greedy and wrongful demands for aid to mark the immorality and the lower status of their accusers.

Most accusations of corruption are several individuals away from the actual event. In other words, stories of wrongdoing are usually related at second or third hand. As stories circulate, they lose accuracy, nuance, and verifiability. And narrators strategically tell and retell stories to enhance their own status, denigrate that of their enemies and rivals, promote the standing of their political party, and (perhaps) position themselves to receive more aid. I do not doubt that people profited unfairly from administering tsunami aid, but I do doubt that corruption at the local level reached the scale that some informants insinuated. I also suspect that perceived shortcomings reflect the complexity of the task at hand and general distrust of government financial dealings (Gamburd 2004) as much as or more than incompetence or nefarious intent of local government officials. A critical reading of narrative politics around class, caste, and political affiliation adds layers of nuance to discussions of the misappropriation of tsunami aid.

Ethnic equity: P-TOMS and national mytho-history

Many people in the Naeaegama area found that as the tsunami waters receded, a sense of unity arose that briefly overrode divisions based on religion, language, and ethnicity. This sense of unity also infused others around the nation. Renner and Chafe note that "Momentary solidarity among the conflict's adversaries triggered hope that post-disaster cooperation would lead to reconciliation. Some Sri Lankans reminisce about the three-week period immediately after the tsunami as a time when there were no divisions" (2007: 28). But this period was all too brief.

Soon after the tsunami, trenchant discussions about the distribution of aid money pervaded not only the local but also the national level in Sri Lanka. In July and August 2005, politicians grappled with how to distribute money equitably to deserving people all over the island in the face of thorny issues of ethnic conflict and civil unrest. Disputes over the Post-Tsunami Operational Management Structure (P-TOMS) agreement illustrated nationalist fears couched in a discussion of state sovereignty (See Frerks and Keenan, this volume). And ethnic chauvinism surfaced in various forms of Sinhala-Buddhist meaning-making, as people reimagined interethnic relations through a famous historical legend (Malkki 1995). Both of the following examples reveal the overt consideration of ethnic identity and citizenship through the discussion of aid distribution and the structure of the Sri Lankan state.

P-TOMS

In June and early July of 2005, then-President Chandrika Bandaranaike Kumaratunga was trying to institute the Post-Tsunami Operational Management Structure (P-TOMS), a "joint mechanism" by which donor aid could be distributed both in the government-controlled south and in the areas of the north and east controlled by the Liberation Tigers of Tamil Eelam (LTTE). The P-TOMS agreement had clear political ramifications. The governing United People's Freedom Alliance (UPFA) and the UNP opposition party supported the P-TOMS agreement as a way to simplify the flow of aid to the north and east. The LTTE supported the P-TOMS agreement and called for as much autonomy as possible from the Government of Sri Lanka (GoSL) in the administration of aid. Although the major parties supported the agreement, Sinhala Buddhist and ultra-nationalist voices objected that P-TOMS would give too much recognition to the Tigers' proto-state organization by empowering their reconstruction wing, the Tamils Rehabilitation Organization (TRO). They also worried that the LTTE would acquire funds and materials for its separatist war efforts under the guise of tsunami aid.

The P-TOMS agreement was signed on 24 June 2005, and was immediately referred to the Supreme Court, which blocked four clauses on constitutional grounds on 15 July 2005. P-TOMS brought grave disunity to the UPFA ruling coalition, and the political debate in the South soon shifted to talk of presidential elections, which were held in November 2005 and won by the UPFA candidate, Mahinda Rajapaksa, whom many perceived as hawkish. Spurred in part by

perceptions of inequitable distribution of tsunami aid, the political situation continued to disintegrate between the GoSL and the LTTE in 2005 and early 2006.
By August 2006, the four-year-old ceasefire between the GoSL and the LTTE
was worth little more than the paper it was written on, though it was not officially
scrapped until January 2008. By that time, tsunami-affected people in the southwest
had long been resettled in new homes, while many tsunami-affected people in the
east still lived in temporary shelters (See Lawrence, this volume).

During the summer of 2005, I asked Sinhala-Buddhist people in Naeaegama
their opinions on the P-TOMS agreement (*yaanthranaya*). To a person, everyone I
spoke with stated clearly that anyone who got caught in the tsunami deserved help.
(De Mel and Ruwanpura (2006: 38) report a similar sentiment among the people
they interviewed.) My informants emphasized that religion and ethnicity should
not affect the distribution of aid. But to a person they also expressed skepticism
about distributing aid through the LTTE or its affiliate the TRO, worrying that these
groups would co-opt the aid and use it for the war effort, without distributing the
needed materials to the tsunami victims. No clear proposals emerged, however, for
a different system of getting aid to the north and east. A minority felt that P-TOMS,
while not perfect, presented a possible way forward. Most people suggested that
the GoSL should distribute the aid – a simple but impractical proposal, given that
at the time, the LTTE held sole control over much of the territory in question.

When I asked whether tsunami-affected people in the north and east should
receive aid, respondents emphasized shared nationality and shared humanity. For
example, Bandara replied, "Why not!? There are also victims in the north and
east. I don't like to talk about Sinhala, Tamil, Muslim, and Burgher. We are all Sri
Lankan. We are all humans." Similarly, the SN Ashok said, "The tsunami went to
all the sides of the island. Sinhalese, Tamils, and Muslims were all affected. We
can't just help the south. So we should give to the north and east too." Everyone
felt that as humans in need and as citizens of the nation, people in other parts of
the island should receive tsunami aid.

Despite wishing to distribute tsunami aid to the north and east, people felt skeptical about P-TOMS. The Naeaegama opinion against P-TOMS was closely tied to
village views of the LTTE. The temple monk made a distinction between giving
equally to all the people, which he viewed as a must, and giving to (vs. "through")
the LTTE. He did not see the LTTE as the legitimate representative of the Tamil
people; rather, he saw the LTTE as using the tsunami to gather a war chest under
the auspices of aid. When I asked Bandara about P-TOMS, he replied, "Aid should
not be given over to the LTTE. Funds and materials would not go to the tsunami
victims. They would go to the LTTE fund. The LTTE will look for Eelam; they
will not help the tsunami victims." A Naeaegama contractor elaborated on a similar
theme: "Yes, we must distribute to the east – but not through the LTTE. They have
committed a lot of crimes and have brought the country down. They have killed
how many master brains and destroyed how many buildings?! Even the Tamils
don't like them." A woman who had clung to her ceiling fan as the tsunami water
washed through her house cautioned against P-TOMS, saying, "The LTTE would
take that money and use it for war. That would be bad. The money needs to go

to the people who suffered damages. It needs to go for food and houses and good things like that. It is not okay to use it for war." These statements emphasize the rights of all tsunami-affected citizens to receive aid, but they reject the LTTE's claim to administer to people under its control.

The fear that the LTTE would use tsunami aid to amass war materials underscores how deeply the Sinhala-Buddhist residents of Naeaegama distrusted the rebel organization. For example, on 26 July 2005, the SNs Ashok and Janaka noted, "Today's paper says that the LTTE is bringing in war weapons [under cover of tsunami aid]." On 1 September 2005, an army soldier, Prasanna, elaborated: "The problem with tsunami aid was that at first no one was checking the goods that went through to the LTTE. Finally they started to check and then they found some airplane parts! They suspect other things went through in the unchecked trucks. About 10 or 15 lorries went through to Trincomalee and Mutur before we got permission to search them." In addition, the soldier suspected that the LTTE would use its distribution of aid to heighten its political claim on the people: "The LTTE didn't let [donor] trucks just go on through. They took the aid themselves and distributed it. Then later the [donor] organizations went back with army escorts so they could distribute their aid themselves. The LTTE probably took what they got from the aid donors and distributed it to 'their' people, their chosen ones. Then they can recruit from that population and get the good wishes of the people. Then those people think that the LTTE is giving them all this stuff, not the government." Instead of allowing the LTTE to take a state-like role, Ashok and Janaka suggested, "The government and the army should go and deliver the goods. This is a government job. Ordinary people can't go to the north and east now because that territory is only for them [derogatory pronoun]. So the government should take the army along." In these statements, Prasanna, Ashok, and Janaka make clear the patron-client relationships between the state and its citizens. Allowing the LTTE to distribute aid would give the organization an undesirable claim to legitimate statehood.

People in Naeaegama did not entirely trust the GoSL, but they trusted the LTTE less. For example, my research associate Siri displayed some mixed emotions regarding the equitable distribution of aid. Siri was an ardent supporter of the political opposition and, like many citizens, he held a cynical view of government use of public funds. Siri started by remarking that the Tigers were distributing aid more efficiently than the GoSL was. But he then said that only 25 percent of the aid distributed by the LTTE got to the needy, and the rest went to the LTTE "army training camps." Since the LTTE was reluctant to let government officials or journalists see what happened with the aid, "There's a big 'question mark' over the distribution." Siri next said that the GoSL should distribute the aid so that it would reach the deserving people. He paused, humorously recognizing the irony of promoting government involvement despite his prior accusations that distribution in the south was more corrupt than in the north. Then Siri suggested that he would rather see foreigners distribute the aid, because "both Sri Lankan sides are going to use it for something else!" Above all, he wanted transparency and accountability, which he imagined foreign donors could provide more ably than either of the governmental bodies on the island.

The retired schoolmaster, Dayawansa, recognized the necessity of a joint system of distribution: "We need something like PTOMS. Without a system, we can't distribute aid. We can't distribute aid to the people in the LTTE area without LTTE consent, cooperation, and help." But he did not trust the LTTE to conform to the agreement and do as they had promised: "Even if we do it with them, they will just do it on their own, without abiding by the terms and conditions." He concluded, "There are a lot of people against the [P-TOMS] agreement. They say not to give aid through the LTTE. They say that if we do that, the sovereignty of the government goes down." In mid-2005, arguments in the Sinhala-Buddhist southwest about the distribution of aid reflected ongoing tensions over how best for the GoSL to minister to the needs of its citizens, including those situated in enemy territory, without ceding political authority or compromising national sovereignty.

Awash in a sea of ethnic meaning: Vihara Maha Devi

Discussions over political legitimacy and ethnic identity played out not only in wrangling over P-TOMS but also in the re-imagining of a popular mytho-history. Numerous informants told me that they had never heard of the word "tsunami" before this one struck Sri Lanka. Nevertheless, the phenomenon has certainly occurred in the past. There is a periodicity to subduction earthquakes; for example, such quakes and their resultant tsunamis ravage the coast of the Pacific Northwest every 300–600 years (Sullivan 2008: 28). In Sri Lanka, a historic tsunami may have been recorded in the story of Vihara Maha Devi, which forms part of the Mahavamsa, a famous Buddhist monastic chronicle (Seneviratne 1999: 21). Most Naeaegama villagers knew this story, but had not in the past recognized in it the risk of a tsunami. Only in hindsight did they equate the recent disaster with the recurrence of a past event.

The Vihara Maha Devi legend remains pertinent to contemporary Sri Lankans because it resonates with current political tensions. The historic tale concerns the Sinhala cultural hero Dutugamunu, the scourge of the Tamils. Tsunami-related retellings of this story inevitably index contemporary ethnic animosities. For example, my research associate translated a short Sinhala book about the tsunami published in 2005. In addition to geological information about undersea earthquakes, the book related the story of Vihara Maha Devi. Siri relayed the tale to me as follows: "A king's wife was having a love affair. Her lover sent her a letter through a friend disguised as a priest attending a ceremony. The king found the letter and ordered all of the priests killed. Because of the king's disrespect for the Buddhist religion, the sea came inland and wreaked havoc on the kingdom. Educated men in the kingdom decided that the solution was to send someone from the king's family into the sea. Vihara Maha Devi, the king's only daughter, volunteered to go in order to save the country. They set her adrift in a small boat. She came safely back to land and married a king in another area. One of her sons was the hero Dutugamunu, who defeated the Tamil king Elara and unified the island under Sinhala rule." In 2005, many of my informants, both in Naeaegama and elsewhere, suggested that the historic disaster must have been a tsunami (Lock

2006: 145). They also drew implicit parallels between historic and contemporary political dynamics.

The Mahavamsa story draws on and reinforces a number of identities. First, it draws clear boundaries around acceptable femininity: bad women cheat on their husbands and cause much chaos in nature and in culture; good women risk their lives to protect their country and give birth to heroes. The dutiful daughter redeems the sins of her adulterous mother. Second, the story reinforces the necessity of proper Buddhist worship to minimize dangers from unpredictable natural events. To prevent further disasters, a good ruler should promote Buddhism and give generously to Buddhist institutions. Third, the story links cultural history, the tsunami disaster, and ongoing ethnic politics. People often read contemporary ethnic identities of Sinhala and Tamil back into the past in a way disturbing to historians but useful to Sinhala Buddhist nationalists (Gunawardana 1990). Furthermore, little imagination is required to equate President Mahinda Rajapakse, a politician from Hambantota in the Sinhala heartland of Ruhunu, with the cultural hero Dutugamunu; likewise, easy parallels equate the Tiger leader Velupillai Prabhakaran with the defeated Tamil king Elara. Through the Vihara Maha Devi story, the Sinhala people I interviewed made sense of the tsunami while simultaneously reinforcing patriarchal gender ideology, Sinhala Buddhism, and a long-standing unwillingness to share the island with Tamil rulers. Sinhala Buddhists in the South reread the Vihara Maha Devi mytho-history against a contemporary background of political tension and natural disaster.

Conclusion

In Naeaegama, the relief and recovery windfall in the aftermath of the tsunami raised questions of accountability and transparency, as people struggled with the morality of aid distribution in a situation where the scale of the undertaking put intense pressure on existing administrative structures. While the deserving received what they needed, some undeserving people also benefited. Local residents' reflections on corruption, sponging, and other perceived inequities in the distribution of aid reveal a complex interpersonal politics. By narrating stories about themselves and others, my interlocutors crafted social prestige using class and caste-based logics. They honored those who gave aid or refused to accept aid (*aeti minissu*, i.e. the middle class or the authoritative patrons) and pitied or scorned those who received it (*naeti minissu*, i.e. the lower class or those from marginal client castes). Government officials used this same cultural logic to counter accusations about their dishonesty and to question the moral integrity and entitlement of those who demanded or received aid that they did not deserve. Through discussions of state policies, citizens thus refined and re-imagined social status in the local area.

Discussion of tsunami relief also provided a space for citizens to revalue ethnic identities. By mid-2005 in the mostly Sinhala-Buddhist South, sympathy for the tsunami-affected populations in the north and east was tempered by distrust of the LTTE. Naeaegama residents supported aid distribution to Tamil populations in Tiger-controlled territories, but uniformly found the LTTE an unsuitable organization to distribute the aid. This judgment rested on their perception that the LTTE would not channel the aid to deserving people but would instead use it to pursue the civil war. They portrayed the LTTE as an illegitimate organization that did not serve the needs of its constituency and furthermore strove to undermine the political stability of the nation. Reflecting long-standing South Asian understandings of the king and the dominant caste as supreme patrons, these people based their understanding of state legitimacy on the fulfillment of obligations to client-citizens. Sinhala people found parallels between the current politically charged context and a widely-known mytho-history of a prior tsunami disaster. The tale of Vihara Maha Devi fed into long-standing anti-Tamil sentiments, reinforcing the perceived need to preserve the unity of the Sri Lankan nation state. Ethnic tension complicated the already draconian political maneuvers around the P-TOMS agreement, making the struggle over this aid-distribution arrangement a microcosm of the ethnic conflict with clear implications for territorial control, political legitimacy, and national sovereignty.

Notes

1 I use pseudonyms for local villages and people to protect the privacy of my informants.
2 CHF stands for Cooperative Housing Foundation International.
3 People I spoke with did not in my hearing identify particular castes by name, or associate particular demeaning activities with characteristics of particular castes. Nevertheless, I feel justified in mentioning caste identities as part of local status struggles due to the importance of giving and receiving in marking out caste relations in South Asia.

4 The Sea Goddess and the fishermen

Religion and recovery in Navalady, Sri Lanka

Patricia Lawrence

Introduction

The iridescent blue and green bee-eaters preening their shimmering feathers in the coconut palms had flown away before the Indian Ocean tsunami visited its devastation upon the fishing village of Navalady at breakfast-time, 26 December 2004. It is also said that hundreds of wild elephants moved away from the eastern shore, while domesticated animals were caught unaware along with their owners, and many perished. However, one young Tamil boy told me that he held on tightly to something that felt like a rope while the waters carried him from his home on the sandy peninsula to the inland side of the lagoon. Only when the current swirling with dogs, goats, people, furniture, parts of broken structures, crushed boats, and other floating objects at last released him, did he realize he had been gripping the tail of a milk cow with all of his might! He assured me that this life-saving cow also survived and still grazed in the area around his home.

In the village of Navalady in Batticaloa District, more than one third of the local population was taken by the sea in the span of just twenty minutes, a catastrophe that further compounded the suffering of two decades of civil war in Sri Lanka's Tamil-speaking eastern region. This village, which received notable coverage in the international press (e.g. Waldman 2005, Ramesh 2005), is home to Karaiyar fishing caste families whose newly reconstructed post-tsunami houses are scattered beneath coconut trees and palmayrah trees along a narrow peninsula between the Batticaloa lagoon and surf-washed beach of the Bay of Bengal. As elsewhere along the eastern coastline, deaths of females in the tsunami were disproportionately high. In Navalady the ratio was five females: one male.

In this vulnerable fishing village, significant concerns about divine protection, religion, and memorializing lost family members emerged during my interviews with surviving family members between 2005–2008.[1] Navalady's main village goddess was found partially buried in the sand 60 meters from the ruins of her temple with her four arms broken and hands severed. Although the tsunami waves swept every building away, leaving only bare foundations of their homes, some survivors – generally middle-aged survivors who had lost many loved ones – insisted upon returning to their original home sites where they had lived with their loved ones prior to the disaster and where some of them constructed new domestic shrines to commemorate their lost family members. I talked with local people under simple palm thatch shelters near fishing boats on the beach. I listened to fishermen while sitting in the sand where fishing nets are woven and cleaned, and heard detailed experiences from both men and women as we relaxed on floor mats in their houses. Through a series of case studies, this chapter explores the reconstruction of social relationships among surviving Karaiyar fishing families, and the simultaneous readjustments in their popular religious beliefs in the aftermath of the tsunami disaster. Although I studied post-tsunami recovery in five locations in Batticaloa District, my research unfolded most memorably in Navalady, where I met interlocutors who could impart a vivid understanding of the tsunami's effects on their lives and community.

An introduction to Navalady's fishing economy and culture

One version of the history of Navalady relates that the original settler was from the Paraiyar drummer caste. He came from Kallar long ago and settled on the peninsula when the place was all jungle. Years later, Karaiyar fishermen saw a large and very beautiful white crane settle close to them on the beach, and they believed the goddess of the sea, Kadalatci Amman, had appeared to them. After sighting the white crane, this small group of Karaiyar fishermen decided to settle at Navalady together. Today, Navalady's landscape features a variety of different fishing activities along the beach, although it is actually only a few kilometers from the bustle of Batticaloa's town center. Still, for some villagers, the trauma of the tsunami has permanently changed their lives and their livelihoods.

Fieldnotes: Navalady, Batticaloa District – 15 July 2007
Saminathan, who lost twenty-six of his family relations in the tsunami, sang fishing songs in a *vadi*, a palm thatch shelter for shade, on the beach at Navalady this evening. He told me that he has not gone out on the sea again since that day. Saminathan explained about their fishing songs: the songs have a lead singer who first sings out a phrase, and then the group of fishermen working together sing the changing refrain in unison. When they need to launch – or beach – a heavy boat, it takes about twenty men to move the hull over the sand, and to pull it in or out of the surf, and they sing during their collective effort. They also sing while they work the nets in beach seine net (*karaivalai*) fishing. The net is U-shaped … A heavy catamaran boat carries the net from the shore out to the edge of the corals … As the boat carries the net out, two lines of fishermen, about ten on each side, carefully let out the long sides of the net from huge baskets in which it is coiled. As they pull the long U-shaped net back into shore, it catches an increasing number of fish, and the men sing as they pull the heavy *karavalai* net in together. Most of the songs fishermen sing on the beach in Navalady are *karaivalai* songs, including some that invoke both the Catholic Virgin Mary and the local Hindu *amman* (mother) goddesses.

Figure 4.1 Karaivalai beach seine fishing, Navalady, Sri Lanka, 2007. Photo by Patricia Lawrence.

The tsunami destroyed ninety *karaivalai* beach seine boats along with their nets in Batticaloa District.[2] In the first weeks after the tsunami, pieces of torn fishing nets were seen hanging from palm trees, or twisted around barbed wire fences (along with women's long sari cloths), or strewn amidst the rubble of houses and broken boats.

Some of the fishermen claimed there were five or six tsunami waves near the end of the narrow, sandy peninsula between the Batticaloa Lagoon and the Bay of Bengal where the village of Navalady is located. Navalady survivors were in agreement that the second of the tsunami waves was the largest, and it was the one that destroyed the houses. With raised eyebrows a fisherman claimed, "The second wave rose high enough so that one man who was lifted on the wave's crest from the beach grabbed the electrical wire along the road and was left hanging up in the air." From the height of a tall tree, six residents who also survived watched this colossal second wave engulf an entire house about 50 meters from the sea so that it totally disappeared from their sight.

This was the house that belonged to Saminathan, my fisherman singer. In the last minutes before the waves arrived, Saminathan asked his wife, who was preparing breakfast, if she would cook *matti* (clam, mussel) curry for the midday meal. She replied that she was going to cook a vegetarian meal since it was Poya Day (Full Moon Day), and there would be a *puja* (ceremony of worship) at the nearby

Kadalatci Amman temple. Those were her last words to him: after the enormous waves subsided, he found her body in the rubble of their crushed house. Of their four children, only two bodies were ever found.

By 2007, three years after the tsunami, the violence of war had escalated around them once again in the form of renewed fighting in Eelam War IV. Those families still living in temporary shelters or transitional camps, of which there still were substantial numbers in the eastern districts, were now surrounded by newly displaced families who were refugees for a different reason. These new families were fleeing the bombing, shelling, and renewed violence of the war in their inland villages. Nonetheless, most of the surviving men who had been fishing earlier had by that time returned to earning their livelihood from the sea in Navalady.

Fieldnotes: Navalady, Batticaloa District – 2 August 2007
At 6 a.m. this morning, when I walked to the part of Navalady beach where the boats come in from night fishing, I passed by a large dead loggerhead sea turtle in the wet sand. The boats on Navalady beach are painted with a kaleidoscope of colored post-tsunami relief organization logos. I photographed a fresh catch laid out on the beach that was valued at more than SL Rs. 100,000 [then worth US $891]. Two or three men go out around sunset in an 18 inch fiberglass FRP engine boat and fish all night with large nets to get a catch like this. They beached their boat at about 7 a.m. A crowd of fishermen gathered around to see their catch, most of which was *mural* (swordfish) along with three large *arukkulameen* (seerfish) and some *kaddaparai* (flat and not as tasty as the others).

Engine boat fishing brings a more lucrative catch than *karaivalai* (beach seine) fishing from the shore. However, I'm told that in the right season the *karaivalai* catch can be very large too, though they get smaller species of fish. There are also a few deep sea divers in Navalady, plus a few who come down from Trincomalee. A decade earlier they used spear guns that are now illegal. Now most of their earnings come from catching several species of sea cucumbers that they sell in the nearby Muslim town of Kattankudy, where they are dried and shipped to the Chinese market. They dive in the corals about four kilometers off the beach, as deep down as a hundred feet, where they swim with schools of colored tropical fish, sharks, and sea turtles. Sometimes they bring lobster home for their own dinner.

Following the tsunami, the people who have chosen to return to live in Navalady are for the most part the eldest in the generation that survived, whose children have reached adulthood. Even though Navalady residents engage in a fishing economy, the majority of families with young children have decided to live seven miles inland where permanent houses have been constructed for them at Tiraimadu, where their children will be protected from the danger of another tsunami experience. In the 1990s, when the Liberation Tigers of Tamil Eelam (LTTE) were a controlling force in Navalady, they constructed a memorial park and shrine on the main beach road for Annai Poopathy, a Batticaloa woman who fasted unto death in 1988 as a martyr for the struggle for Tamil Eelam.[3] By 2007 the Tamil Tigers had vacated Navalady following prolonged and intense fighting between the government and the Tigers in the interior of Batticaloa District, but I continued to hear complaints and fears about pro-government paramilitary groups in the area.

The best time for interviews was usually early evening, stretching into nightfall. As my research continued, the raspy sounds of the bicycle tires turning over the sandy, gritty surface in the darkness was coupled in my mind with the details of thoughts, emotions, and rich descriptions that Navalady people offered. This was especially true the night I rode home after meeting Rubasingam Parwathy, because she offered a story that was an interweaving of local religious understanding of "protection" and the catastrophic consequences of the tsunami.

Parwathy's story of the village Sea Goddess

There were three young children frisking about in front of Rubasingam Parwathy's house when I parked my borrowed bicycle on the sand there early in the evening of 8 August 2007. What she told me that evening tied together what I was learning about temples, shrines, and religious practices in Navalady after the tsunami. She spoke in the style of a Batticaloa female *kathai colluvar* ("story teller").

The village of Navalady's main Hindu temple is dedicated to Kadalatci Amman (*kadal* "sea" + *atci* "ruling" + *amman* "mother" or "goddess" = Sea Ruling Goddess), known as a fierce and protective goddess to whom the local fishermen sing songs as they launch their boats into the Bay of Bengal. I first visited Navalady in 1992 during the annual propitiation of Kadalatci Amman, even though I had been advised that Navalady was a dangerous place that I should keep away from during my field research. When I asked why it was dangerous, people told me that the LTTE came and went from Navalady by sea, therefore I should avoid the possibility of being caught between the Tigers and the government Security Forces during frequent armed clashes there.

With her silver hair pulled back from her weathered face, Parwathy studied me with her steady, wide-set eyes as we both settled into comfortable positions on the floor of her main room. She asked one of the children to bring her *vettilai pakku* (betel leaves and areca nut). When I asked her whether there was enough betel for me to chew with her, she relaxed into a big smile that made her cheeks round under her high cheek bones, and I knew it was going to be a good conversation. Her forehead wore lines of hardship, but her physique was still strong, and the traditional gold and ruby studs in her ears matched the sparkle of this grandmotherly storyteller's eyes and red betel stains on her lips. "These children lost their mother so they are here with me. Their father lives next door, but he is off fishing," she explained as she handed me a small square of betel leaf that she had neatly folded with shavings of areca nut tucked inside. The children explained that a boat service takes them across the lagoon to school on the mainland everyday. There was a heavy brass lamp next to her that was about five feet tall. Otherwise the large main room of her new two-story post-tsunami house, built by Caritas EHED, was bare. I asked Parwathy if the brass lamp was used at the Kadalatci Amman temple, which was only a stone's throw from her house. "Yes, we keep it here when the festival is finished." We chewed our betel, and I waited to see what she would say.

> I truly trusted Kadalatci Amman before the tsunami, and I trust her now. My belief in her has been strong all of my days. The day before the tsunami came, a lady in a white sari with a large staff came walking around the village. We didn't know who she was. People saw her and some people spoke with her, but no one knew her. My daughter (who lives two houses away) was washing dishes when she saw that lady walking toward the house, in her dirty white sari with her staff to help her walk. She passed along the lagoon road behind the house. The neighbor there was also washing dishes. The old lady asked, "What are you doing?" and the neighbor replied, "I'm washing dishes." Then the old lady said, "Don't do this. Tomorrow the sea will come. Don't stay here. You must go somewhere else." My neighbor laughed and scolded her, "Don't tell lies!" Then she queried, "Who are you?" In that instant the old lady's white sari changed into a beautiful silk sari with lots of gold threads in it, although she still had her large staff. With her next breath, the lady vanished into thin air. My sister's daughter, who was setting out on her way to a private tuition class, encountered her next. The old lady asked her, "Where are you going?" So the girl explained that she was going to her class. The old lady commanded, "Don't go to class. Tomorrow water will come!" Then the old lady went on her way. My sister's daughter was frightened, so she turned around and went home. The next morning both my sister and her daughter died in the tsunami. After that the old lady met some boys who were picking *ilanir* (green coconuts). They called down from the tops of the trees, "*Aachchi*, do you want *ilanir* to drink?" She replied in a serious tone, "I don't need young coconuts." The boys answered, "Well, if you don't want young coconuts can we give you *panakam*?" (*Panakam* is a sacralized drink of green coconut water and other fruits given to devotees at the temple.) The lady staunchly answered, "I can't take *panakam* from you." The boys laughed. They didn't take her seriously. Suddenly, she dissipated into nothingness – she simply vanished before their eyes. So we can't blame the *amman* (goddess) because she tried to protect us. She warned us beforehand, but we didn't take her seriously.

Above all, Tamil goddesses are believed to offer protection (*pathukappu, kapparru,* or *kaval*) to the devotees who live around them, and who propitiate them during an elaborate annual ceremony for at least one week every year. Each *kudi* (matrilineal clan) of the village is assigned one day of the annual festival rituals and the families of each *kudi* provide what is needed for the *puja* (ceremony of worship) on their day. Parwathy's "family puja" is on the fifth day, and her son is the treasurer of the Kadalatci Amman temple. The festival is well-known in the area, and it is particularly known for the *kampakamatci* ceremony when one performer climbs to the top of a very tall pole in a state of possession-trance and spins around on a sacred trident. Children are delighted by the appearance of another performer who becomes Hanuman, the monkey god, during possession-trance. He hops up into a tree where small bags of candy are tied to the branches, and throws them down to the children.

This temple is the main temple for the village, so everyone in Navalady customarily participated in the annual festival. However, during the tsunami the temple was broken into pieces, most of which were washed away in the ferocious waves, while sparing a part of the innermost sanctum with its lamps and other sacred objects. A statue of the goddess that was positioned over the entrance to the temple was carried about sixty meters away and badly damaged. In fact, all four of her hands were severed from her arms.

Before the tsunami, three *mukakalai* (metal face icons) of the goddess – the central face of Kadalatci Amman, and on either side of her two other goddesses, Kali Amman and Pecci Amman – were worshipped inside the temple sanctuary. They were adorned with yellow sandalwood paste and red *kunkumam* powder atop brass pots surrounded with white, red, yellow, and rose-colored flowers, green coconuts, fruits, leaves of mango and margosa trees, fragrant incense, burning camphor, and brass oil lamps. After the tsunami, these three faces of *sakti* – the sacred, active female energy of the universe – were stolen by a man from Kallady. This was when there were people going through the ruins after the tsunami looking for valuables. The thief of the goddesses' faces buried them in the sand in his house compound, and after three days he became ill and quite mentally disoriented. Or so says Rubasingam Parwathy. At that point, she says, the president and the secretary of the Kadalatci Amman temple went to the thief's house and dug up the three goddesses' faces. They took them to another temple in the area where they would be safe until the Kadalatci Amman temple was rebuilt.

I noted in 2007 that the broken statue of the goddess once mounted on the front of the temple roof had been propped up under a palm thatch shade in front of the temple. Studying this battered and armless statue, I wondered how the survivors of Navalady, whose lost family members had toiled and kept religious vows for Kadalatci Amman during annual propitiations, could still have faith in this goddess of the sea who had failed to protect them from the tsunami waves (Fig. 4.2).

In June 2007, reconstruction of the temple was sufficiently completed for the annual festival to be held once again through the support of a grant from the Foundation for Co-Existence. Many local people had told me that there was a significant reduction in the numbers of devotees who attended the temple festival after the ritual re-opening. Apparently not everyone from Navalady shares Parwathy's enduring trust and deep belief in Kadalatci Amman after the deaths of so many loved ones in the tsunami. Parwathy commented on the lack of participation in the temple festival this year, stating that all of the main families sponsored their puja on their assigned day but with only two or three family members present. On the final day that always draws the greatest crowds, more people came to Navalady from Tiraimadu, the large tsunami camp for displaced families where many people who survived the tsunami are now living. When I asked her why people didn't come on every day of the festival as they used to before the tsunami, she was reluctant to suggest a reason for their neglect.

As the light in the room had dimmed with the setting of the sun, the eldest girl

Figure 4.2 Tsunami-damaged statue of the sea goddess, Kadalatci Amman, Navalady, Sri Lanka, 2007. Photo by Patricia Lawrence.

from the family next door brought a kerosene lamp and lit it on the floor next to us. We continued talking in the glow of the lamp, but I didn't want to press Parwathy with more questions about Navalady's decline of communal devotion to Kadalaatci Amman as it was clearly disturbing to her. She offered one final piece of information, sadly saying that one of the temple *pusaris* (priests) lost his life in the tsunami waves. The other priest survived, although his wife and four children did not.

Nagapucini Amman: the Virgin Cobra Goddess

I had discovered a small shrine for another goddess in Navalady several weeks earlier while traversing the narrower sandy roads on my bicycle. Although I thought I was familiar with all the forms of the goddess in Batticaloa District, this goddess who lived under a *naval* tree, in a shrine yet to be repaired after tsunami damage, was called Nagapucini Amman, who is understood to be a virgin cobra goddess.[4] I asked Parwathy to tell me about her. Her immediate response was:

It's dangerous to have an unrepaired temple in ruins. We have to fix the temple and do the pujas. Nagapucini Amman is a *naga kanni* (a sacred virgin female cobra). Last week my son, who is a fisherman, saw that *naga kanni* swimming over here from Mamangam (the site of a large temple on the mainland side just across the Batticaloa lagoon) while he was out in his boat, so she is here in Navalady now. This is the time for her *catanku* (annual festival). Since the tsunami the most they have done for her is to boil *ponkal* (coconut rice) for her on the day of the *catanku*. They used to have *teyvam adumakkal* – people who perform trance-possession by a deity – and couples that wanted to conceive a child would come and give offerings to Nagapucini Amman.

Parwathy's response is an affirmation of the Tamil belief that temples for the *ammans* must be carefully maintained and the proper rituals consistently observed. Tamil goddesses are said to lose their benevolent, protective personalities when they are neglected. For example, in 1991 there was a violent event at a temple for the goddess Kannaki Amman in Makaladittivu, Batticaloa District, where Tamil women were raped and murdered by soldiers in the Sri Lankan army. This was explained to me by local people as an instance in which the goddess had taken offense at the disrepair of her temple, and had removed her protective power from the village.[5] I noticed that someone had recently started making a palm thatch roof over the broken shrine for Nagapucini Amman, most likely in preparation for worshipping her in this season. I made a mental note to visit the families living around the shrine. Then Parwathy was moved to tell more about the local goddesses.

Matrilocal sisters: divine and human

There were three sisters, all of whom were *ammankal* (goddesses). They were Pattini Amman (also known as Kannaki Amman), Kappalenthi Matha, and Mari Amman. They came here by boat from Kerala. Pattini said she had to live in the jungle, so she went to a place inland near Morakkottanchenai called Koralaimadu, where there is now a Kannaki Amman temple under a margosa tree. Mari Amman preferred to stay here in Navalady under a banyan tree, but the people changed her name to Kadalaatci Amman ("Sea Queen Mother"), because they are fishermen. Kappalenthi Matha (known in English as "Our Lady of Good Voyage") turned into a Christian and lives across the lagoon from here. Our people believe she is one of the sisters. The ship she holds in her hand is the ship she and her sisters came on.

On the residential relationships between human sisters in Navalady, and on marriage, Rubasingam Parwathy had this to say:

Before the tsunami there were so many sisters living together here. I am an example. I was living next to two sisters. But now it's not like that. Some are living in Tiraimadu, or somewhere else inland, and many died. When their children grow up they will live like that. Now they prefer property in other places because they are still scared after the tsunami. Some girls have their own deeds to property; before the tsunami it was like that here. Now they're all spread out. The tsunami divided them. Before the tsunami, sisters living together was commonplace (*akka tankaicci onraka kidaittal*, "elder sisters and younger sisters getting together"). That has changed. The tsunami changed that because many died. Now, old ladies will come here. Old people who don't have children can live here because it is a simple life for us here.

What Parwathy was stating, in other words, was that the well-established matrilocal system of marriage residence will now be enacted in different places. In her vision it will take a generation to have sisters living next to one another again in Navalady. Next, Parwathy asserted the importance of her own perceived duty to see that her youngest, and only unmarried, son is married in her lifetime.

My son was about to marry a girl when the tsunami came. They would have married in a month. She was his *maccal* (female cross cousin and ideal marriage partner in local Dravidian kinship) but she died in the tsunami. He won't marry now. She lived next door and was Maheswaran's wife's younger sister's daughter. Maheswaran lost eleven close family members in the tsunami … One of my daughters died in the tsunami. One lives in Kallady, and another lives in Tiraimadu. They are all divided. I also have three sons. One is a dental surgeon in Batticaloa town. One is abroad, and one is here fishing. He has an engine boat and runs a fish exporting business. This one must get married. It's been three years now. After the tsunami we had to take him to the hospital because he drank poison after his *maccal* died. I'm getting old. He has to get married.

Although Parwathy's son was still not married when I returned in 2008, there were two marriages that took place in nearby houses. One of those marriages was a *maccan-maccal* (cross-cousin) marriage.[6] This Dravidian-type kinship practice, common among Tamils in eastern Sri Lanka, establishes close relations (McGilvray 2008) and retains rights to work on stretches of the beach for *karaivalai* beach seine fishing within tight family groups.

Family tsunami shrines

The next afternoon I visited with Maheswaran, who lives next door to Rubasingam Parwathy, and whose classificatory "daughter" (wife's sister's daughter) had been betrothed to her son. It was the saddest household interview I experienced during my field research in 2007. I had known that Maheswaran lost all of his immediate family members for some weeks, so I arranged for Ann Terry, a brilliant psychiatric nurse from the U.K., to join me. Ann had been working in the mental health unit of the Batticaloa Hospital for several years following the tsunami, so she was familiar with post-tsunami psychosocial circumstances in Batticaloa District. Maheswaran, like his next door neighbor Rubasingam Parwathy, lives in a new large two-story house built by Caritas EHED. These houses are valued at SL Rs. 12.5 lakhs and are the largest and most well-designed houses I have seen of all the post-tsunami housing designs in Batticaloa District. At the EHED office I was told that a conscious decision was made to give additional assistance to the people of Navalady who suffered such extreme losses.

A man in his late fifties, Maheswaran wore a blue and white plaid cotton sarong and a stained yellowish shirt, and he looked tired, although he welcomed us in a sincere manner. As at Parwathy's house, we sat on several thin mats that were rolled out on the concrete floor of the large, empty main floor room. First, he explained to us that he had owned a successful beach seine fishing business for twenty years before the tsunami, but he doesn't fish anymore. His elder brother who lives next door continues to go out fishing for a livelihood, and so does his deceased wife's brother who lives across the street. Maheswaran said he feels he doesn't have anyone to earn a livelihood for anymore. His family was a strong group at the time the tsunami came. Before the tsunami his eldest son was studying math and engineering at a good secondary school (Shivananda Vidyalayam) and his other three sons were studying in Kalladi Vipulananda school. All of his sons were good students, and his wife was a teacher. Maheswaran explains that he is in poor health now because he is always thinking about his wife, his four sons, his younger sister, his aunt and uncle, cousins, nephews and nieces, and other relations who all died in the tsunami. We were quiet, and then Maheswaran spoke into the silence: "Now I'm living with their memory. I am only living for their memory."

All of his family members were at home when the tsunami came. Maheswaran was spreading out nets to dry on the beach with other beach seine fishermen. The sea began to "boil" in a way that was strange and ususual. When they saw that they were afraid. The water level of the sea rose, reaching the place where boats are pulled up onto the wide stretch of sand, normally out of the water's reach, and they didn't know what was happening. Then the first wave came and Maheswaran was swept up in it. The force of the water lifted his body over the beach with great speed, carrying him toward the inland side of Batticaloa lagoon. When he tried to swim he got tangled in barbed wire and cactus. He clung tight to the cactus until he lost consciousness. The wire and the cactus covered his body with cuts, some quite deep, especially around his abdomen. Several Sri Lankan Army soldiers found him where the waves deposited him, naked and bleeding, on the shore in front of the Kappalenthi Matha Catholic Church at Amirthakali, Batticaloa. Maheswaran remarked that this church has now become the place where he goes to pray at the 7.30 a.m. Mass on Sundays, even though he remains a Hindu.

Maheswaran brought an article from the *Virakesari* Tamil newspaper from the bedroom. In the newspaper interview, which he gave to S. Gunaratnam five months after the tsunami, he described his experience, and how he worried about his wife and children (Gunaratnam 2005):

> … crowds were running towards the town in a disorderly haste. Many vehicles heaped with dead bodies were running towards Batticaloa town. I went to check whether my wife and children were with them. I could not see any

of them. I ran to my house in Navalady again like someone possessed by the devil. The house was flattened. I could not see even the corpses of my wife and sons. I beat my head and cried running the length of the beach. There were lots of dead bodies along the beach. I looked, turning them over. I did not see my wife and children. Weeping, I went back to Batticaloa town and searched for them in the General Hospital. There were the remains of my relatives like my uncle, aunt, and female cousin with the other dead bodies. But my wife and children were not to be seen.

While holding a framed composite photograph of all of his family members that he had also brought from the bedroom, Maheswaran continued his description of what he endured at the time of the tsunami. "While I was being cared for in the hospital, I tried to get the bodies of my family. I went to mortuary several times to look for the bodies but never found them. My relations never found them. They were never found." He touched the photo of them in a prayerful gesture and cried. After some minutes he stated, "God has saved me for the memory of them."

After the tsunami most of the former residents of Navalady who survived lived together in Central College, which was transformed into a refugee camp. They lived there together for half a year, grieving the loss of loved ones, family homes, livelihood, neighborhood, interactions and activities of everyday life – often in states of suicidal contemplation. In the fifth month of living there as a refugee, Maheswaran decided that he would build a memorial shrine for all of his family members who died. When he was interviewed by the journalist five months after the tsunami, the government was enforcing a 200 meter buffer zone in which reconstruction of houses was not permitted along the coast. Maheswaran was nevertheless adamant that he would return to Navalady to live on his family's land, and that he would construct a monument for his lost loved ones on that spot. Maheswaran also believed that if he committed suicide, he would not be able to join his loved ones after death, for Hindus believe it is a sin to take one's own life. As he stated in the Gunaratnam (2005) interview:

> I too had decided to give up my life. However, God did not let me make a decision like that. He made me think. I was the only one remaining in our lineage. If I die there would be no one to carry the name of our family. I braced myself, deciding that I had to live and perform certain things. They are the powers given to me by God and nothing else.

Navalady residents who wished to return were eventually allowed to go back on 21 April 2005. The original buffer zone of 200 meters was reduced to 50 meters along Navalady's coastline. With the help of his wife's surviving relations, Maheswaran pulled together SL Rs. 5 lakhs (approx. US $4900) to build his monument to his family on the site of their original family home. He said he built it "to connect with them." Sadly, looking into the photograph he held, Maheswaran sighed, "They don't visit me in dreams."

Finally I asked, "It is human to make sense of our experiences. How do you make sense of the tsunami?" Maheswaran replied, "The bad people are living now and the good people went to God. God gets all of the good people. The decent people are gone but the bad bad people are living." After a pause, he added, "It was because of *kannnuru* (effects of the evil-eye)." Another survivor who had joined us had a different theory, "I think bad activities had increased, so God had to punish the people."

Then, Maheswaran got a surge of energy at the thought of showing us the shrine that stands next to his house (Fig. 4.3). It is a beautifully designed octagonal building with a peaked red tile roof. There is a gate and walkway up to it with lights along the entrance pathway. He said that he keeps these lights turned on all day and all night. As we stood in front of the building admiring it together, Maheswaran said, "An *achari* [temple craftsman] named Ananthan from Kallady designed it. It is so well-built that if a tsunami comes again it won't destroy it." I wasn't sure if I should enter into the inner room, but Maheswaran encouraged me to enter. The space inside is meticulously clean. A white-tiled case with sliding glass windows surrounds the inner space. The walls above are painted like frothy tsunami waves. Inside the case are large gold-framed photographs of his family members who died in the tsunami. Glowing lamps and colorful bouquets of artificial flowers are placed between the photographs. We looked respectfully at each picture as he talked about his family, and we praised the design and the beauty of what he has done for the memory of his family. Maheswaran ritually cares for the shrine every day. I asked if he would like me to take a photo of him in the shrine, so he buttoned up his shirt in preparation and stood quite still in a formal pose as I fumbled to

Figure 4.3 Maheswaran's commemorative family shrine, Navalady, Sri Lanka, 2007.
Photo by Patricia Lawrence.

find my camera. As we walked out, Maheswaran began to describe his thoughts for further landscaping around the shrine. He said he plans to plant coconut trees all around it. Several neighbors standing nearby remarked, "Even strangers can appreciate what he's done."

In Navalady people no longer expect to recover their loved ones who were pulled into the sea, but they may hope to recover a relationship with them in their dreams, as Maheswaran does. Many Navalady residents, the majority of whom are fifty years or older, believe another tsunami will come, and that they may very well die in it, which is not so different from their experience of living in a war zone for almost three decades. "Death is the surest thing," they will say; it has a central presence in their everyday lives. Maheswaran's shrine is one of many along the coast – some are quite visible to the passerby (Fig. 4.4). Strung along the sandy roads of Navalady, I noted half a dozen family shrines built by other fishermen as I made my way around the village by bicycle.

Post-tsunami anger toward the Sea Goddess

Maheswaran's house stands very near the main Navalady village temple for the Hindu sea goddess Kadalatci Amman, however, he explained to us that he decided not to attend her annual propitiation when the festival at the reconstructed temple was celebrated for her in June 2006. When I asked Maheswaran why he didn't go, he explained:

Figure 4.4 Fisherman's shrine with photo and birthdates of deceased wife and two sons, and date of the tsunami, Navalady, Sri Lanka, 2007. Photo by Patricia Lawrence.

All of my family was always there at the temple, cleaning, sweeping, and helping – but she [the goddess] didn't help them when the tsunami came. Following the tsunami, I have no belief in Kadalatci Amman. Since then I go to the other side to Kappalenthi Matha Catholic Church and pray to Mother Mary. [Note: When Maheswaran regained consciousness after the tsunami waves pulled him into the lagoon, this is where he found himself.] I'm not a Catholic, but I go there. I paddle a *thoni* boat over to the church. Everyone is going to that church since the tsunami. The [Saiva Hindu] people haven't become Christians, but they go to that church. Most people didn't come to the Kadalatci Amman temple for the annual festival last month because they have changed their minds about that temple. Even the Navalady people who are living [in newly constructed post-tsunami houses about 6 km inland] in Tiraimadu now didn't come for the festival. They are angry.

Anger is a part of the grieving process, and who better to be angry at than a local goddess who should have protected her devotees? The Hindu goddesses essential to the social life of Batticaloa's Tamil villages are worshipped almost as family members. Goddesses are not distant deities; they are cared for and treated as an intimate presence in the home. They have their own shrine-rooms in a central part of the house where they are awakened every morning with the light of a lamp before sunrise. The room for the goddess is often constructed with margosa (*veppumaram*, or *neem*) wood, which is the tree that cools her inherent divine heat (McGilvray 1998b). Some families have a weekly gathering to sing devotional songs in their domestic shrine room, and many Hindu Tamils in Batticaloa make references to conversing with goddesses in their dreams. However, Tamil goddesses are deities of extremes who have the capacity to both protect life and to take it away, so people also have arguments with their goddess, particularly when family members face difficult challenges. My 1992 fieldnotes record a conversation with a Tamil mother in an interior village in Batticaloa District who deliberately withheld her annual *cakkarai ponkal* (sweetened milk-rice) offerings from the goddess because she was angry that her son was "missing" in clashes between the government Special Task Forces and the LTTE. Elsewhere, I observed grief-stricken individuals who directly confronted the powerful gaze of a Kannaki Amman temple goddess, angrily taunted her, and pleaded for the life of their lost children (Lawrence 2003).

Rituals of protection

There are many protection rituals associated with Batticaloa's local Hindu goddesses such as: *ur valam*, a procession of the icon of the goddess around the village or neighborhood to protect all the houses in that area; *valavu kaval* or "house compound protection" rituals that may employ techniques such as *villukkuri* divination with a margosa wood bow to reveal unseen dangers, or *vittu kaval* rites at a Vairavar guardian deity shrine at the house compound entrance; *kappu nul* threads tied around wrists or arms for protection; *pali catanku* or "sacrifice rituals" sometimes still employing goats or chickens that are enacted as part of the annual propitiation ceremony; *kannimar* or *kannipillai catanku* which is a beautiful set of rituals for young pre-pubertal girls during the annual temple festival (and which are also said to keep guns and killing outside the village); and a whole range of individual self-mortifying bodily vows including *mullu kavadi*, *paravai kavadi*, and *ankapirathatcanam*. Placing the round red vermillion dot (*pottu*) between the eyebrows can also be viewed as a daily act of protection, which is applied to statues of the goddess as well. Another common protection ritual in association with goddesses is the keeping of a copper *yantiram* or abstract geometric pattern that represents the metaphysical power of the goddess. Sharing a communal offering of *ponkal* milk-rice from the newly harvested paddy fields is another powerful ritual of protection. The "new" rice is cooked with coconut milk either directly in front of the goddess, or sometimes at a smaller shrine on the temple grounds for the male cobra god Nagatambiran.

Having said all this, we now revisit the Virgin Cobra Goddess, Nagapucini Amman, who lives under a *naval* tree in Navalady. This is the goddess that Rubasingam Parwathy's son saw swimming toward Navalady in the form of a female cobra on the waters of the Batticaloa lagoon in August 2007, portending danger for everyone living near her shrine, which was still at that time in a state of post-tsunami ruin.

I parked my bike next to the *naval* tree and the goddess' un-repaired shrine, and began taking photos of the battered statue of Nagapucini Amman, who did not even have a roof over her head. The mother in the closest house came over and told me that her grandmother, who had died in the tsunami, was the one who had built the shrine for Nagapucini Amman. Yes, it was a big problem that the shrine was still damaged. "We don't know what she will do. Now it's the time for her festival (*catanku*). We think she has already made some problems for those families over there on the other side (of the shrine). Those families have moved away (even though they have new post-tsunami houses). We want to repair the shrine. Our house is closest to the goddess, and we don't know what she will do." This mother seemed so deeply fearful that the next day I wrote to several international aid organizations and asked whether they had funds for the shrine's repair. There is a consensus in Batticaloa among Hindu Tamils that whenever temples are damaged by bombing or shelling in the war, they must be repaired so that the *amman* goddesses will offer their protection to the people – otherwise they become offended, wrathful, and withdraw their protection. Before I could get a pledge from an organization to help the neighborhood rebuild the Virgin Cobra Goddess' shrine, I rode my bicycle that way and saw that someone was already building a new palm thatch roof over Nagapucini Amman, and just in time for her annual propitiation. Perhaps she would now be a more benevolent and protective goddess for Navalady.

New fishing nets: new beginnings

The fishing village of Navalady is navigating its recovery in its own good time. The desolation of the village as a place where "the tsunami took everything" is slowly giving way to reclaimed home sites and renewed fishing livelihoods, moments when fishermen have a good catch, renewed aspirations for arranging marriage alliances, a new roof for the potentially dangerous Virgin Cobra Goddess, a festival revival for the armless Sea Goddess – and moments of comradely weaving of new nets.

My friend Neelakantan, who first helped me in Batticaloa in 1991, joined me in some interviews. His pre-existing interest in fishermen gradually took us toward the eastern tip of Navalady's sandy peninsula. We spent some time in a *vadi* beach hut getting to know nine men who were concentrating on weaving the complicated central part of a *karaivalai* beach seine net, using colorful nylon instead of the tree bark fiber, coconut fiber, and cotton used in earlier times. Before the days of nylon it took three years to make a net.

Our meeting with them was auspicious and friendly. They completed their steady work on the net while we were with them the next evening. They had been living and weaving it in the *vadi* for the last three months. After hours of conversing with them and watching their nimble fingers and toes – for they also used their toes – the time had come to drag the newly woven net to the beach. Most of these men lost their wives and children in the tsunami. They now have houses in Tiraimadu, the tsunami resettlement seven miles inland, but it is too far for them to come and go from Tiraimadu every day. They have all chosen to cook, work, and sleep together in the *vadi* – as a close, all-male family of fishermen. When I commented on their coordination and teamwork, saying that it impressed me, they explained, "We are together because we all lost our families in the tsunami." They were all related by kinship to one another as well. After listening to the personal accounts of fishermen who survived their wives and children, I am aware of the persistence of grieving in this especially hard-hit coastal community. For this group of men, working and living closely together makes it possible for them to live with their grief.

The men had made enough progress on the new net to put it into the sea that very night. Their excitement and anticipation of the first catch with the new net increased as we stayed with them in the spreading darkness. The sea eagles and brahminy kites had found their roosting places for the night. One man brought a bright Petromax kerosene pressure lamp to the beach. In the light of the lamp, they wove together the long attachment nets to the central net that they had just finished after months of weaving together. Then they coiled the nets into large baskets. One basket went into the boat with the new part attached to it, and the other long parts with weights and floats were coiled into two baskets that remained on the beach. Then more men came walking through the darkness to the light by the boat. They were chided for showing up at the last moment, but they took it quietly – showing respect to the elders of the team – and did not start an argument. Then one man filled a plastic jug with seawater and put turmeric powder in it. He sloshed the turmeric water (*manjal tannir*) over the new net that lay coiled in the basket on the boat. Then he sprinkled some on the bow and the stern, and then on the fishermen themselves. They said they should have the net properly blessed in a temple cere-mony, but when they are in a hurry a little *manjal tannir* will do. They gathered around the boat, and the men sang as they pushed it across the sand and into the waves. This was a moment of combined emotional and economic recovery – of recovered hope and aspiration for the *karaivalai* fishermen themselves. We wished them good luck. It was late by then, so we rode our bicycles over the sandy beach road in the darkness of the night.

A popular Catholic shrine: Kappalenthi Matha

From the east-facing doors of the church of Kappalenthi Matha (literally "Mother who protectively clasps the ship," conventionally Our Lady of Good Voyage) at Amirthakali, Batticaloa, there is a view across the lagoon to the tenacious coconut trees still standing on the Navalady peninsula. People living near this historic church described the sight of the largest wave as it crashed over Navalady, and how the entire stand of coconut trees completely disappeared from sight when the low-lying peninsula was engulfed by the wave. By an accident of Batticaloa geography, the tsunami first destroyed Hindu beachfront shrines in Navalady and then deposited the survivors across the lagoon before an unscathed Catholic church.[7] Kappalenthi Matha is where Maheswaran of Navalady was deposited by the tsunami waves, clinging to a large cactus which offered enough buoyancy in the surging waters to keep him from drowning.

The Kappalenthi Matha church, like the Portuguese-Dutch fort in Batticaloa town, was alleged to have originally been constructed of lime powder mixed with honey, large chunks of coral, and local rock containing a high level of iron. Local people often commented upon the strength of colonial era structures, saying that even the ferocious cyclone of 1978 and the tsunami couldn't destroy them. In a local legend about Kappalenthi Matha, it is said that a Portuguese ship sailing from Goa in India in the early 1600s was caught in a terrible storm on its way to Trincomalee. The captain of the ship had a statue of Our Lady of Good Voyage on board, to which he, his mate, and the ship's sailors prayed, fearing for their lives. They were blown way off course, but they miraculously survived, safely landing at the mouth of the Batticaloa lagoon where they vowed to build a church for Our Lady of Good Voyage. Legend says that the hut in which the captain enshrined the statue was enlarged when they returned on their next voyage and the substantial church was built that stands there today.[8]

Before the tsunami, the statue of Kappalenthi Matha stood in a shrine directly in front of the church, looking out to sea, holding and protecting a three-masted ship in her right hand, and cradling the baby Jesus with her left arm. Both Mother and Son wear crowns of gold and red velvet, and the baby Jesus holds the palm of his right hand upright facing the worshippers, in the *abhaya mudra*, a gesture which signals "fear not" in Hindu and Buddhist iconography. I was told that even prior to the tsunami, it was an everyday ritual for local Hindu and Catholic fishermen alike to ask Kappalenthi Matha for protection just before setting out to sea. For as long as anyone remembers, Navalady fishing families have played a role in the Kappalenthi Matha Feast Day which is held annually on the last Sunday of September. The festival of Kappalenthi Matha is celebrated for nine days, and on the final day her statue is carried around the lagoon on a decorated fishing boat. The final event is said to "belong" to the families of Navalady, and on that day they provide rice and curry for all the people. Although local Tamil Hindus had participated in the final Feast Day for Kappalenthi Matha long before the 2004 tsunami, their numbers have swelled at the church's Sunday mass and during the annual festival in this post-tsunami period.

An opportunity to speak of death in Batticaloa

In the immediate aftermath of the tsunami, many people mentioned the entanglement of bodies in razor wire, which had been widely deployed around Sri Lankan Army and STF installations during the last quarter century of civil war. I was struck by the way they offered detailed descriptions of the appearance of drowned corpses. This led me to ponder whether such gruesome story-telling in the initial period of collective shock was an emotional release from the self-censorship imposed during the protracted ethnic conflict. Previously, to speak knowledgeably and frankly about the human-made deaths of the civil war was to endanger one's life and the lives of other family members. Thousands of unofficial "disappearances" or deaths were unspoken in order to protect the still-living family members of those who had disappeared. The tsunami natural disaster was different: unlike political violence, it didn't require the censoring of death and the silencing of trauma. In the collective state of societal rupture immediately after the tsunami, the people who had been silenced by fear of death could finally speak openly of it – at last they had a way to express it. For the first time in several decades, graphic descriptions of death were freely voiced.

However, by the time I returned in 2008, the fog of political censorship and silent terror had once again settled over the population, along with a rise in the systematic use of torture, abductions, disappearances, targeted killings, and deaths of civilians, primarily at the hands of pro-government Tamil paramilitaries.[9] The media also encountered a period of extreme censorship, intimidation, and assassination of journalists that was island-wide. Local people once again retreated into a culture of silence, returning to the safety of their local rituals and prayers for protection. Political silencing was back, and along with the renewed requirement for self-censorship, the Hindu goddess Kadalatci Amman, enshrined at the edge of the sea in Navalady, began to recover her powers of protective agency in the minds of most people in Navalady.

The Sea Goddess recovers her protective agency

As soon as I arrived in 2008, I rode a bicycle up the beach road to Navalady. For a long stretch in front of the Kadalatci Amman temple, the side of the road was completely covered with very small fish that the fishermen were spreading out in the sun to dry. I looked to see where the old statue of the goddess had been wrenched and mutilated by the tsunami in 2004. A new image of Katalatci Amman had been installed over the temple entrance, with multiple arms intact and a fresh coat of paint!

When I cycled up to Parwathy Rubasingam's house, the three children whose mother had died were still there with her. It had always been Rubasingam Parwathy's

Figure 4.5 Local post-tsunami representation of the goddess, 2008. Photo by Patricia
Lawrence.

position that the people of Navalady shouldn't blame their village deity for the loss
of lives in the tsunami waves, because she tried to protect them by warning them
the day before, although they couldn't understand her message. Parwathy told me
that this year many more people had come to express religious devotion during the
annual celebration of Navalady's Sea Goddess. The post-tsunami grieving process
was now gradually restoring the protective relationship between the goddess and
her devotees. As for Navalady's Virgin Cobra Goddess, Nagapucini Amman, she
is enjoying spruced-up premises with a new roof that has been constructed over
her dwelling place, and people are no longer so worried that she might be offended
by the people not taking sufficient care and notice of her. A fisherman living
nearby was recently abducted and ill-treated by a local Tamil paramilitary group
then eventually released, and in gratitude his family has vowed to contribute to
Nagapucini Amman's annual festival in the month of August. Both of Navalady's
Hindu goddesses were once again receiving the respect local *ammans* are believed
to require to do their work of protecting the people and the well being of the Tamil
village as a whole.

On the other hand, Maheswaran, who had lost everyone close to him, was still
paddling across the lagoon in a small canoe every morning to light a candle at the
Kappalenthi Matha Catholic church. He returns to Navalady each morning with
flowers that he places in front of the photos of his lost loved ones inside the family shrine he has constructed for them. At night, he sleeps inside the shrine. He
was still angry with Kadalatci Amman, he stated, but I was relieved to see that he

looked much healthier and more energized. While I was still pedaling my bicycle, Maheswaran was now riding a powerful new motorcycle.

Walking on the beach at Navalady early one morning, I noticed for the first time that many fishermen in Navalady had given Catholic names to their boats that often contain the word "mother."[10] This resonates with local Tamil cultural assumptions closely connecting mothers with the notion of protection and well-being. Having suffered decades of civil war even as they recover from the loss of loved ones in the aftermath of the Indian Ocean tsunami, how fortunate, I thought, that the fishing families of Navalady – in the continuing decades of gradual recovery – will still have three protective mothers to turn to: Kadalatci Amman, Nagapucini Amman, and Kappalenthi Matha.

Notes

1 In January 2005, during the second week following the tsunami, I arrived on the east coast of Sri Lanka to assist organizations I had previously worked with in responding to the disaster. In 2006 I concentrated on the largest tsunami camp, Tiraimadu, which housed survivors from Navalady, Dutch Bar, Thiruchentheur, and Palameenmadu. In 2007 I began assessing recovery by living in the new post-tsunami settlement of Pannaichaiyadi. Thereafter, I moved to the original village of Dutch Bar on the sea beach, concentrating on family interviews for three months. In between consultancy work, I revisited families in these villages in 2008. A grant from the National Science Foundation (SES 0525260) supported my research trips in 2006–2007. I wish to grate-fully acknowledge the fieldwork and translation assistance provided to me in Batticaloa by N. Dharmaretnam.

2 District Recovery Plan, Batticaloa District, DRDU, District Secretariat, Batticaloa, Sri Lanka, 2006.

3 Not everyone who actually knew Poopathy would agree with this account of her life and death, and some local women are extremely resentful of this account.

4 The possibility of a connection with the famous Nagapooshani Amman temple on the island of Nainativu in Jaffna deserves to be explored. The village name of Navalady itself means "at the foot of the *naval* tree."

5 This Kannaki Amman temple is now beautifully repaired with a powerful wall mural that depicts how Kannaki righteously incinerated the city of Madurai in the Tamil *Cilappatikaram* epic. In this painting, people are running from flames that are engulfing them. One cannot help remembering that this very temple and the surrounding village of Makaladittivu was burned when local people endured ten hours of killing and burning of their homes at the hands of the government security forces in June 1990 (Lawrence 2000).

6 The Tamil kinship terms *maccan* and *maccal* refer to male and female cross-cousins, the opposite sex children of a brother and a sister, who are culturally approved marriage partners in the Dravidian-type kinship classification system followed in Sri Lankan Tamil and Muslim communities.

7 Farther north, in Mullaittivu, the Catholic church was obliterated by the tsunami except for its ornamental façade.

8 I have not been able to corroborate the early founding of this church. Canagaratnam (1921: 40) states: "The church at Amirthagali was built in 1822."

9 Between November 2005–May 2008, there were 7,477 war-related killings in Sri Lanka. The Foundation for Co-Existence Situation Report, 30 May 2008. FCE Colombo Information Centre, Sri Lanka.

10 For example, Madu Matha ("Mother of Madhu," a Catholic shrine in the North Central

Province), Annai Velankanni ("Mother – or Our Lady – of Velankanni," a Catholic pilgrimage center near Nagapattinam, Tamilnadu), and Arokkiya Matha ("Mother of Good Health," another title for the Velankanni Virgin Mary).

5 Dreaming of dowry

Post-tsunami housing strategies in eastern Sri Lanka

Dennis B. McGilvray and
Patricia Lawrence

Introduction

The east coast of the island was the region hardest hit by the 2004 Indian Ocean tsunami (Fig. 5.1). After the initial relief phase was over, and survivors had been provided with temporary shelter of one kind or another, attention was directed to the long-term challenge of constructing new permanent dwellings for those families who had lost everything. Many were prohibited from rebuilding on their original beachfront house sites because they fell within the government-designated "buffer zones," varying in width from 200 meters to 65 meters depending on the location. The fact that the dimensions of the buffer zone were repeatedly altered added an element of anxiety and confusion that has been widely noted (Shanmugaratnam 2005; Hyndman 2007; Ruwanpura 2008b; Silva 2009; Boano 2009). Along the eastern coastline of the island, where many Tamil, Muslim, and Portuguese Burgher communities live in a narrow belt of land close to the sea, the buffer zone rule immediately erased many generations of women's property in the form of matrilocal dowry houses passed down from mothers to daughters at marriage (McGilvray 1989, 2006, 2008). In the haste and confusion associated with the provision of temporary shelter, and as construction programs for permanent housing projects were initially implemented, the fact that mothers, wives, and daughters had traditionally held sole title – or joint title with their husbands – to domestic dwellings in Tamil and Muslim communities was largely overlooked by government and foreign NGO relief agencies, who never imagined that women might legally have been the primary or joint property holders. In tsunami housing programs island-wide, it was widely assumed that the "head of household" and the "owner" of a damaged dwelling would be the same (male) person – typically a father, a husband, or a son. The comments of a donor organization official in 2005–2006 candidly acknowledged this cultural myopia (quoted in Ruwanpura 2008b): "... at the time of handing over the new house, a legal title is done for each block of land and house. This is usually in the man's name ... We didn't think about instances where the house before belonged to women."

On the east coast, where two decades of civil war and local ethnic rivalry had badly stressed the civilian populations (International Crisis Group 2008, de Silva 2009), the urgent plight of tsunami victims led many to accept reconstruction

Figure 5.1 Tsunami devastation in Maruthamunai, Ampara District, Sri Lanka, as seen on 5 February 2005. Photo by Patricia Lawrence.

grants and NGO housing in the name of a man in the family as a pragmatic way to obtain shelter quickly. As long-term reconstruction programs got underway, however, a potential threat to women's traditional property rights was recognized, and concerns were voiced by women's social service organizations, such as the SURIYA Women's Development Centre in Batticaloa and the Muslim Women's Research and Action Forum in Sainthamaruthu. The same worry was voiced recently by Ruwanpura (2008b), who warned that such changes in women's customary property rights "… can all too easily be read as the entrance of patriarchal power through the back door." By the time we conducted the core of our fieldwork in Batticaloa and Ampara Districts in 2007–2008, more than three years after the tsunami, almost all victims had moved from temporary shelters into permanent dwellings, and the overall patterns of post-tsunami housing and resettlement had begun to emerge. Our research reveals that the pre-existing system of matrilocal residence and transfer of dowry-house property to daughters is being restored and "re-built" by tsunami-affected Tamil, Muslim, and Portuguese Burgher families, despite the fact that many post-disaster aid programs initially placed housing reconstruction resources at the disposal of men.[1]

The east coast matrilocal household and dowry system

The Tamil-speaking Hindus and Muslims of the Eastern Province, especially in Batticaloa and Ampara Districts, but also to some extent in the southern parts of

Trincomalee District, share a system of exogamous matrilineal clan (kudi) membership that – while shared by both men and women – is transmitted only through women. This distinctive descent pattern may have originated with an influx of mercenary soldiers of the Mukkuvar caste from the matrilineal regions of Kerala in the 13th century (McGilvray 2008: Chap. 2). In some places, such as Akkaraipattu, the matrilineal clan system still plays a role in temple and mosque management and in annual festivals, but it does not entail the matrilineal inheritance of wealth or domestic property as some authors have seemed to imply (Ruwanpura 2008b). In modern east coast households today, the key factor is not matriclan identity but rather a matrilocal rule of post-marital residence and a radical system of pre-mortem transfer of family property to daughters as dowry at the time of marriage. The system is "radical" because, unlike dowry in most patrilineal and patrilocal family systems in South Asia where women receive only jewelry and moveable forms of wealth at marriage, here the bride's parents transfer real property – typically both a house and paddy lands – to her as part of the negotiated marriage agreement. In its ideal or prototypical form among the east coast Tamils and Muslims, the dowry system transfers virtually all of the family's real property to daughters prior to the death of their parents, leaving sons with access only to the dowry property of their wives, or to property deeded jointly to the couple as dowry. In families where no daughters are born, the property is often bestowed upon a sister's daughter or upon a more distant female cousin or niece, since there is a cultural presupposition that women need a house to get married. The rituals of female puberty, marriage, and childbirth all take place in the girl's dwelling, further reinforcing the matrilocal theme (McGilvray 1982a).

The corollary of this dowry system is a rule of matrilocal post-marital residence in which a new bridegroom is expected to join the domestic household of his wife, which initially includes his wife's parents and unmarried siblings. In a sense, the new son-in-law is given an opportunity to prove himself as a breadwinner under the tutelage of his wife's parents, while the daughter is acquiring experience as a cook and homemaker, and soon it is hoped, a mother. After several years, the eldest daughter and son-in-law will take sole occupancy of her dowry house while the wife's parents and unmarried children shift their domicile to a new house constructed as future dowry for the next daughter in line. Typically, but not always, the eldest daughter inherits her mother's original dowry house, and additional houses are constructed for the younger daughters in the immediate vicinity if vacant land is available or affordable.

Obviously the provision of a dowry house for every daughter imposes a heavy burden, and the least fortunate families sometimes cannot meet this expectation. In these cases, a future bride may work overseas to earn the money to build her own dowry house, or a groom may agree to build his bride a house with his own labor. However, the typical expectation is that sons will assist in earning money to build houses for their sisters before they accept an offer of matrilocal marriage – including a dowry house – from another family. Once married, a son's economic allegiance is expected to shift to the family of his wife, but brothers and sisters remain emotionally connected throughout life. In the Dravidian-type kinship system to which both Tamils and Muslims belong, the children of brothers and sisters ("cross-cousins" in anthropological jargon) are eligible marriage partners, thus reinforcing these bonds between siblings even if separated by distance. However, the matrilocal dowry-house system also encourages residential propinquity among married sisters, since daughters' dowry houses are often constructed on subdivided sections of their mother's original dowry-house compound or on a neighboring lot if it is vacant. Clearly, there are limits to such dense in-fill construction, and eventually some daughters' houses will have to be sited elsewhere.

However, the impulse to form matrilocal clusters of married sisters in adjacent household compounds is both culturally valued and emotionally appealing, since it allows for shared childcare and sociability, and affords the women at least some deterrence against domestic violence. In the older streets of a town like Akkaraipattu there are houses and domestic compounds that have been passed down from mother to daughter over multiple generations. However, while this matrilocal dowry pattern is relatively advantageous to married women in comparison with the patrilineal patrilocal households found in many parts of South Asia (McGilvray 1989: 230–232), no one has ever plausibly characterized it as a "feminist nirvana" (c.f. Ruwanpura 2006, 2008b). Matrilocal husbands may acquire coercive authority in the household after their wives' parents have moved out, drunkenness and domestic violence occurs, and the plight of widowed or abandoned wives in female-headed households has intensified as a result of both the Eelam Wars and the tsunami (Thiruchandran 1999, de Mel and Ruwanpura 2006).

The transfer of houses to daughters at marriage takes two main forms. Among many Tamils (and some Muslims) the preference is to execute a dowry deed (*citanam uruti*) that legally transfers undivided joint ownership of the house to the daughter and son-in-law, and identifies the property as "dowry" (*citanam*) in a legal sense. Increasingly these days, the groom may insist upon this form of transfer, because it gives him a legal "stake" in the marriage as a co-shareholder in the dowry estate, and it prevents his wife from expelling him from the house in the event of a quarrel or dispute. Also, in the case of a divorce, a dowry deed will entail a laborious division of the property and the costly services of a lawyer, a threat some parents say promotes marital stability.

However, the use of a dowry deed is disapproved by conservative Muslim clergy as un-Islamic, because it recognizes a concept of dowry that is found nowhere in the Quran or Hadiths. The only form of marriage payment recognized in Muslim law is the brideprice, or *mahr*, a nominal sum of money paid or pledged to the bride by the groom as part of the marriage contract. Apart from the inhabitants of a few specific towns such as Nintavur, where dowry deeds are the norm, most Muslims practice the second mode of dowry-house transfer: an outright gift from the parents to their daughter either before or after the wedding. Such female gift property is not "dowry" (*citanam*) in a strictly legal sense, but it is colloquially referred to and is recorded as dowry in the local mosque marriage registers. Since Muslim law in Sri Lanka – unlike in some Muslim countries – places no limitation upon the gift of property *inter vivos* to those who are not one's customary heirs according to Sharia law, the rules of Islamic inheritance only come into play when there is property remaining to be disposed of after death. The simplicity of this flexible gifting procedure also appeals to many Tamils. Sometimes a house and paddy lands are bestowed upon a daughter long prior to marriage. However, there are also families, both Tamil and Muslim, in which the daughter receives her dowry gift long after the marriage has been solemnized. A matrilocal son-in-law would be reluctant to insist upon an immediate transfer of the house, since it would make him appear to have doubts about the trustworthiness of his wife's family. This exemplifies the common faith among both Tamil and Muslim husbands that houses and property will ultimately flow through their wives, and that they can count on the matrilocal dowry system to provide for them in the long run.

The third ethnic group in this study, the Portuguese Burghers (*parankiyar*), are Eurasian descendants of Portuguese and Dutch colonists who controlled the island between the 16th–18th centuries (McGilvray 1982, 2007). They do not share the matrilineal clan system or the Tamil caste system, but in other respects their marriage and household patterns are quite similar to those of the Tamils and Muslims, including the expectation of a dowry house for each daughter and a tendency for married sisters to reside in close proximity. Our fieldwork with Burgher families who survived the tsunami revealed many commonalities with the long-term housing strategies of the Tamils and Muslims.

The question of post-tsunami impact on women's property

In the Sri Lankan post-tsunami environment, how do the various newly-built permanent housing schemes fit into the pre-existing matrilocal residence pattern on the east coast? Have the after-effects of the tsunami caused families to change their traditional priorities and goals for matrilocal marriage and the inter-generational transfer of dowry property? Has the unthinking bestowal of new houses and government reconstruction funds upon men significantly diminished women's rights and control over domestic real estate in the long run? We explored these questions through a set of ethnographic case-studies in three post-tsunami reconstruction areas on the east coast. McGilvray focused on Tamil and Muslim families in Tambiluvil, Sainthamaruthu, and Maruthamunai (all in Ampara District), while Lawrence traced Burgher families who had lost their homes in Dutch Bar near Batticaloa Town. By tracing the history of post-tsunami housing solutions for individual families – from emergency shelter, to temporary housing, to permanent dwellings – we documented a wide variety of reconstruction patterns in these three different locations.[2] In almost every case, however, we discovered the resilience of the matrilocal dowry house system as families developed strategies to promote the residential proximity of married sisters and planned for the future dowry-house marriages of their younger daughters. This historically-rooted matrilocal tradition seems likely to restore the domestic property rights of Tamil, Muslim, and Burgher women in the next generation if not sooner.

Tamils in Tambiluvil: moving toward the beach

Assisted by a local Grama Niladhari, we made personal acquaintance with five tsunami-affected families in the Tamil village of Tambiluvil located south of Akkaraipattu in Ampara District. This coastal Hindu settlement of paddy farmers and lagoon fishermen located on the eastern-most arc of the island was utterly devastated by the tsunami, and the threat of violence between the Sri Lankan security forces and the LTTE in nearby jungle areas created additional hazards and misery for the community. When we first visited Tambiluvil in summer 2005, many survivors were temporarily housed in hot, crowded, corrugated tin-roofed sheds on the inland side of the village. By 2007, however, only a few tin sheds were still visible and most of the permanent houses were in place. In Tambiluvil there are two solutions for those who completely lost their homes: (a.) new single family dwellings built by international NGOs on private plots of land privately acquired by displaced families in scattered locations within the village beyond the 65 meter buffer zone, and (b.) densely laid-out housing colonies containing hundreds of new homes designed and constructed by multiple NGOs located inland from the village on dry rocky land that is deemed unsuitable for agriculture.

Two families in our Tambiluvil sample have the first type of permanent housing. The seaside home of one couple was completely washed away, but with the financial help of kinsmen and relatives they were able to acquire a vacant building plot inland, beyond the 65 meter buffer zone. A new home for the second family could be constructed on their original house site, which was also beyond the buffer zone. With residential land in their possession, an international Christian-related NGO agreed to build brand new, brightly painted houses for both of these families. People in Tambiluvil saw this as an optimal outcome from the tsunami tragedy: for each family, the new location is close to the old one, and the new NGO house is far superior to the one they lost.

Example 1. Rati and Karu

Rati and Karu were moderately well-off to begin with. Rati's husband is a lorry and tractor driver, and so is one of her brothers. Her married elder sister still lives in a dowry-deeded house once belonging to their mother that was untouched by the tsunami. Rati's original house was built on land provided by her brother, who still retains half of the property to build a future dowry house for their remaining younger sister who is still unmarried. Because Rati's original house was beyond the 65 meter buffer zone, she qualified for a completely new NGO house that was constructed on the lot she already owned. The new brightly painted house is quite satisfactory except for the cramped indoor kitchen, which has been converted into a Hindu shrine room (Fig. 5.2). A cheaply constructed but more spacious cooking shed has been erected in the front of the yard. Rati's parents, who still cultivate some orchard lands outside of the village, share the NGO house with their daughter and son-in-law. Judging from the new television set and solid furniture, Rati's family appears to have done quite well in the tsunami reconstruction process. Her

Figure 5.2 Kitchen of a new Tamil NGO house converted into a Hindu shrine room in Tambiluvil, Sri Lanka, 2007. Photo by Dennis McGilvray.

younger sister is still living in a temporary tent shelter, but her brothers intend to build a dowry house for her immediately adjacent to Rati, eventually forming a matrilocal residential cluster of two married sisters and their parents.

Three of our other case-study families have been allocated brand new NGO homes in the Mandanai project, a large permanent housing colony located on the only vacant land said to be available, a dry rocky site about two miles inland from the beach. The 440 houses at Mandanai were built in separate phases by four different NGOs using four different architectural designs and four different budgetary criteria, and as elsewhere in Ampara District (Hasbullah and Korf in press), this has generated lots of envy and complaints. For example, the very last houses to be completed were especially well-designed and well-built by a Scandinavian NGO, but their superior quality now benefits those families who had been assigned the lowest priority in terms of post-tsunami needs. The real problem with the Mandanai housing project, however, is that it is located in an inconvenient, dry, rocky, treeless site far from the main road, public schools, temples, churches, and markets. Water must be trucked in to fill the central cistern that feeds the pipelines to each house. There is no suitable mode of livelihood at Mandanai: agricultural work is located elsewhere, and meager hand-net fishing in a swampy neck of the lagoon is the only alternative. Bus service over the unpaved road is infrequent and unreliable, and yet government security forces have restricted the food supplies that families are allowed to bring in, fearing these provisions will end up in the hands of militant Tamil rebels. On top of everything, there have been STF commando round-ups, as well as marauding elephants who wander into the settlement from the forest, frightened by artillery shelling and aerial bombardment. The even greater flaws and shortcomings of the nearby Kudinilam housing colony was cited in a critical report by the Sri Lankan Human Rights Commission in 2007, and people were skeptical that it would attract any tenants by the time it is completed. A few miles farther inland, along the main road to Pottuvil, an earlier tsunami housing project lies vacant like a ghost-town (Fig. 5.3), a fate predicted for other poorly-sited housing schemes in the east as well (Boano 2009).

Despite these many disadvantages, the current residents of Mandanai took up occupancy of their new NGO houses because they represented the best option available: a spacious new house with no strings attached. Our research suggests, however, that the Mandanai colony may ultimately become a residential community of last resort, as parents calculate the future dowry prospects for their daughters and as younger married couples independently move back to more desirable neighborhoods closer to the sea.

Example 2. Lini and Deepan

Lini and Deepan had a "love marriage" even before Lini's elder sister's marriage had been arranged, but both families seem to have accepted this deviation from Tamil custom. A third sister and a younger brother are still unmarried and living with their mother in a new NGO house in the Mandanai housing colony west of Tambiluvil. Lini's father, a cement block maker, abandoned his wife and family long ago, leaving her mother with sole responsibility for raising their three

Figure 5.3 Abandoned post-tsunami housing project on the Pottuvil Road south of Tirukkovil, Sri Lanka, 2007. Photo by Dennis McGilvray.

daughters and one son. In the post-tsunami reconstruction process, she chose to accept a free new house in Mandanai as the most expedient solution. However, her two married daughters and their husbands are now diligently rebuilding on her original beachfront dowry property, which lies just beyond the 65 meter buffer zone. Using government and NGO grants together with their own money and labor, Lini and Deepan have already dug a new well and have partially erected a new masonry house of their own that they hold in joint title (Fig. 5.4). Lini's elder sister owned a portion of the family lot prior to her marriage, so the new house she and her husband are building is already deeded exclusively in her name. These two married women seem likely to be joined eventually by their younger sister, for whom a final portion of her mother's property has been reserved for her future dowry house. When all three daughters have reconstructed a new cluster of matrilocal households near the beach, their mother and younger brother seem likely to join them, leaving the ultimate disposition of the NGO house in Mandanai an open question.

This couple resembles several other young Tamil families we documented in Tambiluvil who were engaged in rebuilding houses on beachfront property originally belonging to the wives' parents. Because in most cases their government and NGO reconstruction grants have been exhausted, these couples are committed to a slow self-help project of gradually rebuilding beachfront homes using their own resources and labor. Two of the couples have children born since the tsunami, and

Figure 5.4 Young Tamil wife inspects progress on the couple's self-built home at her mother's original beachfront dowry property, Tamibiluvil, Sri Lanka, 2007. Photo by Dennis McGilvray.

another couple is trying to conceive their first child. In the latter case, the young husband and wife own a spacious newly-built NGO house in the Mandanai housing development, but they are dissatisfied with the many problems at the site. They seldom stay there, even though the wife's three sisters and parents live immediately next door, because of the dry, dusty, and isolated situation at Mandanai. Instead, they have chosen to live in a tiny two-room hut they have erected on the beach-front foundations of the wife's mother's original house, because they consider the familiar location, the seaside climate, and the convenient access to schools, work, and shopping more important in the long run.

These advantages of living in the more established parts of Tambiluvil appear likely to lead an increasing number of tsunami-displaced families to move back toward the beach, although some survivors retain a deep terror of the ocean that may never allow them to do so. Strategically, there are also advantages to living in a more central part of the village: such a preferred location might persuade a future son-in-law to accept a matrilocal dowry offer. Based on what we have seen in Tambiluvil, the long-run viability of the massive Mandanai resettlement colony may be weakened by the pragmatic desire of Tamils to reconstitute mat-rilocal family groups in more salubrious coastal locations that could also prove advantageous for the dowry-based marriages of their daughters. Conversations with a number of Tamil community leaders suggests that the entire coastal front-age of Tambiluvil will gradually be rebuilt and repopulated by younger families no longer fearful of the tsunami and willing to invest their private resources and labor in the endeavor.

Muslims in Sainthamaruthu: building up

All of our Muslim family case-studies were identified with the help of local Muslim NGO staff members in the Kalmunai area. Two of these families reside in the relatively more affluent and densely built-up town of Sainthamaruthu, and three families live in the poorer fishing and weaving settlement of Maruthamunai, which was one of the worst-hit towns on the east coast.

The seafront road running south from the famous Beach Mosque (*Kadakkaraippalli*) shrine for the Nagoor Andavar saint at Kalmunaikkudy, through Santhamaruthu, and on to Karaitivu and Nintavur, largely demarcates the buffer zone within which post-tsunami construction is prohibited along this part of the coast. East of the road, the abandoned walls and empty foundations of former shops and homes lie very close to the edge of the sea, while to the west of the road there is a great deal of household repair, reconstruction, and expan-sion underway. The middle-class Muslim neighborhoods in Sainthamaruthu are extremely dense and built-up, and although the tsunami waves took a deadly toll in lives, they did not flatten or demolish all the structures. Perhaps the high masonry walls surrounding many homes here deflected the force of the water. In any case, the provision of permanent housing in Sainthamaruthu has clearly followed a path of private repair and rebuilding, funded by "owner driven" governmental and NGO construction grants to individual families. In the tsunami-affected streets, the height of the brick and mortar edifices would suggest that additional floors have been added to a number of the older homes, along with a florid profusion of new ornamental railings, colorful balconies, and roof gardens (Fig. 5.5). There could also be a certain rationality to this vertical construction boom, since a number of tsunami survivors told us stories of being saved by clinging to the very highest window ledges and rooftops.

Example 3. Muttamma and her daughter Fina

Muttamma and her daughter Fina occupy two separate single-story brick houses that are jammed tightly up against each other on a narrow street in the Malikaikkadu district of Sainthamaruthu. It seems clear that Muttamma's small urban compound had earlier been subdivided to build the house for Fina, her only daughter, leaving little room for a garden or even much direct sunlight. Muttamma is a courageous grandmother who single-handedly rescued the youngest of her eight grandchildren, a baby girl only six days old, from the rising tsunami waters and delivered her to the emergency hospital in Sammanturai, where she was reunited with Fina and her husband. When we met this family in 2007, they were living in their original dwelling, but an entire 2nd storey had been added to Fina's house as well as to Muttamma's immediately contiguous dwelling. Fina's husband is a mason, so he

Figure 5.5 Visible trend toward post-tsunami enlargement and beautification of Muslim homes, Sainthamaruthu, Sri Lanka, 2007. Photo by Dennis McGilvray.

helped to build the new walls and stairs which were as yet unfinished and unplastered. The post-tsunami construction boom has provided steady work for him, while Fina has launched a new NGO-sponsored home enterprise grinding rice flour and steaming stringhoppers (*idiyappam*) for sale in the neighborhood. The enlarged homes of mother and daughter share a common wall, and it would not be difficult to combine them into a single living unit if desired. Muttamma's house will eventually provide a dowry for the eldest of Fina's four daughters, and Fina's own house will go to her next youngest daughter. Given the physical impossibility of further subdividing this lot, it seems inevitable that Muttamma's youngest granddaughters will be married in other dowry houses, but perhaps not far away.

To a casual observer, the Muslim reconstruction process in Sainthamaruthu has the appearance of a huge middle-class home-improvement project, with many families taking advantage of government and NGO funding to refurbish and enlarge dwellings that were badly damaged but not destroyed by the tsunami waters. Interestingly, in a second Sainthamaruthu family we visited, the grandmother's badly damaged house has not been repaired, and in an exception to the matrilocal rule, the eldest daughter has shifted over to live with the family of her husband, who is a single child living with aging parents. We learned, however, that the grandmother's house will eventually be torn down and replaced with a brand new dowry house for her senior granddaughter (i.e. the eldest daughter's daughter), situated immediately next door to the homes of the grandmother's two other married daughters in the original maternal compound. The long-range goals of this family remain the same: to enhance the marriage prospects of daughters and granddaughters, for whom a well-situated dowry house remains an essential requirement for a respectable marriage.

Muslims in Maruthamunai: a new start

Some of the most catastrophic images of the tsunami emerged from Maruthamunai, a coastal Muslim town whose poor, densely populated seaside neighborhoods were utterly demolished by the tsunami waves (Fig. 5.1). By the time our research team first visited the town in 2005, most of the brick rubble had been scooped up to form an elevated roadbed along the beachfront. Only random concrete well-casings and cement floors remained where the modest homes of fishers and handloom weavers once stood. Here, unlike in Sainthamaruthu, the only practical way to provide permanent housing was to start from scratch erecting hundreds of brand-new houses, as well as the region's first multi-storey apartment buildings, in the former neighborhoods just adjacent to the buffer zone. Even so, there remained a shortage of new housing units, a situation complicated by Muslim and Tamil ethnic rivalries and local territorial politics (Korf, *et al.* 2008, de Silva 2009, Hasbullah and Korf in press). By summer 2008, an expanse of identical, bright blue NGO-constructed houses built right up to the 65 meter mark were finally being occupied by families who had been waiting more than three years for permanent shelter. Two case studies in Maruthamunai nicely illustrate the older tradition of matrilocal house construction as well as the contemporary strength of kinship ties between sisters.

Example 4. Kaleel's wife and her five sisters

Kaleel's wife and her five sisters were the daughters of a well-known leader (*Tandel*) of the Muslim sea fishermen in Maruthamunai, whose house once stood at an intersection directly across the road from the beach. The dowry house of the eldest daughter was situated near the center of town and was not touched by the tsunami, but the houses of the Tandel and three of his five younger daughters – constructed in a neat row along the same street immediately behind his – were totally destroyed by the tsunami (see house plan Fig. 5.6). The Tandel and his wife died instantly, as did his third daughter, her husband, two children, and another daughter's child. Altogether seven family members died in the tragedy. The original house belonged to the Tandel and his wife, but the three other demolished houses had been constructed with money individually earned by the Tandel's daughters who worked in the Middle East as housemaids in order to acquire a dowry for their own marriages. Under the government's rules, the Tandel's former house site and the house sites of two of his daughters now fall within the 65 meter buffer zone, so they are ineligible for reconstruction. Only the youngest daughter's original seaside lot can legally be reoccupied, and a new bright blue NGO home has recently been erected upon it.

However, in the intervening three-year period, Mr. Kaleel (an energetic NGO staffer) and his wife (the Tandel's second daughter) were asked to share their house

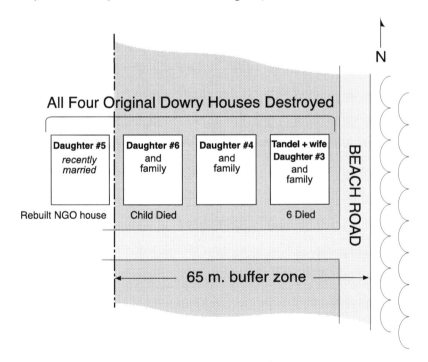

Figure 5.6 Layout of original dowry houses of the Tandel and his daughters, Maruthamunai Sri Lanka.

in the center of Maruthamunai with the Tandel's three tsunami-displaced daughters and their children while two of their husbands worked abroad in Qatar and Kuwait (Fig. 5.7). Kaleel grumbled good-naturedly to us about having to sleep on the floor in his own living room or on the concrete verandah throughout this period. Finally, in 2008, Kaleel and his wife built a new dowry house next door for his youngest sister-in-law and her new husband. The couple were unwilling to occupy the new blue beachfront NGO house that is rightfully hers, because it is too close to the menacing ocean and too far away from her married sisters. Kaleel's wife's other two married sisters have happily moved into a new multi-storey apartment building financed by an Islamic NGO, although they are not sure if rituals such as domestic funeral preparations will be feasible in such a high-rise structure. This example illustrates the strong matrilocal tendency in pre-tsunami house construction as well as the solidarity and support of married sisters in the post-tsunami period. As a well-placed senior son-in-law, Mr. Kaleel was called upon to provide two of his wife's married sisters with temporary accommodation for several years, as well as build a dowry house for his recently married youngest sister-in-law.

Example 5. Raffiq and Bibi

Raffiq and Bibi lost two of their three children in the tsunami, as well as their modest dowry house, which was situated next door to Bibi's mother on the beachfront in Maruthamunai. A mason by trade, Raffiq has had no difficulty finding work in

Figure 5.7 Three surviving Muslim sisters live with their sister and brother-in-law during post-tsunami reconstruction, Maruthamunai, Sri Lanka, 2007. Photo by Dennis McGilvray.

the aftermath of the tsunami, but he and his wife were among the very last of the homeless to receive permanent housing. After a series of short-term solutions – including an emergency tent camp and living for several months with relatives of his mother-in-law – Raffiq and his wife ended up building a temporary wood and canvas shelter in the front yard of his own sister, who also happens to be married to his wife's brother. This is a so-called "exchange marriage" (*marrukkaliyanam*) in which a brother and a sister marry a sister and a brother, an arrangement that appears in this case to have bolstered the patience and forbearance of all parties concerned. The original dowry house that Raffiq and Bibi occupied near the beach, legally owned by Bibi's mother at the time of the tsunami, cannot be rebuilt now because it lies within the buffer zone. Raffiq strongly feels this has placed the worst-affected people such as himself at the end of the queue in the reconstruction process. His mother-in-law, who once managed seven textile handlooms in her beachfront house, now assists her youngest daughter and son-in-law – and her divorced middle daughter – with weaving chores in a new NGO house they share some distance away from the beach. In 2008 we found Raffiq and Bibi still living with his sister and brother-in-law, awaiting a permanent home in a government-sponsored housing colony currently under construction on recovered marshlands to the west of the main road in Maruthamunai.[3]

Among the east coast Muslims, as among the Tamils, it is assumed that a wife will receive her promised dowry property in due course, and in some cases the legal transfer only occurs when a married daughter needs to pledge the dowry property for her own daughter's marriage. In Maruthamunai married daughters and sons-in-law did not always possess legal title to the dowry houses they were occupying at the time of the tsunami, because dowry deeds are rare and no one thought it was urgent to register a maternal gift of dowry property. In order to be eligible for new permanent NGO houses, therefore, some Muslim women had to secure the informal cooperation of local-level officials to pre-date the legal gift of dowry houses from their mothers.

Burghers in Batticaloa: hard choices

Like their cousins in several eastern towns, the Burghers of Batticaloa had shifted their residence several decades ago from the center of town to a less cramped and more economical neighborhood closer to the beach (McGilvray 2007). Their new settlement was at Dutch Bar, a narrow, low-lying isthmus of sand and coconut trees separating the Indian Ocean from the northern outlet of the Batticaloa Lagoon. The tsunami easily swept over Dutch Bar and the nearby fishing village of Navalady, simultaneously destroying Burgher houses and Tamil fishing huts, and pouring a gruesome mixture of dead bodies and debris into the lagoon (see Lawrence chapter in this volume). The church of St. Ignatius, the center of the Burgher parish in Dutch Bar, was quickly repaired, but most Burgher survivors were left utterly homeless. After receiving emergency shelter in a series of churches and schools, most of the Burghers were given temporary housing at the large Tiraimadu refugee camp located north of Batticaloa Town. Tiraimadu had been poorly planned from the very start, so inevitable problems of seasonal flooding and lack of amenities plagued the Burghers in their temporary corrugated tin huts while they waited for a permanent new all-Burgher housing settlement to be built at nearby Pannichaiyadi. The misery and delays the Burghers endured while waiting for permanent houses at Pannichaiyadi presented many families with the difficult choice of whether to stay or to migrate back to their original house sites at Dutch Bar, where a Christian NGO had promised to speed the construction of a limited number of new houses beyond the 125 meter buffer zone that was enforced at the time.

Example 6. Emma

Emma (age 40) is the only daughter in her family never to marry. Her three sisters (one older, two younger) have husbands and children, and prior to the tsunami disaster, all members of her family had been living in Dutch Bar. For many years Emma had taken the responsibility of caring for their widowed father while also earning money in Colombo to assist her sisters to build their dowry houses on his property in Dutch Bar. Eventually, Emma took employment as a housemaid in Saudi Arabia and used her foreign earnings to build a house in Dutch Bar for herself as well. Then, in an instant, the tsunami destroyed every one of the sisters' houses, and all four women eventually found themselves sharing the misery of the Tiraimadu camp while waiting for new permanent homes to be erected at nearby Pannichaiyadi. Unexpectedly, as delays and uncertainties concerning the Pannichaiyadi construction schedule were mounting, the parish priest from St. Ignatius invited Burgher families in Tiraimadu to move back to Dutch Bar. The number of new NGO houses would be strictly limited, he explained, so families had to act quickly to get on the list. Two of Emma's brothers-in-law, a tailor and a carpenter, decided the Dutch Bar location would provide them with better access to work in Batticaloa Town. So, despite their fear of the sea and their regret at being separated, two of the sisters moved back to Dutch Bar, leaving Emma, her youngest sister, and her married brother behind in Pannichaiyadi, where they have permanent homes today. The former matrilocal household cluster of sisters is now evenly divided between Dutch Bar and Pannaichiyadi, and they feel their physical separation acutely. While Emma insists she could never live near the sea again, she pays visits to her two sisters in Dutch Bar as frequently as possible.

A final case-study from our fieldwork among the Burghers of Batticaloa serves to illustrate the principle of inter-generational transmission of dowry property by focusing on an exception that proves the rule. When demographic odds, or marital fate, leaves a woman with no daughters, no sisters or sister's daughters, and no matrilateral female parallel cousins (i.e. mother's sisters daughters, classified as "sisters" in Dravidian kinship) to receive her dowry property, the system channels dowry property to granddaughters instead of transferring disposable wealth to sons.

Figure 5.8 Three tsunami-displaced Burgher sisters in Dutch Bar, Batticaloa, Sri Lanka, 2007. Photo by Patrica Lawrence.

Example 7. Angela

Angela (age 45) is the only daughter in a Burgher family of five children. Her marriage was childless, ending in divorce many years ago, and since then her life has focused on church-related work and caring for her aged parents. She fondly remembers an earlier time when the entire family lived in Dutch Bar, but now several of her brothers are married outside of Batticaloa entirely. After her parents narrowly escaped death in the tsunami at Dutch Bar, they ended up living in a new house with Angela in the Pannichaiyadi Burgher resettlement colony on the north side of Batticaloa. However, legal title to the new Pannichaiyadi house was written in her brother's name, not Angela's, and she stands no chance of inheriting it because she has no children. Instead, it will become a dowry house for her brother's daughter. The only house that Angela ever stood a chance of owning was her original dowry house in Batticaloa Town, but her mother failed to legally transfer the deed prior to Angela's divorce. Today the house is still legally owned by her mother, and it is occupied by Angela's fraternal niece – her elder brother's daughter and her husband – who pay Angela a nominal rent for the accommodation.

When Angela's elderly parents are gone, her brothers have suggested she could build a small house on their property in Dutch Bar, but Angela – who barely makes ends meet by teaching sewing classes – is unlikely to have sufficient resources to do this by herself. If Angela had remained married and borne a daughter, her mother's house would have been transferred to her, but in the absence of any female descendants in the female line, the maternal dowry property as well as the new NGO house in Pannichaiyadi have been arrogated by her elder brothers to provide dowries for their own daughters. This is a bitter dimension of the Batticaloa matrilocal property system, which penalizes unmarried women and those without the promise of offspring. Angela is understandably resentful, but her parents and brothers are following a basic cultural axiom: houses should be given to married women who are likely to bear children themselves.

Conclusion

As we talked with Tamil, Muslim, and Burgher families who had survived the tsunami and experienced the perplexities of the post-tsunami shelter and reconstruction process, we heard a number of familiar problems voiced. The government's erratic and delayed readjustments of the coastal buffer zone created huge problems for families who needed to decide quickly whether to rebuild on the beach or to resettle in large-scale housing projects inland. Many Burghers, for example, felt they had made the wrong choice to abandon their coastal property when the 200 meter buffer zone was later reduced to between 125 meters and 65 meters, retroactively permitting reconstruction of houses at Dutch Bar in Batticaloa and at 40th Milepost in Akkaraipattu. On the other hand, as Thurnheer (2008) notes, the buffer zone policy provided a new – and often much better – house to many impoverished fishermen who owned no legal beachfront dwellings in the first place. The same would have been true of war-displaced IDPs living on the beach when the tsunami struck, but this was not a common occurrence in Ampara and Batticaloa Districts.[4]

In many places, too, the shortage of available land for new inland resettlement schemes led to construction delays and questionable planning for long-term viability. In both the Mandanai colony west of Tambiluvil and the Pannichaiyadi colony north of Batticaloa, residents complained of a lack of reliable transportation, good schools, employment opportunities, public security, even drinkable water. The influx of new motorbikes after the tsunami – many, it is said, purchased with household reconstruction funds – has provided mobility for some families in these isolated resettlement projects. The variety of architectural designs and the uneven quality of building materials used in the construction of permanent housing was commented upon by some of the families in our sample, but it did not seem to be a preeminent concern for most of them. Many people tacitly acknowledged that virtually all of the new NGO and government-constructed permanent housing was superior to what they had owned before the tsunami.

Normally, however, houses in eastern Sri Lanka are planned with sisters, daughters, nieces, and granddaughters in mind, and the location of a house is a strategic factor in the dowry equation. Among the Tamil, Muslim, and Burgher households we surveyed, the long-term goal of restoring and maintaining the traditional matrilocal dowry house pattern for the younger generation seemed quite evident, a finding perceptively corroborated by Thurnheer (2008) among Batticaloa fisher families. Although reasonable concerns were raised in the aftermath of the tsunami as to whether women's dowry assets and property rights would suffer permanent diminishment, or outright extinction, when relief agencies hastily placed reconstruction grants and property deeds in the hands of men, our research suggests that any post-tsunami reduction of women's domestic property rights will be temporary. Even where fathers, husbands, and sons have monopolized reconstruction funds, or have acquired exclusive title to new post-tsunami houses, it is still their married daughters and sisters who are destined to receive this property in the long-run. Displaced, dispossessed, and dispirited families have endured a variety of unfamiliar and stressful conditions since December 2004, but the matrilocal marriage and dowry house system of the Batticaloa region seems to have survived the tsunami.

Notes

1 This project was supported by a team-based interdisciplinary grant from the National Science Foundation (SES 05625260). We wish to gratefully acknowledge the field-work assistance provided by N. Hamead, K. Kanthanathan, K.N. Dharmalingam, M.A. Phakurdeen, K. Shanmugampillai, Y. Shanmugampillai, M.S. Jaleel, S.A. Wahab, and N. Dharmaretnam.
2 Specific individuals are identified by pseudonyms.
3 Korf, *et al.* (2009) have pointed to this government-sponsored housing project as an example of how the "pure gift" of post-tsunami relief was transformed from a religious duty in the hands of the local mosque federation to a channel of patronage in the hands of Muslim politicians.
4 Several authors have expressed concern for impoverished IDPs who fled the violence of the Eelam Wars and would have been camped on the beaches of Sri Lanka when the tsunami hit (Grundy-Warr and Sidaway 2006, Hyndman 2007). Actual instances of this happening, however, appear to have been rare (Timmo Gaasbeek, personal communication).

6 Actors in a *masala* movie

Fieldnotes on the NGO tsunami response in eastern Sri Lanka

Timmo Gaasbeek

> You see, in these [disasters], things get confused out there: power, ideals, the old morality, and practical [humanitarian] necessity. But out there, with these natives, it must be a temptation to … be God.
>
> (After *Apocalypse Now*)

Introduction

After the tsunami hit Sri Lanka, a flood of foreign volunteers, aid workers and NGOs followed who joined those already involved in providing relief to the survivors. They in turn were followed by journalists, evaluators and researchers who documented the tsunami and its aftermath, in a pattern that has been common to major disasters since at least 1883, when the eruption of the Krakatau volcano caused a tsunami that killed thousands on the shores of Java and Sumatra (Winchester 2004).

Many have concluded that the humanitarian response to the Indian Ocean Tsunami was chaotic (Forced Migration Review 2005; Frerks and Klem 2005c; Stirrat 2006). An Indian government official whom I interviewed for a project evaluation succinctly summarized this discourse when he stated that "relief is like a *masala* movie" (interview, Thirunelveli, June 2007). In this popular Bollywood cinema genre, there is a thin overall storyline, but the film is primarily a chaotic and colourful jumble of a large number of standard elements.

Although in general I agree with the *masala* movie metaphor, I contend that three crucial aspects of the tsunami response have been misrepresented or ignored in the common discourses on the topic. First, the initial response in the East of Sri Lanka was actually effective and, though hectic, not chaotic. Many years of near-annual flooding and twenty years of violent conflict meant that most of those living in the East knew exactly what to do when they had to flee their houses. A pre-existing NGO co-ordination mechanism and efficient sharing of resources were in place; the government managed to restore roads and fuel and electricity supply within days; and the response capabilities of the various actors that were on the ground when the tsunami hit formed an almost natural symbiosis. Chaotic scenes of "competitive humanitarianism," as were documented by Stirrat (2006: 11–16) and many others, did take place, but only after new aid agencies started arriving from the second week onwards.

Second, there is much to say about the way in which international NGOs operated. Caught in a struggle for reputations at home, NGOs engaged in open competition and in sometimes unnecessary high-visibility projects. This chapter shows that in the process, the normative debate on international standards of disaster relief delivery became a strategic weapon for agencies that were unable to mount a quick response.

Third, I believe that the role of expatriates in the *masala* movie has not received sufficient critical attention. Many either had insufficient experience, or were used to operating in "failed states." Due to the language barriers, they often worked with a very poor understanding of the local dynamics. Together with highly visible but culturally inappropriate ways in which they spent their leisure time, this led to cross-cultural misunderstandings and misgivings.

I contend that these three aspects have not received the attention they deserve because the vast majority of scholars writing on post-tsunami assistance lack familiarity with the pre-tsunami situation (including Sri Lanka's history of violent conflict), with aid work in general, and with the NGO scene in Sri Lanka in particular. This chapter provides an emic correction of the discourse on the tsunami response.

In the following sections, I will re-tell my own experiences of being involved in the humanitarian response to the tsunami, and reflect on the aspects described above. I mainly focus on the Eastern Province of Sri Lanka, which is where I have lived, worked and studied most of the eight years that I have spent in the country, and where my wife and I found ourselves when the tsunami hit. This chapter is intended to complement the picture painted in Stirrat's insightful paper on the response in Sri Lanka's southwest (Stirrat 2006).

Immediate response and the end of the emergency

When the tsunami hit, my wife, who is Sri Lankan, and I were in our house in the eastern Sri Lankan town of Batticaloa. We lived about one kilometer inland from the beach and directly west of the mouth of the large lagoon that has given Batticaloa (*Mattakalappu* or "muddy lagoon") its name. My wife managed a project for an international humanitarian agency that I refer to as "ABC."[1] I spent most of my days shuttling between Batticaloa and Trincomalee, where I was conducting field work for my PhD on everyday inter-ethnic interaction in a part of Sri Lanka's conflict zone. The rest of my time was spent working as a consultant for "DEF," another international NGO that supports war-affected communities in the north and east of Sri Lanka. I had worked for this NGO since late 2000 (mostly in the Eastern Province).

Within minutes after the first tsunami caused the clocks on the beach to stop ticking (at 9.05 a.m.)[2] our neighbor warned us to put our things as high as possible, because "the water was coming." As the weather was calm and sunny, we did not take this warning seriously. However, since two of my wife's colleagues were staying in a guesthouse on the beach, we figured we should go to have a look, help them carry their suitcases to a dry place and then have breakfast together to have a good laugh about it all. So off we went, in our rickety old van, to the beach – a trip that normally would take about ten minutes. When we got to the approach road of the bridge to the beach, we saw water on the road, and got stuck in a massive crowd of panicking people. Realizing that our van would not take us through the water, we turned around, loaded up the van with fleeing people, and drove towards the hospital, which was also the highest point in town. On the way, we met a colleague, who told us that the staff members of DEF were gathering in the manager's house to plan a response. After dropping our passengers off, we went there in the hope of borrowing a 4x4 vehicle with which we could reach the beach to look for my wife's colleagues. No vehicle was available, so we went to my wife's office to look for one. After obtaining permission from her boss in Colombo, I took the keys of a Land Cruiser and, together with a colleague who had made her way to the office, drove back towards the beach. My wife stayed in the office to maintain radio communications with Colombo and with the vehicle. By this time, the water level on the road had gone down, and the bridge was passable. Because crowds of panicking people blocked the road to the guesthouse, we tried an alternative road that took us straight to the beach. The first sight we saw there was a weeping father, walking towards us with the dead body of his little daughter in his hands and despair written all over his face. We inched forward, but soon got stuck. Debris, barbed wire and bodies that lay strewn all over made the road impassable. I barely managed to swerve around a mat on the road, and then I noticed that it was covering a corpse. Seeing the destruction, both of us wept and sat in shock for a little while. Then I turned the vehicle, and, loading up injured and scared people on the way, we joined in the mad rush of going from the beach to the hospital, and back to the beach, and back to the hospital. Everybody who had a vehicle or motorbike did the same. Civilians spontaneously organized the traffic into an efficient loop that enabled the vehicles to race through the crowded heart of town without too many problems. Along the road, frightened people sat on rooftops, higher than any tsunami could ever come. Some stayed there for an entire week.

A little after eleven o'clock, sitting in the car in front of the office, we had a sip of coffee – our first nourishment for the day. After a brief discussion, we concluded that the response at Batticaloa's beach front was pretty much covered. Because we had no idea how the situation was elsewhere, we decided to check out a coastal village just north of town. Unfortunately, the village was inaccessible because a bridge had collapsed, and we had to return to base. By this time, a number of my wife's colleagues had found their way to the ABC office. Because the person responsible for emergency response[3] had himself lost his house and was in no position to take the lead, my wife formally took charge.

I realized that there had been a tsunami,[4] but I still thought that the epicenter of the earthquake had perhaps been about ten kilometers offshore. It took a couple of hours before we figured out that the damage was probably more widespread. When, around noon, the news came by SMS that the epicenter had actually been in Indonesia, we decided to check out the coastline north of Batticaloa since the situation in Batticaloa town seemed to be under control, and we had heard that other agencies had moved south. Colleagues had told me that DEF had already moved its staff and vehicles to the town of Valaichchenai, thirty kilometers north of Batticaloa, so we split our reconnaissance team into two. One vehicle was to scour the coast between Batticaloa and Eravur, and the other the coast between Eravur and Valaichchenai. After hurriedly eating a few mouthfuls of instant noodles, we went on our way. Along the way, we collected information on which villages had been hit, where people had sought refuge, how many people were in each camp, and what urgent needs they had. It must be noted here that, ironically, a long history of violent conflict and near-annual flooding proved to be an advantage. Almost everybody knew the drill when they had to flee from their homes: you go to the nearest school, temple, mosque or church, get yourself registered, and wait for assistance. Cooked meals will be distributed in the first few days, plastic sheets, mats, pans, *et cetera* will come after a week, and dry rations will come after two weeks.

Around this time, it suddenly hit me that the emergency was over and there was no more need to drive like a maniac. Those who had died had died,[5] those who had been injured were in the hospital or on their way to the hospital, and those who had fled were in schools and temples and had a place to sleep, however basic. There was nothing more that could be done to save people. Racing would only endanger others on the road, and excessive adrenaline levels impede sharp thinking after a while. From then on, there still was an incredible amount of hard work to be done, but it was all basically mopping up. Despite this, one could still hear expatriates talk about doing life-saving emergency relief a year after the tsunami. This rhetoric impressed the home audience (and the high-adrenaline aid workers themselves), but was a misrepresentation of the facts.

After completing my half of the reconnaissance, I drove on to Valaichchenai to exchange information with my colleagues there, and to have a look at the hospital, in front of which eighty bodies lay covered under white sheets and surrounded by a crowd of mourning relatives. Just outside Valaichchenai, we passed a lone funeral procession, complete with the customary firecrackers. It was the only proper funeral that I witnessed in the weeks after the tsunami.

NGO coordination

After we had compiled all our information into a table, I went around town at midnight to see which NGO offices might still be open. Somewhat to my surprise, everybody was still up, busy with the preparations for the next day.[6] We learnt that a first co-ordination meeting had already been organized in the evening by the deputy chairman of the INGO coordination committee, but for some reason not all big NGOs had been invited. The next day, another co-ordination meeting was held with the UN agencies and international NGOs that had offices in Batticaloa, as well as the International Committee of the Red Cross (ICRC), the Sri Lanka Monitoring Mission (SLMM), and representatives of the biggest local NGOs. In that meeting, we moved beyond sharing information to jointly planning the response for the following days. A map of the district was sketched on a whiteboard, onto which every agency indicated where they had been and what they had learnt about the situation.

Thereafter the group decided to allocate specific areas to each agency, depending on their logistical capacities and geographical preferences. Several agencies preferred to work in those areas where they were already working, because they had an existing network of contacts with local government, community leaders, and local NGOs.[7] After that, sector-specific committees were organized that would meet on specific issues: shelter, water and sanitation, food, psychosocial issues, health, and non-food relief items. These are the standard sectors that are generally dealt with in any immediate emergency response in Sri Lanka; education and gender are two sectors that generally follow a little later.

From 28 December 2004 onwards, these committees met daily in the morning and afternoon at various offices in Batticaloa town. All agencies working in a particular sector would attend the respective meetings, in which details were discussed. Needs assessment forms were jointly developed, a joint table of needs and available stocks was made, and activity plans were shared and fine tuned. In the overall meeting in the evenings, general issues were then discussed. When necessary, vehicles, staff and stocks were exchanged as needed. For the first two weeks after the tsunami, this system worked efficiently. New agencies that came into the district were referred to the meetings whenever people who were already attending the meetings came across them, and most newcomers attended the meetings. Since there was more work than the agencies on the ground could handle, any new agency was quickly asked what its capacity was, and given suggestions of areas and sectors to work in that would best suit the needs and existing gaps in aid. The price paid by incoming agencies for non-coordination was silence from those agencies with experience in the area, and without information the newcomers could not work effectively.

In parallel with the NGO coordination mechanism, starting on the day after the tsunami, the district administration also organized coordination meetings with government departments, politicians and humanitarian agencies. Although this may look like duplication, it was in fact a division of tasks. The government itself had a limited emergency response capability, but a great deal of information. Once the supply of emergency food stocks by the World Food Programme was up and running, the government began to actively distribute food, but this effort took about two weeks to get organized. Therefore, in the initial phase the government coordination meetings dealt with sharing information and setting priorities, and the NGO coordination meetings dealt with practical implementation matters.

Based on these observations, I argue that Stirrat's assessment that "the overall picture of relief in the period immediately after the tsunami is one of chaos" (2006: 14) was not valid for the north-east of Sri Lanka, where a district-level humanitarian emergency response infrastructure was already in place. District-level NGO consortia had been in existence for many years. Following the introduction of the "humanitarian charter and minimum standards for disaster response" (Sphere 2000) in late 2000, many people in Sri Lanka had received training, district-level contingency plans had been drawn up,[8] and some emergency stocks were put in place. The plans themselves were largely ignored, but the fact that key NGO staff in the district had spent time together thinking about how to respond to natural and man-made disasters made it easy to put their heads together when the tsunami hit. On top of that, the near-annual flooding in the Eastern Province and a number of conflict-related displacements had provided excellent opportunities to practice, and to keep the emergency coordination mechanisms alive in people's minds.[9] Coincidentally, the two weeks immediately preceding the tsunami had brought unusually heavy floods to the Trincomalee and Batticaloa Districts. In both districts, those local and international NGOs that had stocks, funds, staff, and vehicles available had pooled their resources for the response. I was in Trincomalee when the floods started, and witnessed how multi-agency assessment teams were formed, uniform family packs of relief items were compiled from the combined stocks and packed with the help of two local organizations with little money but many volunteers, and distributions were jointly undertaken. There was no pressure to generate publicity, and the whole exercise was implemented in an atmosphere of great camaraderie. The flood response ended on 24 December 2004. The next day was Christmas and those involved were able to rest, only to be jolted back into action on 26 December 2004. The action taken in response to the flood had worked well. The NGOs and UN agencies simply followed the same approach when responding to the tsunami.

From the end of the second week onwards, the number of newcomers became so large that things descended into the chaos that Stirrat and others have described, but by this time the most immediate needs had been met. Critics often ignore this important fact: within a week, all tsunami-affected people in the Eastern Province had access to a minimum of food, shelter and health care, and by the end of the second week the vast majority of affected people had access to elementary levels of drinking water supply, sanitation, and non-food relief items. This feat was largely achieved by those who were already on the ground when the tsunami hit.[10]

In the weeks that followed, the UN took over the humanitarian coordination, sometimes displacing functioning local mechanisms. For example, in Ampara district, a local NGO consortium together with a small INGO had done a splendid job in organizing NGO coordination, only to be nudged out in a rather hostile take-over by the UN system, which had had no significant presence in the district before the tsunami. While co-ordination was absolutely needed, it became something of a self-sustaining and expanding universe that continued to hold meetings and produce documents long after the bulk of the tsunami-related needs had been met. Interestingly, once the excessive amounts of money had been spent and the journalists had gone home, co-ordination improved. When, in 2006–7, a massive army offensive against the LTTE caused the displacement of tens of thousands of people in the east, agencies reverted to the local co-operative practices that had been used before the tsunami.

The important and neglected roles of other actors

Despite their domination in the rhetoric surrounding tsunami relief and recovery, the international NGOs were certainly not the only actors responsible for the initial response (Telford, Cosgrave and Houghton 2006). The government, private individuals, and local NGOs fulfilled key roles that have not received the attention they deserve. I address each of these groups here in turn.

The Sri Lankan government's response to the crisis deserves both criticism and praise. On the negative side, the government displayed little authoritative leadership in the response to the tsunami, often complicating things by setting unrealistic deadlines that raised people's expectations and ultimately their frustrations. Rash decisions such as the imposition of a much-contested "buffer zone" that, without much explicit reasoning, was twice as wide in the Muslim and Tamil-dominated north and east as it was in the Sinhala-dominated south and west raised many problems. Nevertheless, the Sri Lankan government must be given credit for re-establishing a fuel supply within two days and for provisionally repairing most roads and electricity lines within two weeks. These often-forgotten government interventions meant that the distribution of relief aid could proceed uninterrupted. Apart from that, local government administrators started the process of registering people almost immediately, which meant that by the time food rations and other government assistance started becoming available (from the second week onwards), the affected people could immediately receive it.[11]

Private individuals also played an important role in tsunami relief. Many of the affected people fled to schools, temples, and mosques, where they survived the first day or two on food and drink that were supplied by people living in the neighborhood. This, again, was what normally happened if people got displaced. However, the resources of these neighborhood people ran out fairly soon, and they were unable to continue their support. At this point, NGOs were generally able to distribute a limited amount of rations with the financial and logistical resources that were available in the coastal belt. After the fourth day, a traffic-jamming flow of vehicles started pouring in from other parts of the country, typically loaded with a small crowd of curious well-wishers and a couple of boxes of food and other items. They generally drove along the main roads, and gave out their goods wherever they thought it fit to distribute them. After that began the journey home, which was usually interrupted by a few stops for photo shoots in affected beachfront settlements: a mix of altruism and local disaster tourism.[12] This form of private distribution went on for a little under two weeks, after which the enthusiasm and resources of this group of people fizzled out.[13] (By then, the government system was in a position to take over.) A problem with this unstructured private distribution was that people staying in camps away from the main roads did not get sufficient assistance, while in some camps along the main roads food was thrown away because there was too much. Also, most well-wishers simply distributed the items to whomever came first, which in many cases meant that those who were weaker missed out, despite being very close to assistance.

So far, I have not paid much attention to local NGOs. The fact that they are often ignored is typical of the written coverage of emergency response in Sri Lanka, but not in line with reality. In Batticaloa District, local NGOs had their own co-ordination mechanism that was entirely separate from the international NGOs. This system had been instituted on orders of the LTTE in 2001, when the LTTE wanted to increase its hold over the work that local NGOs were doing. While this local NGO consortium did become active after the tsunami, I am fairly sure that for many local NGOs the links with international NGO partners that funded their work were more important for day-to-day planning and co-ordination of work. In the case of an emergency, local and international NGOs each have capacities that in combination can produce a highly effective response: local NGOs generally have manpower, a local-level network and knowledge of the ground situation, while international NGOs have funds, stocks of goods, and vehicles to move things around. While it would be hard to call these partnerships equal, the symbiosis does generate a win-win situation for local and international NGOs, and ultimately for the affected population. Such symbiotic networks were already in existence in the Eastern Province of Sri Lanka, and they were utilized whenever there was displacement. The claim that local NGOs were ignored, while definitely relevant in the rehabilitation and reconstruction phase (see Hilhorst and Fernando 2006 for an insightful description), is in my opinion also a strategic discourse that was used by local NGOs for staking their own claims. Not only INGOs, but also many local NGOs wanted a "piece of the cake," and ignored their formal mandate in order to gain access to funds and an opportunity to build a reputation. Viewed more positively, it may well have been that in the urge to "do something," many people simply got involved with available resources. It is however questionable why agencies with no relief and reconstruction mandate subsequently continued looking for funds to expand their work. There was no shortage of agencies, and there was no need to stay involved. Even an NGO coordination body that had been set up years earlier with the sole objective of facilitating the co-ordination of humanitarian assistance started implementing its own projects.

While there are a number of highly capable local NGOs around, many others are very small and have very limited resources. On top of that, one gets the distinct impression that some of the local NGOs that mushroomed after major influxes of humanitarian aid money (such as after the 1978 cyclone, the 1990 violence, and the 2002 ceasefire) were primarily established as a tool for the founders to earn an additional income, and/or to earn a reputation.

Corruption

Stirrat's assertion that "few people if any get rich through working in disaster relief" (Stirrat 2006: 16) needs to be qualified. There are rotten apples everywhere, and among expatriates there was quite a bit of hypocrisy: many enjoyed lives of considerable luxury while they were in Sri Lanka. It was not surprising to come across articles in local newspapers accusing NGOs of spending too much money on their expatriates, who spent their days shuttling in air-conditioned luxury vehicles between air-conditioned houses, air-conditioned offices, and air-conditioned high-class restaurants in the capital.

As far as local staff members are concerned, I have come across many truly genuine and committed Sri Lankans in NGOs. But in Sri Lanka's war zone, international NGOs offer among the best-paid jobs available. Also, the exorbitant availability of funds and the lack of knowledge about prices among expatriate managers created opportunities for abuse. For example, a Sri Lankan friend recounted his horror when he went to a shop to buy some supplies and the shop owner insisted that he put the retail rather than the wholesale price on the bill, and then split the difference. According to my friend, this had become standard practice in his hometown after the tsunami. Another friend was in a big shop in Colombo several days after the tsunami, when the (Sri Lankan) procurement officer of one of the biggest organizations in the country walked in to order a large number of blankets. He followed the same procedure of billing the retail price, paying the wholesale price, and splitting the difference with the salesman. The procurement officer made about US $10,000 on that single purchase – where his regular salary would probably have been around US $500 per month. For the organization, which had received several hundred million dollars, this was a negligible amount; for the procurement officer, it was enough to build a decent house.

In the immediate aftermath of the tsunami, NGOs often stressed in the media that all expenses were made with full accountability, and many expatriates whom I spoke to genuinely believed that there was no fraud in their organization. However, by late 2007, I suddenly started hearing stories from friends in a wide range of NGOs that staff had been fired over corruption charges. In a context where the reputation of the humanitarian sector was already fragile, this seems to have been deliberately kept out of the press (and understandably so!).

In walk the specialists

In the days after the tsunami, a team of 30 people under my wife's leadership with six vehicles and about US $10,000 at their disposal had managed to provide three-day food rations plus some supplies of firewood, candles, and sanitary napkins to about 30,000 people over a 100 kilometer stretch of coastline in Batticaloa and Ampara districts. As this operation was winding down on 31 December 2004 and we were planning further activities, my wife was suddenly told that she had been relieved of her duties. Her immediate supervisor, who was jealous that my wife had been the only one in the organization to proactively set up an emergency response, had made a string of false allegations, and the expatriate leadership never bothered to verify them. A little after sunset, two foreign members of her organization's international Emergency Response Team arrived to take charge of the operations. Something interesting happened at this point. The experts got out of their Land Cruiser, walked into the office, sat down on two chairs in a prominent place, called a meeting, and straight away started telling the team members what they should be doing. Not one question was asked about who had been in charge, what had already been done, and how the team was doing. All the relief work was to be put on hold until "proper assessments" were done. Thus started a massive flow of "emergency experts," all of whom had their own bit to add. Even expats who had been on the ground prior to the tsunami were sidelined. For example, an expatriate colleague and friend of my wife who barely survived the tsunami herself got to work as soon as she could find a change of clothes, and after a day or two took on the responsibility for the response in Ampara District. By the time she was "accidentally" written out of the staffing plan three months later, nearly fifty "emergency experts" had passed through ABC's Ampara office. Not one of them ever tapped this person's wealth of knowledge and experience of having lived and worked in the country for nearly a decade (Gaasbeek 2005). Not surprisingly, it took ABC half a year before any substantial work was implemented again. The work that my wife and her team had done was blacked out from all of ABC's public reports.

Though not always so extreme, the same process was at work in other agencies, where emergency relief specialists were sent in who took over the management responsibilities without understanding the existing team dynamics, rather than putting their expertise to use in an advisory capacity and allowing existing managers to continue in their roles. Particularly in a situation where there is a high turnover of expatriate staff, this approach can lead to total chaos – the ultimate "*masala* movie." Most of the die-hard emergency relief experts whom I have come across are dominant, high-adrenaline people – characteristics that are useful to get a lot of work done under stressful circumstances, but counterproductive in a context where existing structures are available. Because these specialists are sent from headquarters and because many among them have impressive credentials, they are the ones whose opinions tend to be taken seriously by those higher up in the organization, even if they are at times dead wrong.

Since we wanted to continue to contribute to the tsunami response, my wife and I volunteered with "GHI," another international NGO in Batticaloa, for a week. We joined GHI because it was mainly involved in water and sanitation, which was the most pressing need at that time. GHI operated in a manner different from ABC. In the first week after the tsunami, an initial planeload of water and sanitation equipment, together with a highly experienced advisor, was sent to support the team in Batticaloa. He did not take over the leadership but functioned as a technical advisor to the existing team, and did a brilliant job in helping to get a substantial emergency water and sanitation program up and running.

Reputations at home

A few days after we joined GHI, the country director received a call from the international headquarters. He was told that another aircraft was airborne with 45 tons of BP5 biscuits (which are meant to provide emergency nutrition to severely malnourished people) and a film crew attached to a television station that had made a substantial donation to GHI. Distribution of these biscuits was to commence as soon as they arrived, so that it could be shown on TV the same day for the evening news. There were, however, no severely malnourished people due to the tsunami, and the biscuits were not needed. GHI's headquarters had decided to send them because images of food being distributed have more media appeal than images of emergency latrines, especially while the people watching the news are having dinner.

The expatriate staff members of GHI in Sri Lanka objected to what they considered to be unethical humanitarian practices. They spoke to the TV crew, which changed its filming plans. In the end, GHI got its TV publicity (and, in a nice collusion of interests, the TV station got its audiences), but the biscuits were still in a warehouse when I spoke to the, by then former, country director almost a year later. The entire team of expatriates resigned after three months of open resistance to pressure from headquarters, and they were replaced by a new team that was less obstinate (interview, October 2005).

Though perhaps a little extreme, this example illustrates the pressures that INGOs were under at home, and the tensions that sometimes arose between head-quarters and those doing the actual work. Starting from about 2000, a discourse had been gaining ground in NGO management circles that growth was essential: medium-sized organizations which fail to grow are at serious risk of collapsing. This NGO considered itself to be at risk of disappearing. The publicity generated by the TV crew was needed to attract more funds and create a good reputation, which in turn might help the NGO attain the critical mass that was considered necessary to survive and continue to provide humanitarian aid.

Open competition and standards

Two weeks after the tsunami, the situation seemed to have stabilized a bit, and I was asked to report back to DEF. Since my wife no longer had a job binding her to Batticaloa, we moved to Colombo, where I became Shelter Coordinator. In that capacity I got involved in the Colombo-level circus of coordination meetings about both transitional shelter and permanent housing. Together with a number of other NGOs, DEF had already been involved in providing shelters to returning refugees and IDPs in Sri Lanka's conflict zones since the beginning of the 2002 ceasefire, and a shelter design was already available. DEF had several hundred shelter kits that were in stock elsewhere trucked to Ampara, and construction started about four days after the tsunami. A team of technical staff adjusted the design to speed up output, and a simple illustrated manual was developed so that we could distribute the materials as a do-it-yourself kit. An initial order was placed for all the materials required for 2,000 shelter kits. To our surprise, we realized that we had bought up virtually the entire stock of galvanized iron pipes and tin sheets that was available in Sri Lanka's wholesale market, as well as much of the supply that was expected for the coming six weeks. Since 50,000 shelters were needed in total, this meant that there was a big problem. Even though alternative designs using other materials were being implemented, and some stocks were available in the retail market, it was clear that material supply was going to be one of the biggest bottlenecks in the process of constructing the shelters.

I raised this point in the national shelter co-ordination meeting six weeks after the tsunami to stress the need to jointly investigate material availability and alternative designs that in combination would generate the highest number of shelters in the shortest possible timeframe, and secondly, to suggest that we explore opportunities for joint importing of materials. There were three responses. Some NGOs interpreted this to mean "there is no point in starting with shelters since there are no materials available anyway." To my surprise, this sentiment was still voiced by some NGOs six weeks later, by which time substantial new stocks had been imported by wholesalers. A few others decided that it would indeed be good to share information to do a joint gap analysis. Over the course of a month, about six agencies hesitatingly shared information on their material requirements with each other, and then the initiative fizzled out due to lack of interest. The other agencies all maintained a stony silence on what they could deliver, but kept making huge and unrealistic pledges to the government and the media. The initial co-operation that existed on the ground during the first two weeks after the tsunami had given way to blatant competition and secrecy, even though this ultimately meant that everybody's work was delayed.

Apart from local competition over territories, there was also some competition about "who was the biggest" in the shelter sector. Thus, when the Government Agent of Trincomalee called a meeting to match shelter requirements and pledges by agencies, he received pledges for 22,000 shelters although only about 8,000 were needed. It took several months to adjust the pledges to more realistic assessments of need and actual capacity of the individual agencies. In Ampara District, interactions were even more competitive. There, a few agencies were in the process of putting up more than 2,000 shelters each. In the beginning, the numbers of shelters pledged were way below what was required, and every time a new shelter agency moved into Ampara District, the other agencies narrowed their project areas and allocated a project area for the new agency. One NGO had put up about 1,000 shelters in one DS Division, and then decided to concentrate on another area, and to give this area over to two large agencies with big reputations that had spare implementation capacity. In order to prevent duplication, copies of the beneficiary lists were given to both agencies. However, both of the other agencies seemed intent on distributing larger numbers than the NGO that had vacated the area, and rather than selecting those families who had not yet received a shelter, one NGO deliberately distributed 800 shelters to families who had already received a shelter, and the other NGO distributed 100 shelters to families who had already received one and sometimes two shelters. The second NGO stopped its work after being informed that duplication was happening, but the first NGO did not (private conversation, NGO staff, Ampara). In the process, nearly a million dollars was wasted.

In the shelter sector, as probably in all sectors, standards were set and continuously debated. However, things were not as straightforward as Stirrat portrays them when he suggests that "well-meaning amateurs" outflanked "the relatively slow dinosaurs of the relief world by undercutting standards" (Stirrat 2006: 14). Stirrat's statement suggests that the big and experienced NGOs and UN agencies did stick to the standards that had been developed over time. In my view, something entirely different happened.

A little over a week after the tsunami, the first suggestions for Sri Lanka-specific shelter standards were drafted by an NGO and shared with other agencies. The draft was rejected by the government and by UNHCR, which assisted the government with co-ordination of the shelter sector. A week later, UNHCR flew in its own expert who almost literally copied the proposed concept with addition of a few details, took the credit (BBC 2005b) and started pushing for agreement among agencies on these standards. There were standards on material quality, shelter size, spacing, safety, site planning, and cost. All of this made sense, but the cost issue proved to be contentious. Before the tsunami hit, donors had capped the amount that NGOs could spend on a shelter for returning refugees at around US $150–200. In order to prevent too much discrepancy with war-affected people, it was decided that the absolute maximum price of a shelter should be US $300. The initial tsunami designs were basically upgraded versions of shelters that were already being built. As demand for materials soared, prices increased, and it was decided to increase the maximum cost per shelter to US $500. Also, some of the other standards were adjusted. It remained possible to put up a decent shelter within this budget right up until the end of 2005, when the last of the shelters were completed. By April 2005 however, disagreement developed among the shelter agencies. Some agencies had already put up hundreds of shelters meeting the original standards, and they were now forced to upgrade their shelters to the newer standards. Other agencies, which had promised large numbers of shelters but were unable to obtain materials, started talking about how beneficiaries should be more involved in a truly participatory design exercise, accusing the agencies that had managed to put up shelters of a top-down approach. The fact that the designs of the shelters that were being put up in the East had been developed over several years in continuous consultation with beneficiaries undermines this argument. In my opinion, standards degenerated into a strategic discourse.[14] To top it all off, some of the slowest agencies worked out designs that were much larger and more luxurious than the standards, and which cost twice the agreed maximum unit cost. When these shelters started coming up, this created problems for agencies that had already started construction with smaller budgets, because over time beneficiaries started increasing their demands.[15]

In order to catch up in the construction race, one of the slower NGOs with a large budget ignored an agreement that had been reached not to inflate laborers' wages too much in order to prevent problems for the laborers after the construction boom ended. This NGO doubled the wages it offered, which triggered a huge inflation in wages, cost overruns for other NGOs, and a paddy harvesting labor shortage in some areas. In response to the last issue, farmers increasingly resorted to the use of combine harvesters; after the construction boom was over, many labourers found themselves permanently out of work. The debate over standards continued for months, defeating the primary purpose of providing transitional shelter as quickly as possible, so that the NGOs involved could proceed with the construction of permanent houses.

The same inflation of standards, and the same debate on stakeholder participation in the design phase, took place with regard to permanent housing. Once again, the question could be asked – Did some agencies spend too much time talking about these things instead of getting to work? However, delays caused by the debates on standards and participation paled in comparison to those caused by other factors. For example, it took the Sri Lankan government a year to develop its housing policy and to finalize the delineation of the coastal buffer zone inside which construction would be banned (see McGilvray and Lawrence, this volume). Since in many areas there was very little land available, large-scale housing construction started late.

In a sense, this nicely dovetailed with the fact that transitional shelter construction took much more time than foreseen. In any case, there was simply not enough sand and other construction materials, and there was a huge shortage of skilled labor. On top of that, the North and East of Sri Lanka were severely affected by resurging conflict from late 2005 onwards. The fact that three years after the tsunami the vast majority of required houses were finally completed remains a major feat. It would have been very difficult to do things faster, but things could well have been done with less hassle and a lot less money.

Prior experience of expatriates

One of the questions that popped up very regularly in conversations with shelter experts of NGOs was "where are all the experienced people?" It was true that a number of highly experienced people came to Sri Lanka after the tsunami, but the majority of foreign aid workers had either very limited experience in the humanitarian field or none whatsoever, and this contributed to the frequent re-inventing of various humanitarian wheels.[16] In that sense, the tsunami was indeed different from other disasters. Not only were there many people who came on their own to implement private initiatives; the NGOs that came to Sri Lanka also needed staff, and many ended up with no other option than to hire whomever was available.

Together with the inexperienced expatriates, many experienced expatriates lacked knowledge of Sri Lanka, its political context, and its cultures. In combination with the sometimes limited English language capacities of Sri Lankan (and foreign) NGO staff and government officials, this led to the development of fairly isolated "in-groups" of expatriates, sharing experiences with each other but sharing little with others. Within such groups, anyone who had been in Sri Lanka even a little longer than the others quickly rose to the status of expert. As someone summarized six months after the tsunami, "In disaster situations, you are knowledgeable if you have flown over the place, an expert if you have landed at the airport, and irreplaceable if you have actually been to the disaster area" (private conversation, Hilversum, the Netherlands, June 2005). Importantly, you do not need to actually know anything to become an expert. Recent geographical proximity and storytelling skills will suffice.

The problem of quite a few experienced expatriates was that they were perhaps too experienced. I came across reunions of people who had met in Iraq (2003–2004), Afghanistan (2002–2003), Liberia (2002–2003), Kosovo (1998), and Rwanda (1994). I even came across a few people who had met each other while working at the Thai border in the late 1970s. In most of these places, they had worked in a context of failed and dysfunctional states, where there is little point in taking the government seriously. Sri Lanka may be viewed by some as a politically failed state (Fund for Peace 2009), but it does have a functioning bureaucracy. This lack of respect for the state and for government bureaucrats at times strained relationships between government officials and NGOs.

Language

In combination with low expatriate expectations of the Sri Lankan state, the language barrier between expatriates and Sri Lankans led many expatriates to treat local government officers and Sri Lankan NGO staff as incapable. Although there definitely was some incompetence around (just as there were incompetent expatriates), many competent people were relegated to the sidelines. About a month after the tsunami, my wife joined an assessment mission in Galle District as a freelance consultant. When she came home, she told me about one of the Divisional Secretaries whom she had met, who had genuinely impressed her with his knowledge, approach, and vision. However, when she attended a district-wide coordination meeting, she heard many expatriates complain about the man, simply because he could not speak English. In the same district, one of the biggest Sri Lankan NGOs was put in charge of NGO co-ordination. However, as the senior staff in Galle had difficulties with English, and as the expatriates did not bother to arrange for proper translators, the expatriates basically worked the NGO out of the co-ordination role and did the work by themselves. I would consider this arrogance, but expatriates whom I spoke to from the district were convinced that they were doing a brilliant job and that the local NGO was at fault.

The arrogance of leisure

In March 2005, I walked to the beach in one of the worst affected areas in the town of Kalmunai, where I found groups of men staring at the horizon. They had heard that another tsunami was going to come the next day and wanted to see the sea one more time before they died. There had been radio broadcasts warning people to be a bit careful around the full-moon day that was coming up. Tides are stronger around full-moon days, and there could be some flooding here and there as the shore topography had changed after the tsunami.[17] As I walked along the beach after having tried to allay the men's fears, I saw two foreign women in their bikinis, taking a swim next to the destruction. In Batticaloa, expats also started swimming in the sea fairly soon after the tsunami. There, the few people who were still living near the beach asked them to move to an isolated stretch of beach because they found the behavior insulting to the memory of their loved ones.

While in the Trincomalee area during 2006, I received an invitation to an NGO party. As I had not visited the town for a while and I wanted to catch up with some of the longer-term expats, I decided to go with a colleague. During this time, an unofficial dusk-till-dawn curfew was in place. With violence escalating, many residents of Trincomalee lived in fear. Because the party was very close to my colleague's house in a calm part of town, we considered it safe to go. The party was held on the rooftop of a four-story building set up by a contractor who had made a lot of money after the tsunami, and it was now rented out at exorbitant rates to a group of expatriates. Music was blaring from huge loudspeakers, so that the entire neighborhood could enjoy our fun. When the song "I will survive" was blasted over the terrified town, my colleague and I left in disgust. A friend in another town told me of an expat party where people were invited to come dressed in mosquito nets: "wear nothing underneath, and the drinks are free." This e-mail had been sent around on a mailing list that included many Sri Lankan NGO staff.

Everybody needs to relax sometimes, particularly if he or she works hard. At the risk of generalizing, I would suggest that the problem here is that many Sri Lankans and expatriates have distinctly different ways of passing their leisure time. In my experience, most Sri Lankans tend to fill their leisure time chatting with friends and relatives, playing or watching cricket, watching TV, and – for men – drinking. In contrast, expatriates tend to go to the beach, go for runs, and organize parties (at which alcohol often flows freely). Both groups have legitimate ways of relaxing, but they generally do not appreciate each other's styles. Cricket, unintelligible television serials, and endless chatting are boring to expatriates, while swims and runs (in often rather skimpy outfits) and expat-style parties are considered uncivilized and indecent by many Sri Lankans.

It was not entirely surprising that in 2006 rumors started circulating about expats organizing orgies with their local female staff, and making pornographic movies about it. These rumors were strengthened when porn VCDs, with obvious NGO logos on them, appeared on the market in Ampara. I am fairly confident that the rumors were false and that the CDs were existing porn movies that someone had decorated with an NGO logo, but the way the rumors gained ground shows that the idea of expatriates having sex with their employees and filming the event seemed entirely plausible in the popular imagination. Although everybody has a right to leisure time, the expats should have been more sensitive in how and where they enjoyed themselves. Culturally inappropriate practices reinforced local people's perceptions of expats as arrogant, rude, and insensitive.

Conclusion

The response to the tsunami was exceptional for the unprecedented amounts of money that became available, facilitated by the fact that it happened right in front of the world's television-watching population during the Christmas season, and – if the observer is more cynical – by the fact that so many Western tourists were caught up in it in front of the cameras. It was also unprecedented for the speed with which the rehabilitation and reconstruction work was implemented. For all the talk about avoidable delays on the part of aid agencies and the Sri Lankan government, there have been few disasters in which nearly the entire affected population found themselves in transitional shelters and with assistance to re-start their destroyed livelihoods within a year, and in which the vast majority found themselves back in permanent housing within three years. At the official third-year remembrance of the tsunami, the tsunami was rightly declared "old news."

My point is not to ignore what has been achieved. I am however of the opinion that the same amount of work could probably have been done with a third of the expatriates, half of the NGOs, and half the money. In this article, I have tried to highlight issues that in my opinion deserve more attention: a remarkable emergency response in areas where disaster response capacity and coordination was already there, the strains that NGOs came under when humanitarian aid became mixed with struggles for reputations, and a number of inherent problems that arise when insufficient attention is paid to the role of expatriates in the dynamics of delivering humanitarian assistance.

Notes

1   I use fictitious acronyms for all NGOs that I refer to in this paper. In late 2004, some 15 to 20 international humanitarian agencies were present in Batticaloa, mostly involved in post-conflict rehabilitation and community development.

2   Unfortunately, even the time at which the tsunami is remembered (9.25 a.m. on 26 December 2004) has become politicized. 9.25 a.m. was the time the tsunami hit Hambantota, the president's home district; the clocks in Batticaloa and Ampara stopped ticking 20 minutes earlier.

3   At the time, most of the international NGOs and UN agencies in the conflict areas of Sri Lanka had some sort of emergency response capability, and specific staff members who were designated to lead any emergency response should the need arise.

4   I had heard of the tsunami that struck Papua New Guinea in 2000, and at the time I wondered what a tsunami would look like. Little did I realise that Sri Lanka might one day be hit by a tsunami as well.

5   Exactly a week after the tsunami, I realized that I had been wrong when, at sunset, I was talking with a colleague of mine. Staring gloomily into the disappearing sun, he told me that at sunset on the day of the tsunami the last people were still dying, suspended in mid-air on barbed wire fences. But with that it really was over.

6   For almost a week, we all worked 20 hours a day; the second week, working days were reduced to 16 hours, and after about three months people were down to 12 hours a day, six days a week. On the day of the tsunami, my wife and a colleague of hers worked non-stop for 42 hours before they had their first sleep.

7   "Carving out territories" (Stirrat 2006: 13; Hilhorst and Fernando 2006) in order to keep other agencies out, rather than to ensure an optimum spread of the response, became an issue only after the second or third week following the tsunami.

8   In September 2001, when there were very strong rumours of an impending LTTE attack on Batticaloa (which never materialized), the agencies present worked out a contingency plan for a scenario in which 100,000 people would be displaced in and around the town.

9   I myself had been involved in five such emergency responses between October 2000 and the tsunami, and observed a sixth. With one exception, all of these involved relatively intense inter-agency coordination. Four of the six involved joint interventions.

10   The absence of epidemics after the tsunami became a major source of self-congratulation among humanitarian agencies, and is regularly mentioned as proof that the humanitarian response was successful (see Nursey 2005 for an example). Rony Brauman, ex-chairman of MSF, has however made the point that epidemics rarely happen after natural disasters (Politique Autrement 2005), and the fears of epidemics that are raised after many disasters are unrealistic.

11   Unfortunately, there were serious delays in the issuing of ration cards, which meant that some of those who were affected were unable to access government assistance for quite some time despite having been duly registered.

12   Interestingly, most people whom I came across did not seem to take any photographs of themselves distributing the items. The only exception was an obviously very wealthy couple who were handing out milk packets in a camp to mothers who had been summarily ordered to line up, while getting themselves filmed by their teenage son.

13   This kind of public response was not a new phenomenon: after flash floods displaced

600,000 people in the south of Sri Lanka in May 2003, similar traffic jams could be observed for over a week.

14 See Nursey 2005 for an assessment of standards that is much more positive than I would consider warranted.

15 By contrast, in Tamil Nadu only one relatively simple design was used. The shelters were put up within a few months (also helped by the much larger volume of the Indian wholesale market), and a time-consuming and frustrating debate over designs never erupted among both beneficiaries and agencies (interview, Kanniyakumari, India, October 2006).

16 I very strongly disagree on this point with Caroline Nursey's statement that the tsunami was a "showcase response" (Nursey 2005:2). In her article, she first gives a hypothetical scenario of what might have happened: "there is a mad scramble to reach the scene … supplies get stuck in customs and a staffing shortage means that some very inexperienced staff are on the ground" (note the subtext here that staff at organization headquarters *were* capable!) "… there are media scandals," aid gets siphoned off by armed forces, a "sex exploitation scandal surfaces." Nursey then claims that this scenario fortunately did not happen, which is actually quite a bizarre claim to make. Every single element of Nursey's doom scenario did become reality in Sri Lanka in some form or other.

17 There actually was a big earthquake near Nias a few days later, and for a while there was a genuine concern that a tsunami might have developed. It caused a huge panic.

7 Principles ignored and lessons unlearned

A disaster studies perspective on the tsunami experience in Sri Lanka

Georg Frerks

Introduction

Disasters often function as a magnifying glass, mercilessly revealing societal ills and weaknesses. In this chapter I discuss the tsunami experience in Sri Lanka by reflecting on it from the perspective of Disaster Studies. Disaster Studies is a multi-disciplinary thematic field of inquiry that tries to explain why and how disasters occur, and how societies deal with them. I shall consider some major recent academic insights and policy trends in Disaster Studies and indicate to what degree they have been relevant to, and were applied in the aftermath of, the tsunami in Sri Lanka. I base my discussion mainly on the contributions made by the social sciences to Disaster Studies, by what sometimes has been called the "anthropology of disaster." I personally believe that a social science perspective has much to offer and indeed can add something valuable to the perhaps all-too-technocratic and top-down approach that characterized disaster studies earlier, when the field was typically referred to as "disaster management." Though my discussion will be mainly based on secondary sources, I shall use illustrations from empirical fieldwork done after the tsunami in Sri Lanka to underline the issues raised (see: Frerks 2008; Frerks and Klem 2005a, 2005b, 2005c and 2006).

Disaster studies

Disaster Studies comprises an inherently complex field of endeavor. It encompasses the hard sciences (seismology, geology, climatology and hydrology) and medicine, but also the social sciences (sociology, economics, anthropology, political science), and a range of applied sciences such as architecture, communication, management and logistics. Whereas in the past technical and engineering sciences dominated the field, since the *International Decade for Natural Disaster Reduction* (United Nations 1999) more emphasis has been put on a people-centered approach providing a boost to social science contributions. Nevertheless, it remains a challenge to muster the different relevant insights from the wide range of relevant disciplinary fields and to bring them systematically together into a coherent and well-balanced approach both conceptually and in terms of applied policy practice. The different paradigms, methodological approaches, concepts, and disciplinary "languages" complicate proper cross-disciplinary communication, let alone a coherent approach in practice. Cardona (2004) identifies in this connection different discourses about vulnerability, risk, and disaster among the natural, applied, and social sciences. Hilhorst (2004) argues that different groups of actors perceive, understand, and deal with disaster in fundamentally different ways. She discerns several domains of disaster response (science and disaster management, government, and local population) and asserts that these responses often contradict or negate each other. On the other hand, one can also clearly distinguish some emerging paradigmatic trends and policy developments in recent years that tend to inform studies of disaster and bring about a certain level of consensus. This has been stimulated by critical reviews of the field as a consequence of the *IDNDR*, the *International Strategy for Disaster Reduction* (ISDR) as well as the First and Second *World Conferences on Disaster Reduction* in 1994 and 2005 and the associated "*Yokohama Strategy and Plan of Action for a Safer World*" and the "*Hyogo Declaration and Framework for Action*" respectively (United Nations 1999; UNISDR 2005 and 2006). Impetus for rethinking the field also came from criticisms and evaluations of disaster response during large-scale disasters such as the Indian Ocean Tsunami (Telford, Cosgrave and Houghton 2006) and Hurricane Katrina (US House of Representatives 2006).

Trends and developments in disaster studies and their relevance to Sri Lanka

Below I outline four major (clusters of) issues that have emerged in current debates within the field of Disaster Studies: (i.) complexity and conflict-sensitivity; (ii.) vulnerability, capacity, and resilience; (iii.) perceptions and discourses; and (iv.) political culture, governance, and patronage. For each of these clusters I shall give an explanation of the issues and then relate them specifically to the post-tsunami situation in Sri Lanka.

i. Complexity and conflict-sensitivity

It has been increasingly recognized that disasters are complex and multi-causal. Many so-called 'natural' disasters are in fact due to weak natural resource management or failing government policies. As argued by Nobel Laureate Amartya Sen (1981), famines can be better explained with reference to government policy and all sorts of economic data than by decline of precipitation or food availability *per se*. Similarly, floods and earth-slides have to do with deforestation on hill slopes by farmers pushed upstream by mono-cropping agriculture carried out by multinational corporations, or are caused by the outright plunder of the rainforest by commercial interests or warlords. The disasters following Hurricane Mitch have been attributed to a push of marginal settlements into high-risk areas by uncontrolled urban sprawl and speculative land markets as well as the expansion of the agricultural frontier (Grunewald, *et al.* 2000). Summing up the debate, the author Alexander (1997: 289) asserts: "[I]t is now widely recognized that 'natural disaster' is a convenience term that amounts to a misnomer. Neither disasters nor the conditions that give rise to them are undeniably natural."

Oliver-Smith (2004: 24) discusses the relationship between disaster, environment, and society and posits the mutuality between the material and social worlds. He raises the question of how to theorize the linkage between the cultural construction of nature, the social production of disaster, conditions of vulnerability, and disaster impact. He states that:

> Today many local problems, including disasters, may have their root causes and triggering agents, and possibly their solutions on the other side of the globe. Through this globalization process problems have become basically non-linear in causation and discontinuous in both space and time, rendering them inherently unpredictable and substantially less amenable to traditional methods of change and adaptation.

Another aspect of this dynamism is the historical construction of disaster, as Hilhorst and Bankoff (2004: 4) remind us:

> Asking why disasters happen is a political question, but understanding how they occur is a social and historical one. Above all, it is the present condition (the outcome of past factors) that transforms a hazard into a calamity and determines whether people have the resilience to withstand its effects or are rendered vulnerable to their consequences.

The tsunami disasters in Aceh and Sri Lanka added another layer of complexity to the above mentioned issues, namely that of violent conflict. Scholars debated whether a disaster of such magnitude would further peace, as it supposedly did in Aceh, or whether it would intensify the conflict, which apparently was the case in Sri Lanka. It is only recently that the overlap of so-called "natural disasters" and conflicts has become a subject of serious analysis. Spiegel, *et al.* (2007) and van Oijen (2009) have looked at the occurrence and overlap of natural disasters and complex political emergencies and found that this was indeed the case in a large number of situations. Discussing the period 1995–2004, Spiegel, *et al.* found that over 27 percent of the largest natural disasters took place in areas with at least one conflict, while 87 percent of the largest complex political emergencies had to deal with at least one natural hazard. Van Oijen has compared several different lists and indexes for the period 2000–2008 and concludes that in about half of the conflict countries, natural disasters occur regularly. This figure rises to 75 percent for the countries having a major armed conflict. An ongoing conflict clearly hampers the provision of aid in many ways, and aid organizations have to work and relate to local parties in a different "conflict sensitive" manner. One major issue that requires special attention in such a situation is the interaction with military actors. Aid providers are deeply divided on whether and how to relate to military actors in conditions of violent armed conflict, as current debates on civil-military cooperation show (Frerks, *et al.* 2006).

It is, on the one hand, to be considered progress that a more sophisticated, multidisciplinary, and dynamic approach to disaster is emerging with different interrelated levels of analysis that are linked to natural, environmental, social, cultural, institutional, and conflict factors. However, the resulting complexity in what Fordham (2004: 178) has called a "messy reality" clearly provides challenges to policymakers and practitioners. Simple disaster typologies have been rendered out of date, while the notion of complexity *per se* is difficult to grasp and may yield major problems when trying to design operational approaches for policy practice. Moreover, the response in the aftermath of the tsunami has shown that even well intended aid may add considerably to the complexity and messiness of the situation, and make it close to unmanageable. Histories of conflict and ongoing armed violence can only compound such problems.

Sri Lankan situation

This general notion of complexity also applies to the situation prior to, during, and after the tsunami in Sri Lanka. In later sections I shall deal with the pre-disaster construction of group and gender-specific vulnerabilities to disaster and highlight the context of regional development and inequity in Sri Lanka, and the prevailing cultural patterns in society. I shall also discuss the pervasive effects of the existing patronage-based, or what Max Weber (1947: Chap. IV) would call "patrimonial," governance regime on aid to tsunami victims. With regard to the discussion on complexity, I will limit myself in this section to the impact of the conflict in Sri Lanka on the disaster and *vice versa*.

As a consequence of over 20 years of civil war, over 80,000 people died and more than 800,000 were displaced, while countless faced loss and destruction of possessions and livelihoods. Many households were displaced more than once. Before the tsunami hit, there were 390,000 conflict-related internally displaced persons in Sri Lanka according to figures by the United Nations High Commissioner for Refugees (UNHCR n.d.). Thousands of them lived in camps that were situated directly along the coast where they easily fell victim to the tsunami waves[1]. Apart from the category of displaced persons, war-affected areas in general proved to be particularly sensitive to the impact of the tsunami. The war had made these populations extremely vulnerable in economic and social terms, while they also often lacked the space and opportunities to develop or maintain coping capacities to avert crisis. The resulting lack of resilience not only reduced their chance of survival, but also affected the likelihood of their successfully overcoming the impact of the tsunami.

A second major consequence of the war was its effect on the delivery of aid. Keenan, Gamburd, and the editors' introduction in this volume have already pointed out some of the issues involved, especially the failure by the government and the Liberation Tigers of Tamil Eelam (LTTE) to design a joint aid management mechanism (Post-Tsunami Operational Management Structure or P-TOMS). Prior to the tsunami, during periods of fighting and the cease-fire agreement alike, development aid had already become involved in the conflict dynamics and, moreover, was used as an instrument for peace-making and peace-building by the donor community, though with limited success (Frerks and Klem 2006). In the process, aid was securitized and became itself a subject of struggle. Hence, it did not come as a surprise that the tsunami aid also became entangled in the political and conflict dynamics at play in Sri Lanka, further compounded by the patron-client functioning of the state, as I shall elaborate further below. The political legitimacy and credibility of both parties depended at least in part on how they managed the humanitarian disaster and this also affected the competing "state projects" of the government and the LTTE. Would the LTTE care for "its subjects" adequately or rather use the tsunami aid for military purposes? Did the involvement of the rebel movement as a partner in aid not inadvertently amount to political recognition of their position and viewpoints? Was the government able and willing to deliver aid "independently" according to humanitarian principles, or would it favor its own Sinhalese constituencies to the disadvantage of minority groups in the island, as was argued by its opponents? It soon became clear that the initial "fraternizing" effect of the tsunami between different ethnic and religious groups and even, to some extent, the conflict parties was to be short-lived. As shown in this volume, they failed to reach a meaningful joint system of aid management and delivery. The negotiations, delays, and juridical arguments about it only served to further antagonize and divide the parties, and effectively contributed to the end of the ceasefire and of whatever chances still remained for a political agreement.

Apart from the political impact of the conflict on tsunami aid and vice versa, the conflict also confounded the possibility for civil-military cooperation in dealing with the catastrophe. Domestic and international military units are usually asked to help out when major disasters surpass the capacity of local civilian authorities. However, the ongoing low-level violence, the geographical division between government and LTTE-controlled areas, mutual suspicions, road blocks, check points, and other limitations on mobility all made the role of the military heavily contested and impeded its effectiveness. As the tsunami-affected regions straddled areas under military control of both protagonist parties, any military aid operation was bound to create suspicion, whether it was construed to be the infiltration of more troops or cadres, the gathering of sensitive intelligence, or the attempt to win over the sympathy of the people (Frerks 2008). The relationship between the two major national military actors in the disaster response was of course already heavily influenced by their politico-military struggle, and the control over and distribution of aid became quickly securitized in this larger framework. Similarly, the prior reputation of the military forces, depending on whether they were seen as "heroes" or "occupying" or "oppressing" forces, also determined the way they were perceived in the aid operation by the local population and their intermediaries. Foreign military personnel also ran the risk of becoming associated with one of the conflict parties. The LTTE was, for example, suspicious of Indian and US troops, as they were believed to collaborate with the Sri Lankan government (Frerks 2008).

In summary, it can be argued that aid in times of conflict has to be delivered in a conflict-sensitive manner to avoid strengthening existing conflict dynamics, and to promote incentives for peace. It thus should take into consideration how conflict affects the vulnerabilities and resilience of the population. Aid itself runs a serious risk of becoming politicized and militarized, and therefore aid organizations and aid workers must seriously reflect on their "positionality" under circumstances of war, in addition to seeking to implement humanitarian principles.

ii. Vulnerability, capacity and resilience

In an overview article about the state of Disaster Studies on the occasion of the twentieth anniversary of the Journal *Disasters* in 1997, David Alexander asserted that the emergence of the notion of vulnerability was one of the most salient achievements in the field of disaster studies over the last decades. The risk of being exposed to disaster had become recognized as a product of hazard and vulnerability that, in turn, was actively created by such factors as bad governance, bad development practice, and political and military destabilization. This emphasis on vulnerability was associated with a shift from seeing disaster as an event caused by an external agent to a more sociologically-oriented interpretation of disaster as a complex, socially (as well as politically, environmentally and economically) constructed process. Wisner, *et al.* (2004: 11) define vulnerability as:

> the characteristics of a person or group and their situation that influence their capacity to anticipate, cope with, resist and recover from the impact of a natural hazard (an extreme natural event or process). It involves a combination of factors that determine the degree to which someone's life, livelihood, property and other assets are put at risk by a discrete and identifiable event in nature and in society.

This "new" understanding of disaster also called into question earlier, ill-conceived ideas of "normality" and "abnormality" that pervaded much thinking about disaster. Disaster was often seen as an abnormality or an aberration from a linear path of progress rather than a chronic condition as much caused by development as impinging on it. Wisner, *et al.* (2004: 20) therefore argue that the phenomenon of disaster should be placed in the mainstream of policy and practice. Lavell (2004: 72) shows that in the Lower Lempa River Valley Project in El Salvador "disaster risk" became combined with "lifestyle" or "everyday" risk: "The sum of their permanent living conditions signify that the poor or destitute live under permanent conditions of disaster." An important policy implication is the emphasis put on reducing everyday risk and vulnerability as a significant contribution to disaster risk reduction. "Vulnerability to disasters and life style vulnerability are part of the same package and must be tackled together in the search to reduce overall human insecurity or risk" (Lavell 2004: 72). Heijmans (2004: 120) also notes that the difference between normal and extreme events has become negligible, as both may be turned into disasters as a consequence of the conditions under which people live.

The great advantage of the idea of vulnerability is that it more easily facilitates policy intervention. Whereas it is difficult or even nearly impossible in many cases to reduce risk by influencing the underlying hazard, vulnerability as the result of socio-economic and political processes is more conducive to policy action. This also applies to its opposite, namely the element of capacity engendered in individuals, groups, and local communities to cope with crisis.

The concept of capacity mediates the relative weight of people's vulnerability, taking into account their knowledge, skills, and organizing capabilities to cope with disaster. The thinking on the role of local capacities and people's coping mechanisms has been influenced by sociological debates on actor-orientation and the role of agency. Actor-orientation is a constructivist perspective focusing on the making and remaking of society through the self-transforming actions and perceptions of a diverse and interlocked world of actors (Long 2001). Actor-oriented approaches form a counter-balance to approaches that basically see human behavior as externally determined by a person's place and role in the social system or by the values and norms that rule society. Long (2001: 16) says:

> The notion of agency attributes to the individual actor the capacity to process social experience and to devise ways of coping with life, even under the most extreme forms of coercion. Within the limits of information, uncertainty and other constraints (e.g. physical, normative or politico-economic) that exist, social actors possess 'knowledgeability' and 'capability'. They attempt to solve problems, learn how to intervene in the flow of events around them, … taking note of the various contingent circumstances.

In the disaster literature, agency is recognized in the growing emphasis on people's capacity and the local coping mechanisms that people employ to face and survive disasters. It tries to move disaster practice away from what has been called the "victimization discourse."

Vulnerabilities and capacities together give a good indication why and to what degree people are at risk. Several practical tools have been developed in order to assess people's vulnerabilities and capacities. Early examples include the matrix developed by Anderson and Woodrow (1989) distinguishing between physical/ material, social/organizational, and motivational/attitudinal capacities. Their matrix can be further specified for gender, different socio-economic groups, and various levels of society, and can also be applied diachronically. In addition, the IFRC developed an early guide to Vulnerability and Capacity Assessment (IFRC 1993). Since then there has been a constant production of more general as well as more specific guides, tools, and manuals in this field. Cannon, Twigg, and Rowell (2005) have made an inventory of over fifty instruments to deal with vulnerability and capacity aspects.

Reflecting the above mentioned discussions, the *Hyogo Declaration and Framework for Action* adopted during the second World Conference on Disaster Reduction called for the integration of disaster reduction measures into the overall development policy, planning, and programming with special attention to disaster prevention, mitigation, and preparedness (DPMP) as well as structural vulnerability reduction. It also asked for attention to be paid to institutions, mechanisms, and capacities at all levels, but especially at the community level, to increase disaster resilience. Finally, it argued that disaster reduction should become an integral part of reconstruction programs focused on the affected communities (UNISDR 2005).

Sri Lankan situation

Even though many people consider the tsunami to be a prototypical example of a destructive natural force that hits all people equally, pre-existing patterns of economic and social exclusion and inequality did, to a large extent, contribute to who fell victim to it and who did not. This fact has already been pointed out by Gamburd and McGilvray, and Kuhn, in this volume. At a macro-level of analysis, the most affected districts in the south and the east represented 26 percent of the island's population, but generated only 17.5 percent of the Gross Domestic Product (GDP). They were on average relatively poor (World Bank 2005, Annex III: 1). It is also documented that within this larger framework the poorest sections of the population were hit especially hard, such as poor fishermen's families living in low-lying areas along the sea or lagoons, or illegal squatters along the railway line. These settlements generally lacked proper spatial planning or local infrastructure, while government regulations had not been observed in what often had been a spontaneous, organic process of growth on the margins of legality. The World Health Organization's (WHO) Situation Report of 14 February 2005 stated that 80 percent of the affected households lived on less than one dollar per day/person before the tsunami struck and that 30 percent of the affected population was living well below the official Sri Lankan poverty line (WHO 2005). Due to many years of war and lack of investment, this proportion no doubt was much higher in the north of the island, but hard data to confirm this are not available.

Another aspect is the bias in terms of gender. Due to deeply embedded and gendered cultural norms, attitudes, and behaviors, women were disproportionately more affected by the catastrophe than men. Fordham (2004) drives home the need to better recognize the gendered nature of vulnerability and the dominant masculine culture manifested in disaster management and humanitarian practice. In this connection, Fordham signals the importance of "gender-fair" approaches in disaster analysis and management. The highly gendered impact of disaster calls for a rethinking of existing practices in the field of DPMP that will have to be recast in a more gender-sensitive way. The gendered impact of the tsunami has already been discussed extensively in this volume, and in a separate study by De Mel and Ruwanpura (2006). For example, McGilvray and Lawrence have pointed out the prevalence of matrilineal patterns of inheritance and settlement on the east coast of Sri Lanka that were ignored by aid providers, but gradually re-established by the actors themselves.

Referring to the Hyogo Declaration mentioned above, it is doubtful whether, apart from the controversial post-tsunami buffer zones, a more structural vulnerability and disaster risk reduction approach has been applied in Sri Lanka during the reconstruction phase. At the time the tsunami hit, the country did not have either a disaster policy, an institutional framework, or a National Disaster Management

Plan, despite having experienced different types of natural disasters in the past. Jayawardane (2008: 18) sums up the situation:

> Although the need for a long term disaster risk management plan was identified after each disaster, the idea soon died with the recovery from such localized disasters. The normal practice was to provide disaster relief by different line ministries with a reactive or relief focus rather than a proactive or risk mitigation and management focus except a few initiatives.

The *Sri Lanka Disaster Management Act* was only enacted after the tsunami in May 2005, followed by a *Road Map* in December 2005. A holistic National Disaster Management Plan is under preparation currently (Jayawardena 2008). Hence, it will not come as a surprise that there has been little evidence of the integration of disaster risk reduction in post-tsunami reconstruction or of the use of community-based approaches and popular participation in reconstruction-related decision-making, as asked for in the *Hyogo Declaration*.

Frerks and Klem (2005c) indicate that in the aftermath of the tsunami many people were in fact completely unaware of the Sri Lankan government policies with regard to both food entitlements and resettlement. This was caused by a lack of communication and information. It led to tensions at the local level, including within temporary housing camps. In Batticaloa the UNICEF office had tried to convince the District Secretary to put out an information bulletin that made clear what the rules and procedures were in order to reduce the confusion. However, this had not been easy because the central government had been slow, indecisive, and deficient in its communication. In this situation, district-level authorities were afraid to put their commitments in writing. After much pressurizing, one bulletin had been issued, and a second one was only under preparation more than six weeks after the disaster hit the Sri Lankan shores. A *kachcheri* official interviewed on 15 February 2005 in Batticaloa stated: "The planning process is completely top-down. There is no consultation with the people or with local groups. This is the nature of the government bureaucratic process." One aid co-ordinator said:

> Information from Colombo doesn't reach the people. Information is an asset that many people don't have. Government servants and LTTE officials don't tell people the truth. This is also a cultural thing. Knowledge yields a kind of power people are not always willing to share. It allows for manipulation. (Frerks and Klem 2005c: 25)

The government's plans for reconstruction and relocation of people were particularly prone to criticism, as they totally ignored local knowledge and were, on top of that, often megalomaniacal, unrealistic, unfeasible, or unsustainable. A local aid worker from an Islamic organization interviewed on 12 February 2005 in the Kalmunai displaced persons' camp astutely observed that all tsunami relief aid was in effect controlled by people who were *not* affected by the tsunami at all. In Batticaloa, civil society members issued a "Call for adherence to established guidelines on provision of humanitarian assistance in post-disaster situations: Statement of concern by civil society members in response to recent post-tsunami development activities in the Batticaloa District," saying that:

> In Batticaloa, we have been extremely concerned that there has been inadequate consultation with community groups, let alone local practitioners and civil society activists. Decisions about large-scale projects affecting the lives of thousands of families are being taken hastily by locally-based officials of international agencies ... in collaboration with district-level representatives of the Sri Lanka government. This has been most alarming in relation to the decisions being made about temporary resettlement of displaced people. A sense of urgency has been created around this issue by the officials of international organisations, and decisions about location and types of shelters are being made without any consultation with the communities themselves. It has been terrible to witness these decisions being implemented, with the displaced people being loaded into trucks to new locations with neither adequate prior information nor any influence in determining where they might wish to be sheltered. The absence of clear and accurate information through reliable channels has created much uncertainty and worry for the displaced people. (reported in Frerks and Klem 2005c: 26)

iii. Perceptions and discourses

Another significant trend in current Disaster Studies is to look at local disaster realities as formed or "constructed" in the everyday life experiences of those affected by them or responding to them. In order to elicit these disaster perceptions and narratives, ethnographic approaches have been applied increasingly to the study of disaster. The notion of discourse is helpful here, as it can convey how reality is socially constructed and deconstructed through discursive practice, and also how particular discourses are shaped in turn by power relations. Discourse refers to the social production of knowledge and meaning, to the ordering of reality, and to how topics are talked about and practices conducted. It frames how we understand and act upon the world around us. Hence, discourse is fundamentally constitutive of social practice. This performative aspect of discourse, including the power and domination it engenders, enables us to see "what discourse does," or as Jones and Norris have called it: "discourse as action" (2005: 9).

The persistence of deep-rooted, one-sided views on disaster and outright myths about disaster (Fisher 1998; Ville de Goyet 2000) among the public at large and sections of academia, the media, and the bureaucracy, illustrates the prevalence of particular discourses in the domain of disaster. As mentioned above, the still popular notion of disaster as a purely natural phenomenon caused by an external agent that is considered to be completely separate from society or from the position of the victims is one example in this connection. There are also many misunderstandings, on the one hand, about the role and necessity of Western aid and, on the other hand, one-sided representations of disaster victims as passive, traumatized, and aid-dependent people that are repeatedly reinforced by the media. Such representations deny them agency and organizational capacity.

Anthony Oliver-Smith (2004: 17) asserts that societal characteristics play a role in the way meanings and explanations of disasters are constructed. They give "broad disclosure to the internal variance of a community and [are] underscoring the difficulty in determining an absolute or objective determination of the nature of the disaster." He concludes that there is a great variability of interpretation of the threat or impact of disaster. Confirming this observation in the context of the conflict in Sri Lanka, Frerks and Klem (2005a) identified at least 10 different local discourses on peace and conflict in that country. They assert that knowledge of the existence and workings of different local discourses is needed in order to understand the stances of the conflict parties and to inform conflict resolution strategies. Criticisms of external mediation in the Sri Lankan conflict have characteristically cited a lack of cultural and historical understanding by non-Sri Lankans. Acquiring knowledge of the prevailing Sri Lankan discourses can therefore help to offset such criticisms. Similarly, Heijmans (2004) stresses in the context of "natural disaster" the importance of knowing what determines the understanding, perceptions, and ways of coping of vulnerable groups. This should also be done for external actors, as these may as well entertain particular disaster discourses. Bankoff (2004: 33) shows for example that: "The Western discourse on disasters forms part of a much wider historical and cultural geography of risk that creates and maintains a particular depiction of large parts of the world (mainly non-Western countries) as dangerous places." Likewise, aid agencies have their own discourses which express their allegiance to humanitarian principles on the one hand, but are often supply-driven, top-down, and paternalistic on the other.

These references show that the existence of different perceptions and discourses about risk, vulnerability, and disaster is a highly relevant issue for policy-makers and practitioners. Discourse is not only important in the construction of disaster itself, but also in the framing and evaluation of aid responses. At the local level, aid is frequently subject to criticisms, reflecting discontent about the amount, type, and delivery of aid. Local discourses of aid often include allegations and accusations of mismanagement, patronage, and corruption, based on existing ethnic, political, and other divisions in society (Gamburd, this volume).

Recognizing the different disaster discourses is a key step to improved practice. A lack of understanding of these discourses will render action inappropriate and ineffective. In this connection, the re-appreciation of local knowledge, including gender-specific and bottom-up approaches, must be welcomed. The conventional condescension toward local knowledge has done a lot of harm irrespective of whether such knowledge was scientifically "true." As the construction of vulnerability and of actions to reduce it are intimately linked to the local perceptions, calculations, and activities of the stakeholders, it is indispensable to take their views into account and therefore to adopt an agency-based and constructivist approach.

Though one may agree on the desirability of incorporating local knowledge into the implementation of relief efforts, existing disaster management models find it difficult to achieve this because of their often top-down, technical, or managerial orientation. Apart from academic work to document differentiated perceptions among involved stakeholders, further work is needed to compare existing practical instruments to engage local perspectives or eventually to design new ones. There are several examples of such tools used in practice, varying from discussion sessions, to diagnostic and training workshops, to popular consultation meetings.

Sri Lankan situation

Sri Lankan examples described in this volume include discourses that interpret disaster as a punishment for "sins" committed by the people, including the ongoing conflict, or as the divine displeasure of local gods or goddesses, as described by Lawrence. Societies that frequently face disasters develop so-called "cultures of disaster." Such cultures imply embedded ways of dealing with disaster, based on either religious interpretations and fatalism or on particular indigenous coping mechanisms, mutual aid, and other forms of local resilience. Moonesinghe (2007: 59) describes how in southern Sri Lanka local cultural institutions played an important role in providing relief and spiritual and psycho-social counseling. Traditional healing ceremonies and ritual blessings (*bahirawa puja*) were performed for the protection of land, house, and property against disaster. *Pirith* chanting was done at public places as a purification ceremony and to offer merit to the deceased. *Thovils* (devil dances) were carried out for the emotional stabilization and support of victims.

Local narratives on the delivery of aid reveal a strong perception among the population that those in control misused and diverted tsunami aid. The press published critical articles, including an editorial titled "A Tsunami of Discontent" (*Sunday Leader*, 6 February 2005: 10). Discontented victims demonstrated against the government in Weligama, Jaffna, and Kattankudy, though government officials alleged that these were organized by oppositional forces. Already in the first weeks after the tsunami several instances of corruption were reported, though it is difficult to prove whether they were based on fact or fabricated for political motives. Examples included allegations of the overvaluation of possible lands for resettlement in the Galle District that were at the time the property of "an active JVP member" (Nanayakkara 2005: 15), as well as fraudulent contracts for the reconstruction of the bus station in Galle. Later, foreign NGOs would become the target of accusations varying from proselytizing activities to inefficiency and profiteering. Some of those criticisms were reportedly orchestrated by the government and by political parties for their own benefit. In the last section of this chapter, I shall discuss the role of the government in the provision of tsunami aid more explicitly.

iv. Political culture, governance, and patronage

The public sector and public policies play a crucial role in attempts to prevent, mitigate, and respond to disasters. Regardless of whatever international aid can be offered, the responsibility to help people in need resides squarely with their own government. It is here that an analysis of the government institutions, the political culture, and the functioning of the public sector can provide insight into the history of a disaster and the disaster response. Ahrens and Rudolph (2006) describe the interdependence between institutional failure and the susceptibility to disaster. They assert that accountability, popular participation, predictability, and transparency of the administration are key factors in the promotion of sustainable development and disaster reduction. However, in many societies facing disaster, governments are weak, failing, or even collapsing. Others are plagued by corruption, "spoils politics," dictatorships, and predatory regimes, or are subject to "economies of violence." Many of them operate through systems of patronage or patron-client politics. Disaster Studies has only recently focused on this type of anthropologically induced analysis. Its earlier a-historical, de-contextualized models of disaster management and engineering approaches to preferred technical solutions hardly took such specificities into consideration. However, work in complex emergencies over the last two decades has put those governance issues forcefully on the agenda.

I already referred above to the absence of a policy framework and a National Disaster Management Plan in the case of Sri Lanka. Having said that, how did the authorities react and how successful were they in carrying out their tasks? How can the governance style of the Sri Lankan authorities be understood? What were the views of the public and the tsunami-affected groups?

Sri Lankan situation

The role of the central authorities at the initial rescue and relief stage was minimal. Some officers were absent due to the holiday season, while others were personally affected by the tsunami itself and were unable to help out. There were also strong indications that the central government was completely overwhelmed by the situation and lacked the resources for a quick and effective response. Consumer Affairs Minister Jeyeraj Fernandopulle acknowledged in a forum discussion held in Colombo that the state apparatus was unprepared and inexperienced to face a tragedy of the magnitude of the tsunami (Chickera 2005). Some observers also mentioned that the government's accountability structures, and rules and procedures, made it "naturally" slow and reactive.

Having said that, in several instances there was also simply blatant inaction, delay, and negligence. The implementation of the standard compensation scheme for all tsunami survivors in the island was highly deficient. The Commissioner General of Essential Services himself said during a press conference that by 1 February 2005 – over five weeks after the tsunami – only 30 percent of the eligible 960,000 people had received state compensation. The Additional District Secretary of the Amparai District admitted that by 13 February 2005 there were 28,000 persons still waiting for the ration card in his district. Batticaloa had received the first cards on 16 January 2005, but there were not enough. Only 179,000 out of the 254,000 needed had been supplied. The Kachcheri had asked for the remaining 75,000 on 20 January 2005, but had received no reply until mid-February 2005. Delays in the issuing of coupons had affected the food distribution process in most districts, especially in the Batticaloa District. Frerks and Klem (2005c: 24) made a "calendar of delays" on the basis of information collected during fieldwork carried out in the affected areas in February 2005:

- After 8 days: a first meeting of MPs, NGOs, and government was convened in Batticaloa.
- After 12 days: the first significant government stocks arrived in Batticaloa.
- After about 20 days: the District Secretary of the Batticaloa published a first report on the situation in the Batticaloa District.
- After 21 days: the first ration cards arrived in Batticaloa with a shortage of 75,000; the government was reminded four days later.
- After 48 days: ration cards were issued in Piriya-Nilawa camp.
- After 49 days: 28,000 people were still without ration cards in Amparai District.
- After 51 days: there was still a shortage of 75,000 ration cards in Batticaloa.
- After 53 days: first ration cards were issued by Grama Niladharis in Mulliyavallai (LTTE-held area).

There was also a conspicuous neglect of livelihood issues in the government's initial actions, such as the provision of tools and implements needed to take up one's job again. Frerks and Klem (2005c: 23) report:

> We spoke to many people idling in the camps who were keen to take up their lives again, but had not been provided with the means to do so. In our interviews we met dressmakers, tailors, beauticians, masons, carpenters and mechanics who expressed a desire to start working again, but did not know to whom to turn. A spokesperson for the Sri Lanka Jamaath-i-Islami said that none of the survivors had gone back to work. Many had no place to carry out their activities, but moreover they completely lacked the necessary information on how to continue with their livelihood. Nobody had also talked to them about this issue. A diplomat said that the issue of livelihood was a blank spot for the government.

These varied experiences and omissions with respect to the tsunami can only be understood when placed in the politico-social and institutional context of Sri Lanka's political culture. The Sri Lankan government as well as many local organizations have the formal trappings of Western institutions and seem to resemble "Weberian" types of bureaucracy (see Mommsen 1974; Giddens 1978) or participatory, democratic organizations at local or grassroots levels respectively. Yet, it would be a mistake to take such organizations and institutions in Sri Lanka at face value, as this is often nothing more than an outer façade hiding a rather different underlying *modus operandi*.

In fact, the tsunami response cannot be grasped when assuming a formal, monolithic, a-political and a-personal type of bureaucracy. It is true that the government has formal structures and a frame of operational rules and procedures, and that

it represents human and material resources, networks, and capacities for (inter)
national resource mobilization. However, the effective operation of these assets
depends on the way political and societal actors are using them, and how they
are linked to their overall political, societal, and ideological interests. It should
be recognized that the Sri Lankan government, as indeed some governments in
other countries, are not agents acting for the common good, but can be structures
through which individual agents operate for their own benefit. Hence, access to
state services, control over state machinery, and proximity to central state authority
are powerful entitlements in Sri Lanka.

As among others observed by Sunil Bastian (n.d.: 9), Sri Lanka's electoral
and political system historically evolved into a system of patronage and operates
through "patronage politics":

> The institutionalisation of a system of patronage politics, that keeps the elected
> members happy, has almost become another mechanism through which the
> elected members are politically managed. The hallmark of this patronage
> politics of the political class is the use of state resources and state patronage
> for personal accumulation as well as distributing patronage to party members,
> family members, the caste network etc. etc. As a result electoral politics is
> dominated by a simple straightforward desire to grab power, so that there can
> be access to resources and influence that state power provides.

In the Sri Lankan context, this patronage network acquired ethnic characteristics, as
most political parties are run and controlled on the basis of ethnicity. Moonesinghe
(2007: 3) states that:

> Relationships in which the "patron" is dominant and exercises control over the
> distribution of limited resources as rewards and favors among clients, typically
> characterise partisan politics, the political processes, public administration and
> service delivery in Sri Lanka.

Unsurprisingly, the distribution of resources and privilege has become a major
issue of contention, with ethnic, regional, and caste differences as the determining factors. Patterns of inequity in the past have led to grievances of the Tamil
population and resulted in separatist Tamil nationalism and armed struggle. The
Muslims have also voiced feelings of exclusion more recently (McGilvray and
Raheem 2007). These conditions provided fertile soil for social dissent. The aid
response directly impinged upon the relations between the different identity-
groups in Sri Lanka, and of those groups with the government. It also reflected
and stimulated the power struggle between political leaders, parties, and factions.
Finally, this "politics of aid" affected the bureaucracy from higher to lower level
functionaries as already described in this volume by Gamburd for southwestern
Sri Lanka. Aid distribution with regard to caste (Goyigama and Vellala versus
coastal castes, mainly fishermen), region (north, east, and south), and ethnicity
(Tamils, Muslims and Sinhalese) all became increasingly an inflammatory issue.

But divisions also emerged within those groups, mostly on the basis of political allegiance and patronage.

After the immediate relief work was over, according to one of my respondents, "politics crept in and messed up the whole thing." This sentiment was broadly shared in Sri Lanka and in the press. Jeyaraj (2005: 17) concludes his article in the *Sunday Leader* as follows:

> The people of Sri Lanka who displayed commendable inter-ethnic solidarity amidst the tsunami tragedy must realise that this government and the politicians running it will ruin things once again. Inter-ethnic dissension will be promoted to divide the people so that the 'corrupt' ones can have a field day as usual. The state that failed its people at their hour of need must not be allowed to disrupt the climate of amity again. The people who did not fail their fellow people must come forward as one nation and prevent the evil machinations of the state. Otherwise, Sri Lanka will be in the throes of a permanent man-made tsunami.

Another illustration is the following anecdote told by the chairman of a local NGO in the east (Frerks and Klem 2005c: 19):

> Politics is certainly a factor. We had proposed to build 100 new houses and we had arranged for the funds. Everything was looking fine. On the day we were going to put the foundations, the whole thing was blocked by the Urban Development Authority. It transpired that they were not against the project as such, but the problem was that the Minister had wanted to open the scheme. Who the Minister is? Please, I'd better reserve my comments. Apart from God's blessing, you need political blessing.

There was a widespread perception that President Chandrika Kumaratunga quickly assumed firm control over major aid flows. With the creation of various Colombo-based co-ordinating bodies, headed by personal confidants, the President even sidelined her own ministers and their machineries. The Prime Minister at that time, Mahinda Rajapakse, took the lead in the specially designed program "Helping Hambantota." His electorate happened to be the Hambantota District. He was able to mobilize aid and official action quickly (Kuhn, this volume). By early February, 18 fishing families from Uruwella had already been issued 20 perches of land located inland, where they now lived in tents, but where houses would soon be built for them, paid for by the Deutsche Gesellschaft für Technische Zuzammenarbeit (GTZ). The leftist-nationalist political party Janatha Vimukhti Peramuna (JVP) had launched a highly conspicuous campaign with volunteers to assist tsunami victims by providing first relief aid, removing debris, and constructing temporary housing. Thousands of JVP volunteers had become active (Moonesinghe 2007: 67; Frerks and Klem 2005c: 19–20). The JVP not only reached out to the southern areas where they traditionally have the most followers, but also to the southeast and the east, helping Sinhalese, Muslims, and Tamils alike. They received much praise for it, though nearly everybody recognized the political motives behind it: to popularize the party further as well as to offer an alternative to the Sri Lanka Freedom Party (SLFP) and perhaps to counter the President's centralizing efforts.

Aid operations clearly reflected differences between the ethnic majority and the minorities. Frerks and Klem (2005c) highlight the experiences in the Amparai District. The Members of Parliament (MPs) representing those minorities (especially the Tamil National Alliance, but the Muslim MPs as well) had no clout at the central level and were unable to put their area on the tsunami relief agenda or to assure the necessary support from the center. Moreover, several district and divisional authorities allegedly acted with levels of indifference, delay, and inertia. This evoked strong criticisms from the population and civil society, who attributed this sluggishness to the fact that the interior side of Ampara District was inhabited by Sinhalese as was the district capital, Ampara town. Two Muslim respondents interviewed on 13 February 2005 in Kalmunai added that many government officials sent to the east are less capable or motivated. "They only send human vegetables to this place," they commented. A humanitarian NGO-worker interviewed on the same day in Kalmunai complained about an eastern Sinhalese District Secretary: "He is really good for nothing, totally inefficient and ineffective and on top of that corrupt." The two Muslim respondents mentioned above called the same official "indifferent, lethargic and not concerned about minority people."

Though the criticisms reported above ignore the demonstrably good works of many government officers, including members of the Sri Lankan Army and Special Task Force, they nevertheless hint at structural factors in the realm of governance and patronage politics that have affected the distribution of aid in Sri Lanka. Moonesinghe's study (2007) confirms virtually all of the observations made above. She among others mentions how "time consuming bureaucratic procedures and centrally issued directives contradict ground realities, cause confusion and prevent efficient delivery of relief aid, assistance and public services in general" (Moonesinghe 2007: 72). She also mentions the entry of divisive, ethnicized, and partisan politics. The resulting politicization of aid hampered, delayed, and "communalized" relief and reconstruction efforts. She also mentions that traditional patronage networks became politicized to the disadvantage of the clients, while in parts of her research area "subterranean forces," underworld gangs, drug gangs, and unidentified armed groups became active (Moonesinghe 2007: 74). Based on detailed district-level studies, Haug and Weerackody (2007: 18) similarly state that:

> As time passed and the initial sense of unity evaporated, political patronage re-emerged in aid distribution as politicians diverted resources to supporters, for instance by including them on beneficiary lists. Politicians became fiercely competitive for control over aid resources through the government machinery.

Conclusion: principles forgotten and lessons unlearned

Though this chapter obviously cannot provide an overall judgement on the tsunami relief and recovery programs in Sri Lanka, the experiences I have described suggest a somewhat paradoxical situation. On the one hand, Telford, Cosgrave and Houghton (2006: 18 and 66) report that by 2006 fishing infrastructure had been repaired for 80 percent of the fishermen, and that 70 percent of people affected by the tsunami had regained a steady income. On the other hand in their comprehensive study for the Tsunami Evaluation Coalition, they also mention many constraints, shortcomings, and flaws in the tsunami response. Despite the availability of an unprecedented amount of funding, the delivery of aid in practice faced many implementation problems. Similar critical observations arose consistently during our own fieldwork (Frerks and Klem 2005c), and in the district-level studies by Moonesinghe (2007) and Haug and Weerackody (2007). All these studies also typically show fairly high levels of dissatisfaction among the recipients of aid. It seems that the way in which aid was distributed – and information-sharing, communication and transparency were handled – determined to a high degree how the aid response was viewed.

In an attempt to influence the distribution and management of tsunami aid, the donors active in Sri Lanka have formulated a set of "guiding principles" as listed below. Though they were never accorded official or enforceable status under the circumstances, they can be considered state-of-the-art with regard to important principles and lessons on humanitarian and reconstruction aid. They reflected a broad consensus forged over the years and based on insights derived from the earlier mentioned IDNDR, ISDR, World Conferences on Disaster Reduction and countless evaluation reports on humanitarian aid and invaluable practical experiences learned in the field.

Guiding principles for a post-tsunami reconstruction strategy (Asian Development Bank, et al. 2005)

- The allocation of domestic and international resources should be guided by identified needs and local priorities.
- There should be no discrimination on the basis of political, religious, ethnic or gender considerations.
- The recovery strategy should strengthen the peace process and build confidence.
- The reconstruction strategy should be sensitive to the impact on neighbouring, but unaffected communities.
- The reconstruction activity should be designed and implemented at the lowest competent tier of government (subsidiarity) to enable locally appropriate solutions, the engagement of sub-national structures, capacity building and the strengthening of different levels of governance and civil society organisations.
- To secure the mid and long-term needs of the victims, solid consultation,

local decision-making and full participation in reconstruction activities is essential.

- Interventions should respect local religion, culture, structures and customs.
- There needs to be adequate communication and transparency in decision-making and implementation. This refers to policies, entitlements and procedures, as well as to resource use, including 'zero tolerance for corruption'.
- Reconstruction should reduce future vulnerabilities to natural hazards by adopting a multi-hazard risk approach.
- Interventions need to be assessed for their impact on prospects for peace and conflict, on gender, on the environment and on governance and human rights.
- Revenues resulting from debt relief should demonstrably benefit the tsunami victims.
- Efforts need to be properly co-ordinated between all relevant stakeholders.

Though perhaps not always phrased in the same language, these principles also reflect to a considerable degree the four trends and developments in the field of disaster studies as outlined in this chapter: (i.) complexity and conflict-sensitivity; (ii.) vulnerability, capacity and resilience; (iii.) perceptions and discourses; (iv.) political culture, governance, and patronage. However, the donors clearly underestimated the deep and real societal problems these issues represented and the counter-dynamics that these principles would provoke. Though it can be debated whether the government was formally obliged to take these guiding principles into consideration as part of its tsunami response efforts, it is sobering to conclude that both domestic and international tsunami recovery agencies seemed to have forgotten these principles along the way and to have unlearned the lessons learned previously.

Whereas in the field of disaster studies a more nuanced understanding of disaster causation, process, and response is slowly emerging, it is not yet easy to translate this into policy practice. This chapter shows that the major trends and developments outlined for this multi-disciplinary field were of relevance to Sri Lanka after it was hit by the tsunami. However, as also corroborated by the other chapters in this volume, local contexts and specificities affected the way those lessons and principles were applied, ignored, or sidelined. It was seen that the presence of the violent conflict had a pervasive and overall negative impact on the aid operations and that struggles over the distribution of aid in turn destroyed any remaining prospects for political agreement and eventual peace. The principle of "Do No Harm" was known, but not systematically applied. With respect to vulnerability and resilience, virtually all insights as outlined in the disaster studies literature were applicable in the Sri Lankan case, yet these did not sufficiently guide or inform aid practice. Opportunities were missed to introduce a disaster prevention and vulnerability reduction approach and to make practice more gender-sensitive.

The research described in this book touches upon the relatively new terrain of disaster perceptions and discourses. It shows the existence of particular cultural responses to disaster and outlines some of the prevailing narratives and perceptions.

These have encompassed both the nature of the disaster and the reasons for it, as well as the delivery of aid that followed. Discourses on aid have tended to emphasize its shortcomings and have been highly critical of aid providers, governmental and non-governmental. A lot of criticisms have been aired against the "aid industry," and many of them contain an element of truth. Apart from the challenges posed by the task at hand itself after the tsunami, agencies have made obvious mistakes, and a number of them were clearly not capable of carrying out their tasks in a responsible and professional manner, as corroborated in the several studies quoted above. A serious omission was a nearly total lack of communication, consultation, and information vis-à-vis the local population, leading to frustrations, misapprehensions, and accusations. In particular, there was a lot of insecurity regarding reconstruction plans for the future, as the government had been slow and indecisive on this issue. Many Colombo-based agencies, including many donors themselves, lacked the capacity to link to the lower grassroots level where the tsunami survivors lived.

A last topic explored in this chapter was the role of governance, political culture, and patronage in the aid delivery to the tsunami victims. Though there are positive exceptions and examples of courageous and altruistic behavior, especially in the initial stages, political dynamics gradually took over, leading to what has been called an ethnicized, politicized, and communalized distribution of aid based on politically charged patron-client relations. This has strained the relations between different ethnic and religious groups locally and nationally, leading to further divisions and also complicating the relations of those groups with the government. The government, both nationally and locally, was subject to heavy criticism for its late, ineffective, and inefficient support to the tsunami victims. The initial hope that the tsunami would lead to mutual solidarity and eventual peace-building among the different sectors of Sri Lankan society was dashed after the serious mismanagement of the aid, the political dissent surrounding it, and the emotions that these aroused.

In summary, despite the availability of generous funding and the achievement of a number of tangible results, the overall post-tsunami situation in Sri Lanka was increasingly evaluated critically by both experts and the public at large. Reconstruction became haunted by a history of mistakes and failures. The prevailing "politics of aid" as well as the conflict between the government and the LTTE made it difficult to provide aid according to professional standards. In this situation, important basic humanitarian principles and lessons learned for improved reconstruction aid in the years before were ignored or sidelined.

Notes

1 *Editor's note*: the actual tsunami death toll among such violence-displaced groups has not been verified. See McGilvray: this volume, note 4.

8 Conclusion

Hybrid perspectives on tsunami recovery

Dennis B. McGilvray and
Michele R. Gamburd

General awareness of tsunami hazards was dramatically heightened by the global media attention given to the 2004 Indian Ocean disaster, and the subsequent deluge – what Sri Lankans have called a "golden wave" – of international tsunami relief and reconstruction aid that ensued (Telford, Cosgrave, and Houghton 2006; Gamburd, this volume). Before that unforgettable event, authors seem to have found the threat posed by tsunamis awkward to classify under the major categories of the natural hazards literature. A widely read textbook on the social causes and impacts of natural hazard vulnerability published just prior to the event (*At Risk: Natural Hazards, People's Vulnerability and Disasters*, 2nd ed., by Wisner, Blaikie, Cannon, and Davis 2004) includes only four brief references to tsunami episodes scattered across three different chapters of the book. The problem is that tsunamis display "hybrid" characteristics. A tsunami is a wall of water, but unlike a conventional flood, it does not inundate lowland areas for a lengthy period of time. A tsunami has a sudden destructive impact, but unlike an earthquake it does not devastate large contiguous regions. A tsunami's closest parallels are with volcanic eruptions, flash floods, and coastal storm surges, all of which permit a small degree of advanced warning and tend to affect narrowly-delineated geographical areas or ecological zones. But unlike tropical cyclones, tsunamis are not seasonal, and the extremely long intervals between tsunami disasters makes it difficult to sustain a collective concern about vulnerability (Wisner, *et al.* 2004: 107, 205, 246, 267–68, 275, 277).

It is perhaps fitting, then, that the research contained in this book was conducted by a hybrid interdisciplinary group with diverse interests and concerns. In the immediate aftermath of the tsunami, faced with the sudden challenge of a looming NSF grant deadline, we proposed a cross-island natural experiment to compare the culturally distinctive Sinhalese Buddhist southwest coast with the ethnic minority Tamil Hindu, Muslim, and Burgher east coast, taking the physical impact of the tsunami as a constant factor in both locations. This represented a rare degree of methodological formalism for the cultural anthropologists on the project, and it induced anxiety about latter-day "culture shock" on the part of at least one of them (McGilvray 2006). However, it also opened the door for a wide spectrum of multi-disciplinary participation and served as a broad intellectual platform to consider impinging political factors such as the LTTE rebellion, the ethno-nationalist tendencies of the Sri Lankan government, and the bureaucratic problems of NGO versus governmental reconstruction efforts. Two authors in the field of disaster studies, Gaasbeek and Frerks, joined the book project after this research was underway, and we are grateful for the additional perspectives they bring to this volume.

It will be obvious from the chapters in this book that in our writing, the temptation to explore particularly rich areas of our research data often supplanted our formal NSF research design. These choices reflect our pre-existing knowledge of specific regions and cultural practices in Sri Lanka, as well as the wish to seize upon opportunities that opened up in our individual research sites. Good social science should leave room for serendipitous outcomes, especially in projects involving intensive first-hand fieldwork and data-gathering. Thus, like the anomalous nature of the tsunami itself, this volume offers a hybrid set of perspectives on Sri Lanka's recovery process approximately five years after the disaster struck, one that represents a diverse combination of political, demographic, ethnographic, and policy viewpoints.

The social and cultural basis of vulnerability to natural hazards has become a commonplace theme in the current literature on disasters. It is therefore worth noting the diversity of factors that made the coastal populations of Sri Lanka so susceptible to the 2004 tsunami. Unlike the inhabitants of U.S. gulf coast retirement communities that were badly hit by Hurricane Katrina in 2005, most Sri Lankan beach-dwellers had not chosen to live by the ocean in a quest for "sun and surf." Indeed, many Sri Lankans are uncomfortable living by the open sea: some cannot swim, some believe the ocean to present supernatural dangers, and the salt spray corrodes household possessions. Instead, most Sri Lankans who were exposed to the tsunami earned their livelihood from fishing (as in Navalady and Maruthamunai as described by Lawrence and McGilvray in this volume), or from jobs associated with the tourist beach resort industry (as in the Ambalangoda area described by Gamburd). Many lived by the ocean because the seaside real estate prices were affordable and there was a shortage of suitable house-sites elsewhere (as in Dutch Bar, Maruthamunai, Sainthamaruthu, and Tambiluvil on the east coast described by McGilvray and Lawrence).

Scholars often examine a disaster's effects on social hierarchies and economic relations. The desire – and the economic necessity – of tsunami survivors to migrate back to house sites near the beach is clearly seen in a number of tsunami-affected communities discussed in this book. In the future, many of these families could be protected by an advanced tsunami-detection and early warning system; such technology could also alert people to the impending impact of the devastating coastal storms that irregularly strike the east coast of the island, such as the cyclone of 1978. As experts have pointed out, however, technological warning systems for floods, coastal storm surges, and tsunamis are only effective if they are timely, locally credible, and permit sufficient lead-time for evacuation (Wisner, *et al.* 2004: 241, 343). Such warning and evacuation systems have proven successful in recent decades in the south Indian state of Andhra Pradesh (Wisner, *et al.* 2004: 253 ff.), but they require adequate funding, active community participation, trust in local authorities, and historical memory of earlier disasters to sustain their long-term effectiveness.

The goal of combining reconstruction with economic change and socio-economic development forms a second theme in contemporary natural disaster studies. Through "sustainable disaster reduction," practitioners hope to combat poverty and build community resiliency against renewed disasters in the future (Wisner, *et al.* 2004: Chap. 9). A key component of this process is the active involvement of community members in planning and carrying out reconstruction projects that strengthen the disaster resistance of the entire community or region, rather than depending upon external authorities and sponsoring agencies to plan and construct the needed housing and infrastructure for a passive population of "victims." Housewives, for example, should have significant input into the design of new housing, since they spend a large portion of their time on domestic labor and childcare in the home (Wisner, *et al.* 2004: 365). Many of this volume's authors suggest that in Sri Lanka the enormous scale of international funding for post-tsunami reconstruction, and the uncoordinated and competitive humanitarian projects of so many different NGOs, positioned survivors as speculators and market shoppers, rather than as collaborative participants in the reconstruction process. Five years after the tsunami, one cannot doubt that the quality of coastal housing stock has greatly improved, but whether these projects have increased the long-term disaster resiliency and economic development of local Sri Lankan communities is not yet clear.

The effect of disaster on diplomacy and political conflict forms a third theme in the disaster literature. As all of the volume's contributing authors note, the distribution of tsunami aid in Sri Lanka unfolded against a backdrop of deep distrust between the various political and ethnic factions on the island. Animosity undermined the timely delivery of aid to the north and east; this delay in turn provided support for claims of bias in the government's approach to relief and recovery operations. Events that unfolded in the aftermath of the tsunami reflected the fractured social structure of 2004 and foreshadowed the defeat of the LTTE and the violent end of Eelam War IV in 2009. Ethnographic data reveal what happened when the tsunami devastated communities already battered by decades of civil war. Years of war-related loss, displacement, and uncertainty made coastal populations in eastern Sri Lanka simultaneously more vulnerable and more resistant to the disaster (Gaasbeek, this volume). The case studies clearly show that patronage politics and ethnic animosity affected the national and international humanitarian response to the tsunami in Sri Lanka. Discussions of how disaster aid influenced diplomacy are likely to dominate scholarly conversations about Sri Lanka for a decade to come.

A complex disaster requires a multifaceted analysis. We feel that this book's interdisciplinary research approach, which combines quantitative and macro-level material with richly textured local ethnography, offers insights to those who wish to acquire a well-rounded perspective on disaster and disaster management in culturally sensitive terms. Through the lens of the tsunami, the contributing authors have not only analyzed the larger ethno-political and demographic context of the disaster, but have also explored village-level ethical discourses of sharing and gift-giving among south-western Sinhala Buddhists, described religious devotion to protective maritime "mother" goddesses among eastern Hindus and Catholics, documented the continuity of matrilocal marriage and women's property rights in Muslim, Tamil, and Burgher tsunami housing schemes, compared the effectiveness of foreign and domestic NGO relief efforts on the ground in the Eastern Province, and provided a broad evaluation of Sri Lankan tsunami recovery efforts by current global standards. We hope these Sri Lankan examples will prove useful to policy makers in Sri Lanka and in South Asia, and to international organizations that are called upon to provide disaster relief in the future.

References

Ahrens, J. and Rudolph, P.M. (2006) 'The importance of governance in risk reduction and disaster management,' *Journal of Contingencies and Crisis Management*, 14(4): 207–220.

Alexander, D.C. (1993) *Natural Disasters*, New York: Chapman and Hall.

—— (1997) 'The study of natural disasters, 1977–1997: some reflections on a changing field of knowledge,' *Disasters*, 21(4): 283–304.

Anderson, G.W. (2008) 'Interagency overseas: responding to the 2004 Indian Ocean tsunami,' in J.J. Carafano and R. Weitz, (eds.) *Mismanaging Mayhem: How Washington Responds to Crisis*, Westport CT: Praeger Security International.

Anderson, M. and Woodrow, P. (1989) *Rising from the Ashes, Development Strategies in Times of Disaster*, Boulder and San Francisco/Paris: Westview Press/UNESCO.

Anonymous (2005) 'Aide humanitaire: les dangers de la surmédiatisation – rencontre avec Rony Brauman, ancient président de Médecins Sans Frontiers,' *Politique Autrement*, No. 35, May 2005. Available online at <http://www.politique-autrement.org/spip.php?article149> (accessed 4 May 2009).

Asian Development Bank, the Japan Bank for International Cooperation and the World Bank (2005) *Guiding Principles of the Needs Assessment and Recovery Strategy. Preliminary Damage and Needs Assessment*, (January 1–28, 2005), Section D, 7–9.

Athukorala, P. and Resosudarmo, B.P. (2005) 'The Indian Ocean tsunami: economic impact, disaster management, and lessons,' *Asian Economic Papers*, Winter 2005: 1–39.

Bankoff, G. (2004) "The historical geography of disaster: 'vulnerability' and 'local knowledge' in western discourse," in G. Bankoff, G. Frerks and D. Hilhorst (eds.) *Mapping Vulnerability, Disasters, Development and People*, London: Earthscan.

Barbier, E.B. (2008) 'In the wake of tsunami: lessons learned from the household decision to replant mangroves in Thailand,' *Resource and Energy Economics*, 30(2): 229–249.

Barnett. M. (2005) 'Humanitarianism transformed,' *Perspectives on Politics*, 3: 723–740.

Bastian, S. (1999) 'The failure of the state formation, identity conflict and civil society responses – the case of Sri Lanka,' Working Paper 2, Centre for Conflict Resolution, Department of Peace Studies, University of Bradford.

—— (2005) 'Limits of aid,' *Polity*, 2(3): 21–23.

—— (n.d.) 'Electoral systems and political outcomes,' (unpublished draft paper).

BBC (2005a) "'Helping Hambantota' probe halted." Available online at <http://www.bbc.co.uk/sinhala/news/story/2005/09/050928_helping_hambantota.shtml> (accessed 5 August 2009).

—— (2005b) 'Mobile homes for tsunami victims'. Available online at <http://news.bbc.co.uk/2/hi/uk_news/england/cambridgeshire/4213243.stm> (accessed 9 August 2009).

Benini, A., Conley, C., Dittemore, B. and Waksman, Z. (2008) 'Survivor needs or logistical convenience? Factors shaping decisions to deliver relief to earthquake-affected communities, Pakistan 2005–06,' *Disasters*, 33(1): 110–131.

Blaikie, P. M., and Brookfield, H. C. (1987) *Land Degradation and Society*, London: Methuen.

Boano, C. (2009) 'Housing anxiety and multiple geographies in post-tsunami Sri Lanka,' *Disasters*. Published online 5 May 2009. Available online at <http://www.ncbi.nlm.nih.gov/pubmed/19459904> (accessed June 12, 2009).

Bohle, H-G. and Fünfgeld, H. (2007) 'The political ecology of violence in eastern Sri Lanka,' *Development and Change*, 38(4): 667–687.

Brodie, J. (2008) 'Effects of the 2004 Indian Ocean tsunami on sea turtle populations in Sri Lanka,' *Chelonian Conservation and Biology*, 7(2): 249–251.

Brubaker, R. and Cooper F. (2000) "Beyond 'identity'," *Theory and Society*, 29: 1–47.

Bryant, R. and Bailey, S. (1997) *Third World Political Ecology*, London: Routledge.

Buchanan-Smith, M.S. and Maxwell, S. (1994) 'Linking relief and development: an introduction and overview,' *IDS Bulletin*, 25(4): 2–16.

Bush, K.D. (1993) 'Reading between the lines: intra-group heterogeneity and conflict in Sri Lanka,' *Refuge*, 13(3): 15–22.

Canagaratnam, S.O. (1921) *Monograph of the Batticaloa District*. Colombo: H. R. Cottle, Government Printer.

Cannon, T., Twigg, J. and Rowell, J. (2005) *Social Vulnerability, Livelihoods and Disasters: Report to DFID*, Kent: University of Greenwich.

Cardona, O.D. (2004) 'The need for rethinking the concepts of risk and vulnerability from a holistic perspective: a necessary review and criticism for effective risk management,' in G. Bankoff, G. Frerks and D. Hilhorst (eds.) *Mapping Vulnerability, Disasters, Development and People*, London: Earthscan.

Cashman, T. (2006) 'Lest the world forget: Sri Lanka's educational needs after the 2004 tsunami,' *Journal of Social Studies Research*, 30(2): 30–37.

Casimir, M.J. (ed.) (2008) *Culture and the Changing Environment: Uncertainty Cognition, and Risk Management in Cross-Cultural Perspective*, New York: Berghahn Books.

Centers for Disease Control and Prevention (U.S.) (2005) *Tsunami Disaster Health Information for Humanitarian Workers*. Atlanta: Department of Health and Human Services, Centers for Disease Control and Prevention.

Centre for Policy Alternatives (2005) 'Report on the workshop on post-tsunami reconstruction of Sri Lanka', *Polity*, 2(3): 26–30.

Cheng, M.H. (2007) 'Health and housing after the Indian Ocean tsunami,' North American edition, *Lancet*, 369: 2066–2068.

Chickera, G. de (2005) 'Opposition parties want tsunami work de-centralized,' *Daily Mirror*, 19 February 2005.

Cliffe, L. and Luckham, R. (2000) 'What happens to the state in conflict? Political analysis as a tool for planning humanitarian assistance,' *Disasters*, 24(4): 291–313.

Couldrey, M. and Morris T. (2005) 'UN assesses tsunami response,' *Forced Migration Review Special Issue: Tsunami – Learning From the Humanitarian Response*: 6–9.

Crawshaw, S. (2009) 'An urgent need for UN action on Sri Lanka,' *The Huffington Post*, 6 May 2009. Available online at <http://www.hrw.org/en/news/2009/05/06/urgent-need-un-action-sri-lanka> (accessed 5 August 2009).

Crespin, J. (2006) 'Aiding local action: the constraints faced by donor agencies in supporting effective, pro-poor initiatives on the ground,' *Environment and Urbanization*, 18(2): 433–449.

Danielsen, F. (2005) 'The Asian tsunami: a protective role for coastal vegetation,' *Science*, 310(5748): 643.

de Mel, N. and Ruwanpura K.N. (2006) *Gendering the Tsunami: Women's Experiences from Sri Lanka*, Colombo: International Centre for Ethnic Studies.

Department of Census and Statistics – Sri Lanka (2001) *Census of Population and Housing*, CD Data for Ampara, Batticaloa, Galle, Hambantota, Matara districts. Available online at <http://www.statistics.gov.lk/PopHouSat/index.asp> (accessed 9 August 2009).

—— (2005) *Census on the Buildings and People Affected by the Tsunami*. Available online at <http://www.statistics.gov.lk/Tsunami/> (accessed 9 August 2009).

Department of Elections – Sri Lanka (2009) *Past Parliamentary Election Results*. Available online at <http://www.slelections.gov.lk/pastElection4.html> (accessed 9 August 2009).

de Silva, K.M. (1997) 'Affirmative action policies: the Sri Lankan experience,' *Ethnic Studies Report*, XV(2): 245–287.

de Silva, M.W.A. (2009) 'Ethnicity, politics and inequality: post-tsunami humanitarian aid delivery in Ampara District, Sri Lanka,' *Disasters* 33(23): 253–273.

Development Assistance Database Regional (2008) *Sri Lanka Reports*. Available online at <http://tsunamitracking.org/undprcb/> United Nations Development Program, Bangkok (accessed 9 August 2009).

District Recovery Plan (2006), Batticaloa District, DRDU, District Secretariat Batticaloa, Sri Lanka, 2006.

Domroes, M. (ed.) (2006) *After the Tsunami: Relief and Rehabilitation in Sri Lanka ... Re-Starting Towards the Future*, New Delhi: Mosaic Books.

Dunham, D. and Jayasuriya, S. (2001) 'Liberalisation and political decay: Sri Lanka's journey from welfare state to a brutalised society,' Working Paper 352 Institute of Social Studies, Netherlands.

Easterly, W. (2003) 'The cartel of good intentions: the problem of bureaucracy in foreign aid,' *Journal of Policy Reform*, 5(4): 1–28.

Fengler, W., Ihsan, A. and Kaiser, K. (2008) 'Managing post-disaster reconstruction finance: international experience in public financial management,' World Bank Policy Research Working Paper 4475, 1 January 2008. Available online at <http://ssrn.com/abstract=1083903> (accessed 10 June 2009).

Forced Migration Review (2005) *Forced Migration Review Special Issue: Tsunami: Learning from the Humanitarian Response*, July 2005. Available online at <http://www.fmreview.org/tsunami.htm> (accessed 9 August 2009)

Fordham, G. (2006) *Tsunami Stories, Thailand: A Collection of Tsunami Stories from Thailand*, Bangkok: Image Asia Events Co.

Fordham, M. (2004) 'Gendering vulnerability analysis,' in G. Bankoff, G. Frerks and D. Hilhorst (eds.) *Mapping Vulnerability, Disasters, Development and People*, London: Earthscan.

Foundation for Co-Existence (2008) *Situation Report, 30 May 2008*, FCE Colombo Information Centre, Sri Lanka.

Fox, F. (2001) 'New humanitarianism: does it provide a moral banner for the 21st century?' *Disasters*, 25(4): 275–289.

Freeman, P. K. (2004) 'Allocation of post-disaster reconstruction financing to housing,' *Building Research & Information*, 32(5): 427–437.

Frerks, G. (2008) 'Tsunami response in Sri Lanka: civil-military cooperation in a conflictuous context,' in S. J. H. Rietjens and M.T.B. Bollen (eds.) *Managing Civil-Military Cooperation, A 24/7 Joint Effort for Stability*, Aldershot: Ashgate.

Frerks, G. and Klem, B. (2005a) (eds.) *Dealing with Diversity: Sri Lankan Discourses on Peace and Conflict*, The Hague: Netherlands Institute of International Relations 'Clingendael.'

—— (2005b) 'Muddling the peace process. Post-tsunami rehabilitation in war-torn Sri Lanka,' *CRU Policy Brief 2*, January 2005, The Hague: Netherlands Institute of International Relations 'Clingendael.'

—— (2005c) *Tsunami Response in Sri Lanka, Report on a Field Visit from 6–20 February 2005*, The Netherlands: Wageningen University and Clingendael Institute.

—— (2006) *Conditioning Peace among Protagonists: A Study into the Use of Peace Conditionalities in the Sri Lankan Peace Process*, The Hague: Netherlands Institute of International Relations 'Clingendael.'

Frerks, G., Klem B., van Laar, S., and van Klingeren, M. (2006) *Principles and Pragmatism. Civil-Military Action in Afghanistan and Liberia*, Utrecht: Universiteit Utrecht; Amsterdam: Bart Klem Research.

Fund for Peace (2009) *The Failed States Index 2009*. Available online at <http://www.fund forpeace.org/web/index.php?option=com_content&task=view&id=99&Itemid=140> (accessed 10 June 2009).

Funk, J. (ed.) (2005) *Tsunami: Hope, Heroes, and Incredible Stories of Survival*, Chicago: Triumph Books.

Gaasbeek, T. J. (2005) 'What remains is sadness – narratives of humanitarian aid workers who left their organizations after the tsunami'. Paper presented at a working conference organized by the Disaster Studies Group, Wageningen University, The Netherlands, November 2005.

Galappatti, A. (2005) Reflections on post-tsunami psychosocial work. *Forced Migration Review Special Issue: Tsunami – Learning From the Humanitarian Response*: 32–33.

Gamburd, M.R. (2000) *The Kitchen Spoon's Handle: Transnationalism and Sri Lanka's Migrant Housemaids*, Ithaca: Cornell University Press.

—— (2004) 'The economics of enlisting: a village view of armed service,' in D.Winslow and M.D. Woost (eds.) *Economy, Culture, and Civil War in Sri Lanka*, Bloomington: Indiana University Press.

Gasper, D.R. (1999) "'Drawing a line': ethical and political strategies in complex emergency assistance," *European Journal of Development Research*, 11(2): 87–114.

Geist, E. (2006) 'Tsunami: wave of change,' *Scientific American*, 294 (1): 56–63.

Giddens, A. (1978) *Politics and Sociology in the Thought of Max Weber*. London: The Macmillan Press Ltd.

Goff, J. (2005) 'Survey of the December 26th 2004 Indian Ocean tsunami in Sri Lanka,' *Bulletin of the New Zealand Society for Earthquake Engineering*, 38 (4): 235–244.

Goodhand, J. and Klem, B. with Dilrukshi Fonseka, Keethaponcalan S. I., and Shonali Sardesai, (2005) *Sri Lanka Strategic Conflict Assessment 2005 – Volume 1, Aid, Conflict, and Peacebuilding in Sri Lanka, 2000–2005*, Colombo: Asia Foundation. Available online at <http://asiafoundation.org/publications/pdf/208> (accessed 5 August 2009).

Goyder, H., Coventry, C., Adams, J., Kaiser, T., Williams, S. and Smillie, I. (2006) *Linking Relief, Recovery, and Development (LRRD) – Policy Study*, London: Tsunami Evaluation Coalition.

Green, D.S. (2006) 'Transitioning NOAA moored buoy systems from research to operations,' *Oceans*, 18–21: 1–3.

Grewal, M.K. (2006) *Approaches to Equity in Post-Tsunami Assistance: Sri Lanka, A Case*

Study, London: Department for International Development. Available online at <http://www.alnap.org/pool/files/ApproachestoEquity.pdf> (accessed 9 August 2009).

Grundy-Warr, C. and Sidaway, J.D. (2006) Editorial: political geographies of silence and erasure, *Political Geography*, 25: 479–481.

Grunewald, F., de Geoffroy, V. and Lister, S. (2000) 'NGO responses to Hurricane Mitch: evaluations for accountability and learning,' *HPN Network Paper 34*, London: Humanitarian Practice Network.

Gunaratnam, S. (2005) 'A monument for wife and children in my own village even if the government prevents,' trans. N. Hamead, *Virakesari*, 12 June 2005.

Gunawardana, R.A.L.H. (1990) 'The people of the lion: the Sinhala identity and ideology in history and historiography,' in J. Spencer (ed.) *Sri Lanka: History and the Roots of Conflict*, New York: Routledge.

Gunawardena, N. (2008) 'Peddling paradise, rebuilding Serendib: the 100-meter refugees versus the tourism industry in post-tsunami Sri Lanka,' in N. Gunawardena and M. Schuller (eds.) *Capitalizing on Catastrophe: Neoliberal Strategies in Disaster Reconstruction*, New York: Altamira Press.

Gunawardena, N. and Schuller M. (eds.) (2008) *Capitalizing on Catastrophe: Neoliberal Strategies in Disaster Reconstruction*, New York: Altamira Press.

Hasbullah, S. and Korf, B. (in press) 'Muslim geographies and the politics of purification in Sri Lanka after the tsunami,' *Singapore Journal of Tropical Geography*.

Hassmiller, S. (2007) 'The 2004 "tsunami,"' *The American Journal of Nursing*, 107(2): 74–77.

Haug, M. and Weerackody, C. (2007) *The Tsunami Aid Delivery System and Humanitarian Principles: A View from Five Districts in Sri Lanka*, Oslo: NIBR.

Hawkins, C.A. and Rao, P.N. (2008) 'CEDER3: a social development response to the tsunami recovery in Tamil Nadu, India,' *Social Development Issues*, 30(1): 29–46.

Heijmans, A. (2004) 'From vulnerability to development,' in G. Bankoff, G. Frerks and D. Hilhorst (eds.) *Mapping Vulnerability, Disasters, Development and People*, London: Earthscan.

Hewamanne, S. (2007) *Stitching Identities in a Free Trade Zone: Gender and Politics in Sri Lanka*, Philadelphia: University of Pennsylvania Press.

Hilhorst, D. (2002) 'Being good at doing good? Quality and accountability of humanitarian NGOs,' *Disasters*, 26(3): 193–212.

—— (2004) 'Complexity and diversity: unlocking social domains of disaster response,' in G. Bankoff, G. Frerks and D. Hilhorst (eds.) *Mapping Vulnerability, Disasters, Development and People*, London: Earthscan.

Hilhorst, D. and Bankoff, G. (2004) 'Introduction: mapping vulnerability,' in G. Bankoff, G. Frerks and D. Hilhorst (eds.) *Mapping Vulnerability, Disasters, Development and People*, London: Earthscan.

Hilhorst, D. and Fernando, U. (2006) 'Everyday practices of humanitarian aid: tsunami response in Sri Lanka,' *Development in Practice*, 16(3): 292–302.

Hines, R. (2007) 'Natural disasters and gender inequalities: the 2004 tsunami and the case of India,' *Race, Gender and Class*, 14 (1–2): 60–68.

Hodgson, R. (2006) "Discussion of 'Lessons learned from tsunami damage in Sri Lanka' by Priyan Dias, Ranjith Dissanayake and Ravihansa Chandratilake," Proceedings of the Institution of Civil Engineers, *Civil Engineering*, 159(3): 104.

Hoffman, S.M. and Oliver-Smith, A. (1999) 'Anthropology and the angry earth: an overview,' in S.M. Hoffman and A. Oliver-Smith (eds.) *The Angry Earth: Disaster in Anthropological Perspective*, New York: Routledge.

—— (eds.) (2002) *Catastrophe & Culture: The Anthropology of Disaster*, Santa Fe: School of American Research Advanced Seminar Series.

Horobin, D. (2005) 'DFID evaluation of tsunami response,' *Forced Migration Review Special Issue: Tsunami – Learning From the Humanitarian Response*: 18.

Houghton, R. (2007) *The Tsunami Evaluation Coalition: Implications for Practice*, London: Tsunami Evaluation Coalition.

Human Rights Center (2005) *After the Tsunami: Human Rights of Vulnerable Populations*, Berkeley: University of California Human Rights Center, and Honolulu: East-West Center.

Hyndman, J. (2007) 'The securitization of fear in post-tsunami Sri Lanka,' *Annals of the Association of American Geographers*, 97(2): 361–372.

—— (2008) 'Feminism, conflict and disasters in post-tsunami Sri Lanka,' *Gender, Technology, and Development*, 12(1): 101–121.

Institute of Policy Studies (2005) *Sri Lanka: State of the Economy 2004*, Colombo: Institute of Policy Studies.

Integrated Regional Information Networks (IRIN) (2009) "SRI LANKA: Tsunami aid 'missing' says anti-corruption group," 28 December 2007. Available online at <http://www.irinnews.org/report.aspx?ReportId=76025> (accessed 5 August 2009).

International Crisis Group (2006) *Sri Lanka: The Failure of the Peace Process*, Asia Report N°124, 28 November 2006. Available online at <http://www.crisisgroup.org/home/index.cfm?id=4459&l=1> (accessed 5 August 2009).

—— (2007) *Sri Lanka's Human Rights Crisis*, Asia Report N°135, 14 June 2007. Available online at <http://www.crisisgroup.org/home/index.cfm?id=4459&l=1> (accessed 5 August 2009).

—— (2008a) *Sri Lanka's Return to War: Limiting the Damage*, Asia Report N°146, 20 February 2008. Available online at <http://www.crisisgroup.org/home/index.cfm?id=4459&l=1> (accessed 5 August 2009).

—— (2008b) *Sri Lanka's Eastern Province: Land, Development, Conflict*, Asia Report N°159, 15 October 2008. Available online at <http://www.crisisgroup.org/home/index.cfm?id=4459&l=1> (accessed 5 August 2009).

—— (2009) *Development Assistance and Conflict in Sri Lanka: Lessons from the Eastern Province*, Asia Report N°165, 16 April 2009. Available online at <http://www.crisisgroup.org/home/index.cfm?id=4459&l=1> (accessed 5 August 2009).

International Federation of Red Cross and Red Crescent Societies (1993) *Vulnerability and Capacity Assessment: a Federation Guide*, Geneva: IFRC.

International Water Management Institute (2005) *Tsunami Impacts on Shallow Groundwater and Associated Water Supply on the East Coast of Sri Lanka*, Colombo: IWMI.

Jayawardane, A.K.W. (2008) 'National disaster management plan and post disaster reconstruction in Sri Lanka,' *International Technology and Knowledge Flows for Post-disaster Reconstruction: Proceedings, Symposium and Workshop*, Surabaya: Department of Architecture, ITS. Available online at <http://digilib.its.ac.id/detil.php?id=2617> (accessed 9 August 2009)

Jayaweera, S. (2005) *The Impact of the Tsunami on Households and Vulnerable Groups in Two Districts in Sri Lanka: Galle and Colombo*, Colombo: Center for Women's Research.

Jeyaraj, D.B.S. (2005) 'Sri Lanka: the state that failed its people,' *The Sunday Leader*, February 2005.

Jones, R.H. and Norris, S. (2005) 'Discourse as action/discourse in action,' in S. Norris and R.H. Jones (eds.) *Discourse in Action: Introducing Mediated Discourse Analysis*, Abingdon: Routledge.

Keenan, A. (2006) 'Building a democratic middle-ground: professional civil society and the politics of human rights in Sri Lanka's peace process,' in Jeff Helsing and Julie Mertus (eds.) *Human Rights and Conflict: New Actors, Strategies and Ethical Dilemmas*, Washington, DC: United States Institute of Peace. Available online at <http://humanrightsandpeace.blogspot.com/2006/03/building-democratic-middle-ground.html> (accessed 9 August 2009).

—— (2007) 'The temptations of evenhandedness: on the politics of human rights and peace advocacy in Sri Lanka,' in Michel Feher (ed.) *Non Governmental Politics*, New York: Zone Books. Available online at <http://www.humanrightsandpeace.blogspot.com/> (Accessed 9 August 2009).

Kelman, I. (2005) 'Tsunami diplomacy: will the 26 December 2004 tsunami bring peace to the affected countries?' Available online at <http://www.socresonline.org.uk/10/1/kelman.html> (accessed 9 October 2008).

Kennedy, J., Ashmore, J., Babister, E., Kelman, I. and Zarins, J. (2009) 'Disaster mitigation lessons from "build back better" following the 26 December 2004 Tsunamis,' in J. Feyen, K. Shannon and M. Neville (eds.), *Water and Urban Development Paradigms: Towards an Integration of Engineering, Design and Management Approaches*, London: Taylor & Francis Group, pp. 297–302.

Kerr, A. (2007) 'Natural barriers to natural disasters,' *Bioscience*, 57(2): 102–103.

Klein, N. (2007) *The Shock Doctrine: The Rise of Disaster Capitalism*, New York: Picador.

Korf, B. (2005) 'Rethinking the greed – grievance nexus: property rights and the political economy of war in Sri Lanka,' *Journal of Peace Research*, 42(3): 201–217.

Korf, B. and Engel, S. (2006) 'On the incentives of violence: greed and pride in Sri Lanka's civil war,' *South Asia Economic Journal*, 7(1): 99–116.

Korf, B., Hasbullah, S., Hollenbach, P. and Klem, B. (2009) 'The gift of disaster: the commodification of good intentions in post-tsunami Sri Lanka,' *Disasters*. Published online 27 March 2009. Available online at <http://www3.interscience.wiley.com/cgi-bin/fulltext/122289349/PDFSTART> (accessed 9 August 2009).

Korf, B. and Silva, K.T. (2003) 'Poverty, ethnicity and conflict in Sri Lanka,' Paper presented at conference, Staying Poor: Chronic Poverty and Development Policy, University of Manchester, 7–9 April 2003. Available online at <http://www.chronicpoverty.org> (accessed January 2008).

Krauss, E. (2006) *Wave of Destruction: The Stories of Four Families and History's Deadliest Tsunami*, Emmaus PA: Rodale.

Kreps, G.A. (1984) 'Sociological inquiry and disaster research,' *Annual Review of Sociology*, 10: 309–330.

Kuhn, R. (2008) 'Tsunami and conflict in Sri Lanka,' Unpublished manuscript, World Bank Research Group.

—— (2009) 'An ethno-political accounting of the Sri Lankan tsunami impact and recovery,' Paper presented at conference, Re-Examining Disaster, Recovery and Reconstruction: Social Science Perspectives on the Tsunami, Jawaharlal Nehru University, New Delhi, January 2008.

Lavell, A. (2004) 'The lower Lempa River valley, El Salvador: risk reduction and development project,' in G. Bankoff, G. Frerks and D. Hilhorst (eds.) *Mapping Vulnerability, Disasters, Development and People*, London: Earthscan.

Lawrence, Patricia (2000) 'Violence, suffering, amman: the work of oracles in Sri Lanka's eastern war zone,' in V. Das, A. Kleinman, M. Ramphele, and P. Reynolds (eds.) *Violence and Subjectivity*, Berkeley: University of California Press.

—— (2003) 'Kali in a context of terror,' in J. Kripal and R.F. McDermott (eds.) *Encountering*

Kali: In the Center, at the Margins, in the West, Berkeley: University of California Press.

Lawrence, Patrick (2008) *Conversations in a Failing State*, Hong Kong: Asian Human Rights Commission. Available online at <http://www.ahrchk.net/pub/mainfile.php/conversations/> (accessed 5 August 2009).

Lazar, S. (2005) 'Citizens despite the state: everyday corruption and local politics in El Alto, Bolivia,' in D. Haller and C. Shore (eds.) *Corruption: Anthropological Perspectives*, London: Pluto Press.

Le Billon, P. (2001) 'The political ecology of war: natural resources and armed conflicts,' *Political Geography*, 20(5): 561–584.

Le Billon, P. and Waizenegger, A. (2007) 'Peace in the wake of disaster? Secessionist conflicts and the 2004 Indian Ocean tsunami,' *Transactions of the Institute of British Geographers, NS*, 32: 411–427.

Leckie, S. (2005) 'The great land theft,' *Forced Migration Review Special Issue: Tsunami – Learning From the Humanitarian Response*: 15–16.

Lock, C. (2006) *Nothing in the World in Tsunami-Affected Southern Sri Lanka*, Colombo: Vijitha Yapa Publications.

Long, N. (2001) *Development Sociology: Actor Perspectives*, London and New York: Routledge.

Lynch, C. (2007) *Juki Girls, Good Girls: Gender and Cultural Politics in Sri Lanka's Global Garment Industry*, Ithaca: Cornell University Press.

McCaffrey, R. (2009) 'The tectonic framework of the Sumatran subduction zone,' *Annual Review of Earth and Planetary Sciences*, 37(1): 345–366.

McCarthy, J.F. (2007) 'The demonstration effect: natural resources, ethnonationalism and the Aceh conflict,' *Singapore Journal of Tropical Geography*, 28: 314–333.

Macrae, J., Bradbury, M., Jaspars, S., Johnson, D. and Duffield, M. (1997) 'Conflict, the continuum and chronic emergencies: a critical analysis of the scope for linking relief, rehabilitation and development planning in Sudan,' *Disasters*, 21(3): 223–43.

McGilvray, D.B. (1982a) 'Sexual power and fertility in Sri Lanka: Batticaloa Tamils and Moors', in C.P. MacCormack (ed.) *Ethnography of Fertility and Birth*, London: Academic Press, 2nd ed., 1994, Long Grove IL: Waveland Press.

—— (1982b) 'Dutch Burghers and Portuguese Mechanics: Eurasian ethnicity in Sri Lanka,' *Comparative Studies in Society and History* 24(2): 235–263.

—— (1989) 'Households in Akkaraipattu: dowry and domestic organization among the matrilineal Tamils and Moors of Sri Lanka,' in J.N. Gray and D.J. Mearns (eds.) *Society from the Inside Out: Anthropological Perspectives on the South Asian Household*, New Delhi: Sage Publications.

—— (1998a) 'Arabs, Moors, and Muslims: Sri Lankan Muslim ethnicity in regional perspective,' *Contributions to Indian Sociology*, 32 (2): 433–483.

—— (1998b) *Symbolic Heat: Gender, Health, and Worship among the Tamils of South India and Sri Lanka*, Ahmedabad: Mapin. Reprinted 2003.

—— (2006) 'Tsunami and civil war in Sri Lanka: an anthropologist confronts the real world,' *India Review* 5(3–4): 372–393.

—— (2007) 'The Portuguese Burghers of eastern Sri Lanka in the wake of civil war and tsunami,' in Jorge Flores (ed.) *Re-Exploring the Links: History and Constructed Histories between Portugal and Sri Lanka*, Weisbaden: Harrassowitz Verlag.

—— (2008) *Crucible of Conflict: Tamil and Muslim Society on the East Coast of Sri Lanka*, Durham and London: Duke University Press.

McGilvray, D.B. and Raheem, M. (2007) *Muslim Perspectives on the Sri Lankan Conflict,* Policy Studies 41, Washington DC: East-West Center.

Malkki, L.H. (1995) *Purity and Exile: Violence, Memory, and National Cosmology among Hutu Refugees in Tanzania,* Chicago: University of Chicago Press.

Mamadouh, V. (2008)'After Van Gogh: the geopolitics of the tsunami relief effort in The Netherlands,' *Geopolitics,* 13(2): 205–231.

Manning, C. (2006) 'After the wave – the Centrelink social work response offshore,' *Journal of Social Work in Disability and Rehabilitation,* 5(3–4): 81–95.

Marsella, A.J., Johnson, J.L., Watson, P. and Gryczynski, J. (eds.) (2008) *Ethnocultural Perspectives on Disaster and Trauma: Foundations, Issues, and Applications,* New York and London: Springer Science and Business Media.

Mommsen, W.J. (1974) *The Age of Bureaucracy: Perspectives on the Political Sociology of Max Weber,* Oxford: Blackwell.

Moonesinghe, S. (2007) *Politics, Power Dynamics and Disaster: A Sri Lanka Study on Tsunami Affected Districts,* Colombo: International Centre for Ethnic Studies.

Morris, A. (2005) *Tsunami: Helping Each Other,* Minneapolis MN: Millbrook Press.

Morris, S.S. and Wodon, Q. (2003) 'The allocation of natural disaster relief funds: Hurricane Mitch in Honduras,' *World Development,* 31(7): 1279–89.

Muricken, A. and Kumar, A. (eds.) (2005) *Breaking Silence: Voices from the Margins,* Mumbai: Vikas Adhyayan Kendra.

Naik, A., Stigter, E. and Laczko, F. (2007) *Migration, Development and National Disasters: Insight from the Indian Ocean Tsunami,* Geneva: International Organization for Migration.

Nanayakkara, S. (2005) 'Cashing in on resettlement,' *The Sunday Leader,* 6 February 2005.

Nursey, C. (2005) 'The international tsunami response: showcase or circus?' *Humanitarian Exchange,* 32: 2–4.

Okal, E. (2008) 'Far-field tsunami hazard from mega-thrust earthquakes in the Indian Ocean,' *Geophysical Journal International,* 172 (3): 995–1015.

Oliver-Smith, A. (1999a) '"What is a disaster?' anthropological perspectives on a persistent question," in A. Oliver-Smith and S. M. Hoffman (eds.) *The Angry Earth: Disaster in Anthropological Perspective,* New York: Routledge.

—— (1999b) 'Peru's five-hundred-year earthquake: vulnerability in historical context,' in A. Oliver-Smith and S. M. Hoffman (eds.) *The Angry Earth: Disaster in Anthropological Perspective,* New York: Routledge.

—— (2004) 'Theorizing vulnerability in a globalized world: a political ecological perspective,' in G. Bankoff, G. Frerks and D. Hilhorst (eds.) *Mapping Vulnerability, Disasters, Development and People,* London: Earthscan.

Oliver-Smith, A. and Hoffman, S.M. (eds.) (1999) *The Angry Earth: Disaster in Anthropological Perspective,* New York: Routledge.

Olwig, M. (2007) 'Using remote sensing to assess the protective role of coastal woody vegetation against tsunami waves,' *International Journal of Remote Sensing,* 28 (13): 3153–3169.

Ortner, S.B. (2006) *Anthropology and Social Theory: Culture, Power, and the Acting Subject,* Durham: Duke University Press.

Peebles, P. (1990) 'Colonization and ethnic conflict in the Dry Zone of Sri Lanka,' *Journal of Asian Studies,* 49(1): 30–55.

—— (2006) *The History of Sri Lanka,* Westport, CT: Greenwood Publishing Group.

Peet, R. and Watts, M. (eds.) (2004) *Liberation Ecologies,* 2nd ed., London: Routledge.

Peluso, N.L. and Watts, M. (2001) *Violent Environments*, Ithaca: Cornell University Press.

Philips, R. (2005) 'After the tsunami: a plea for responsible reconstruction,' *Polity*, 2(3): 8–9.

Phillips, B. (2008) 'Mass fatality management after the Indian Ocean tsunami,' *Disaster Prevention and Management*, 17 (5): 681–697.

Phongsuwan, N. (2007) 'Re-orientated coral growth following the Indian Ocean tsunami of 2004,' *Coral Reefs*, 26 (3): 459.

Preston, C. (2008) 'Cultivating loyalty after a disaster,' *The Chronicle of Philanthropy*, 20(6): 7.

Raheja, G.G. (1990) 'Centrality, mutuality and hierarchy: shifting aspects of inter-caste relationships in North India,' in M. Marriott (ed.) *India through Hindu Categories*, New York: Sage.

Rainford, C. and Satkunanathan A. (2009) *Mistaking Politics for Governance: The Politics of Interim Arrangements in Sri Lanka 2002–2005*, Colombo: International Centre for Ethnic Studies.

Rajapakse, S.K. (2007) *Gone with the Wave: A Collection of Short Stories*, Colombo: Wijesooriya Grantha Kendraya.

Rajkumar, A.P., Titus S. and Premkumar, P.T. (2008) 'Coping with the Asian tsunami: perspectives from Tamil Nadu, India on the determinants of resilience in the face of adversity,' *Social Science and Medicine*, 67: 844–853.

Ramesh, R. (2005) 'Six months on, tsunami survivors still wait to go home,' *The Guardian*, 25 June 2005.

Renner, M. and Chafe, Z. (2007) *Beyond Disasters: Creating Opportunities for Peace*, Washington, DC: Worldwatch Institute.

Richardson, J. (2005)*Paradise Poisoned: Learning about Conflict, Terrorism, and Development from Sri Lanka's Civil Wars*, Colombo: International Centre for Ethnic Studies.

Rigg, J., Grundy-Warr, C., Law, L., and Tan-Mullins, M. (2008) 'Grounding a natural disaster: Thailand and the 2004 tsunami,' *Asia Pacific Viewpoint*, 49(2): 137–154.

Routray, B.P. and Singh, A.K. (2007) 'The pawns of war,' *South Asia Intelligence Review*, 5(12). Available online at <http://www.satp.org/satporgtp/sair/Archives/5_12.htm> (accessed 9 August 2009).

Ruwanpura, K.N. (2006) *Matrilineal Communities, Patriarchal Realities: A Feminist Nirvana Uncovered*, Ann Arbor: University of Michigan Press/Colombo: Social Scientists' Association.

—— (2008a) "Temporality of disasters: the politics of women's livelihoods 'after' the 2004 tsunami in Sri Lanka," *Singapore Journal of Tropical Geography*, 29(3): 325–340.

—— (2008b) 'Putting houses in place: rebuilding communities in post-tsunami Sri Lanka,' *Disasters*, 33(3): 436–456.

Ruwanpura, K.N., *et al.* (2000) *Structural Adjustment, Gender and Employment: The Sri Lankan Experience*, Geneva: ILO.

Samarajiva, R. (2005)'Mobilizing information and communications technologies for effective disaster warning: lessons from the 2004 tsunami,' *New Media and Society*, 7(6): 731–747.

Sampson, S. (2005) 'Integrity warriors: global morality and the anti-corruption movement in the Balkans,' in D. Haller and C. Shore, (eds.) *Corruption: Anthropological Perspectives*, London: Pluto Press.

Sarvananthan, M. (2005) *Post-Tsunami North and East Sri Lanka: Swindlers Hold Sway*, Point Pedro, Sri Lanka: Point Pedro Institute of Development.

Sarvananthan, M. and Sanjeewanie, H.M.P. (2008)'Recovering from the tsunami: people's experiences in Sri Lanka,' *Contemporary South Asia*, 16(3): 339–351.

Schmidt, K.J. (1995) *An Atlas and Survey of South Asian History*, Armonk NY: M.E. Sharpe.

Schuller, M. (2008) 'Deconstructing the disaster after the disaster: conceptualizing disaster capitalism,' in N. Gunawardena and M. Schuller (eds.) *Capitalizing on Catastrophe: Neoliberal Strategies in Disaster Reconstruction*, New York: Altamira Press.

Sen, A. (1981) *Poverty and Famines: An Essay on Entitlement and Deprivation*, Oxford: Clarendon.

Seneviratne, H.L. (1999) *The Work of Kings: The New Buddhism in Sri Lanka*, Chicago: University of Chicago Press.

Shanmugaratnam, N. (2005) "'Tsunami victims' perceptions of the buffer zone in Eastern Sri Lanka," *Polity*, 2(4): 13–16.

Shaw, R. (2008) 'Environmental aspects of the Indian Ocean tsunami recovery,' *Journal of Environmental Management*, 89(1): 1–3.

Silva, K.T. (2009) "'Tsunami third wave' and the politics of disaster management in Sri Lanka,' *Norwegian Journal of Geography*, 63: 61–72.

Slim, H, (1997) 'Doing the right thing: relief agencies, moral dilemmas and moral responsibility in political emergencies and war,' *Disasters*, 21(3): 244–57.

Smillie, I. (2001) 'From patrons to partners?' in I. Smillie (ed.), *Patronage or Partnership: Local Capacity Building in Humanitarian Crises*, Bloomfield: Kumarian Press.

Smillie, I. and Minear, L. (2003) *The Quality of Money: Donor Behavior in Humanitarian Financing: An Independent Study*, Somerville, MA: Tufts University.

South Asia Terrorism Project (2009), *Sri Lanka Assessment 2009*. Available online at <http://www.satp.org/satporgtp/countries/shrilanka/index.html> (accessed June 2008.)

Sphere Project (2004) *Humanitarian Charter and Minimum Standards in Disaster Response*, Oxford: Oxfam Books.

Spiegel, P.B., Le, P., Ververs, M.T. and Salama, P. (2007) 'Occurrence and overlap of natural disasters, complex emergencies and epidemics during the past decade (1995–2004),' *Conflict and Health*, 1(2): 9. Available online at <http://www.conflictandhealth.com/content/pdf/1752–1505–1–2.pdf> (accessed 19 May 2009).

Srinivas, H. (2008) 'Environmental implications for disaster preparedness: lessons learnt from the Indian Ocean tsunami,' *Journal of Environmental Management*, 89(1): 4–13.

Steele, P. (2005) *Phoenix from the Ashes? Economic Policy Challenges and Opportunities for Post-Tsunami Sri Lanka*, Colombo: Institute of Policy Studies.

Stewart, G.B. (2005) *Catastrophe in Southern Asia: The Tsunami of 2004*, Detroit: Lucent Books.

Stirrat, R.L. (2006) 'Competitive humanitarianism: relief and the tsunami in Sri Lanka,' *Anthropology Today*, 22(5): 11–16.

Stokke, K. and Shanmugaratnam, N. (2005) 'From relief and rehabilitation to peace in Sri Lanka?' *Polity*, 2(3): 10–11.

Sullivan, W.L. (2008) *Oregon's Greatest Natural Disasters*, Eugene, OR: Navillus Press.

Sunday Leader (2005) 'A tsunami of discontent,' Colombo, Sri Lanka. 6 February 2005.

Tambiah, S.J. (1986) *Sri Lanka: Ethnic Fratricide and the Dismantling of Democracy*, Chicago and London: University of Chicago Press.

Tamilnet (2005) 'LTTE suspends negotiations with Sri Lanka pending implementation of agreements reached'. Available online at <http://www.tamilnet.com/art.html?catid=13&artid=8824> (accessed 5 August 2009).

Telford, J. and Cosgrave, J. (2007) 'The international humanitarian system and the 2004 Indian Ocean earthquake and tsunamis,' *Disasters*, 31(1): 1–28.

Telford, J., Cosgrave, J., and Houghton, R. (2006) *Joint Evaluation of the International Response to the Indian Ocean Tsunami: Synthesis Report*, London: Tsunami Evaluation Coalition.

Thangaraj, M. (2005) 'Tsunami: women and children,' in A. Muricken and U. Kumar (eds.) *Breaking Silence: Voices from the Margins*, Mumbai: Vikas Adhyayan Kendra.

Thiruchandran, S. (1999) *The Other Victims of War: Emergence of Female-Headed Households in Eastern Sri Lanka Volume II*, New Delhi: Vikas.

Thurnheer, K. (2009) 'A house for a daughter? Constraints and opportunities in post-tsunami eastern Sri Lanka,' *Contemporary South Asia*, 17(1): 79–91.

Tomita, T. (2006) 'Damage caused by the 2004 Indian Ocean tsunami on the southwestern coast of Sri Lanka,' *Coastal Engineering Journal*, 48(2): 99–116.

Tong, J. (2004) 'Questionable accountability: MSF and Sphere in 2003,' *Disasters*, 28(2): 176–89.

Turner, V. (1974) *Dramas, Fields, and Metaphors: Symbolic Action in Human Society*, Ithaca: Cornell University Press.

United Nations (1999) *Final Report of Scientific Committee of the International Decade for Natural Disaster Reduction, Addendum to International Decade for Natural Disaster Reduction, Report of the Secretary-General*, 18 June 1999, A/54132/Add. 1 – E/1999/80/Add. 1

United Nations High Commissioner for Refugees (2005) *UNHCR Outlines Post-Tsunami Role in Sri Lanka*. Available online at <http://www.unhcr.org/42038a474.html> (accessed 19 May 2009).

United Nations International Strategy for Disaster Reduction (UNISDR) (2005) *Hyogo Declaration, World Conference on Disaster Reduction, 18–22 January 2005, Kobe, Hyogo, Japan*. Available online at <http://www.unisdr.org/wcdr/intergover/official-doc/L-docs/Hyogo-declaration-english.pdf> (accessed on May 9, 2009).

—— (2006) *Strengthening the ISDR System*, Background and Discussion Paper, 31 December 2006.

United Nations Office for the Coordination of Humanitarian Affairs (UNOCHA) (2005) *Humanitarian Situation Report – Sri Lanka: 13 – 19 May 2005*. Available online at <http://www.reliefweb.int/rw/RWB.NSF/db900SID/VBOL-6CJHBG?OpenDocument> (accessed 5 August 2009).

UNOCHA Somalia office (2005) 'Tsunami worsens existing vulnerability in Somalia,' *Forced Migration Review, Special Issue: Tsunami – Learning From the Humanitarian Response*: 51. Available online at <http://repository.forcedmigration.org/show_metadata.jsp?pid=fmo:4495> (accessed 9 August 2009).

United States (2005a) *Tsunami Response: Lessons Learned, Hearing Before the Committee on Foreign Relations, United States Senate, One Hundred Ninth Congress, first session, February 10, 2005, (0–16–075146–2, 978–0–16–075146–2)*, Washington: U.S. G.P.O. Available online at <http://foreign.senate.gov/hearings/2005/hrg050210a.html> (accessed 14 March 2009).

—— (2005b) *Emergency Supplemental Appropriations Act for Defense, the Global War on Terror, and Tsunami Relief, 2005: Report*, (to accompany H.R. 1268). Washington D.C.: U.S. G.P.O. Available online at <http://frwebgate.access.gpo.gov/cgi-bin/

getdoc.cgi?dbname=109_cong_bills&docid=f:h1268enr.txt.pdf> (accessed 14 March 2009).

United States House of Representatives (2006) *A Failure of Initiative: Final Report of the Select Bipartisan Committee to Investigate the Preparation for and Response to Hurricane Katrina*, Washington DC: US Government Printing Office.

University Teachers for Human Rights (UTHR) (2002) *Towards a Totalitarian Peace: The Human Rights Dilemma*, Special Report No: 13, 10 May 2002. Available online at <http://www.uthr.org> (accessed 5 August 2009).

—— (2009) *A Marred Victory and a Defeat Pregnant with Foreboding*, Special Report No. 32, 10 June 2009. Available online at <http://www.uthr.org> (accessed 9 August 2009).

Uvin, P. (1998) *Aiding Violence: The Development Enterprise in Rwanda*, West Hartford, CT: Kumarian Press.

Uyangoda, J. (2005a) 'Ethnic conflict, the state, and the tsunami disaster in Sri Lanka,' *Inter-Asia Cultural Studies*, 6(3): 341–352.

—— (2005b) 'Post-tsunami recovery in Sri Lanka,' *Polity*, 2(3): 4–7.

—— (2005c) "Ethnic conflict, the state and tsunami disaster in Sri Lanka," unpublished manuscript, shortened version published in *Forced Migration Review*, Special Issue, July 2005, pp. 30–32. Available online at <http://www.fmreview.org/FMRpdfs/Tsunami/14.pdf> (accessed 5 August 2009).

van Oijen, P. (2009) "Civil-military interaction in 'double' affected areas: complex emergencies and natural disasters," The Hague: Netherlands Institute of International Relations 'Clingendael.'

Ville de Goyet, C. de (2000) 'Stop propagating disaster myths,' *Lancet*, 356: 762–764.

Waldman, A. (2005) 'Torn from moorings, villagers from Sri Lanka grasp for past,' *The New York Times International*, 6 March 2005. See also video clip by Waldman. Available online at <http://www.nytimes.com/2005/03/06/international/asia/06lanka.html?scp=13&sq=&st=nyt> (accessed 10 June 2009).

Walton, O. (2008) 'Conflict, peacebuilding and NGO legitimacy: national NGOs in Sri Lanka,' *Conflict, Security and Development*, 8(1): 133–167.

Waters, T. (2001) *Bureaucratizing the Good Samaritan: The Limitations to Humanitarian Relief Operations*, Boulder, CO: Westview Press.

Weber, M. (1947) *The Theory of Social and Economic Organization*, New York: Oxford University Press.

Weiss, T.G. (1999) 'Principles, politics and humanitarian action,' *Ethics and International Affairs*, 13: 1–32.

Wijetunge, J. (2008) 'Indian Ocean tsunami on 26 December 2004,' *Journal of Earthquake and Tsunami*, 2(2): 133–155.

Wilson, A. J. (2000) *Sri Lankan Tamil Nationalism: Its Origins and Development in the 19th and 20th Centuries*, Vancouver: University of British Columbia Press.

Winchester, S. (2004) *Krakatoa: The Day the World Exploded, August 27, 1883*, New York: HarperCollins.

Winslow, D. and Woost, M.D. (eds.) (2004) *Economy, Culture, and Civil War in Sri Lanka*, Bloomington: Indiana University Press.

Wisner, B., Blaikie, P., Cannon, T., and Davis, I. (2004) *At Risk: Natural Hazards, People's Vulnerability and Disasters*, 2nd ed., London and New York: Routledge.

World Bank (2005) *World Bank Response to the Tsunami Disaster*, 2 February 2005. Available online at <http://www-wds.worldbank.org/external/default/WDSContentServer/WDSP/

IB/2005/05/03/000160016_20050503112017/Rendered/PDF/321540tsunamireport1020 20501public1.pdf> (accessed 20 May 2009).

World Health Organization (2005) *Situation Report*, released on 14 February 2005 Colombo: WHO.

Zhang, J. (2006) 'Public diplomacy as symbolic interactions: a case study of Asian tsunami relief campaigns,' *Public Relations Review*, 32(1): 26–32.

Zinn, D.L. (2005) 'Afterword – anthropology and corruption: the state of the art,' in D. Haller and C. Shore, (eds.) *Corruption: Anthropological Perspectives*, London: Pluto Press.

Index